DATE DUE

Landscapes of Fear

To Rossana

Landscapes of Fear

*Perceptions of Nature and the City
in the Middle Ages*

Vito Fumagalli

Translated by Shayne Mitchell

Polity Press

First published in Italy as follows: Part I, *Quando il cielo s'oscura* © Il Mulino 1987; Part II, *La pietra viva* © Il Mulino 1988; Part III, *Solitudo carnis* © Il Mulino 1990.

First published in 1994 by Polity Press
in association with Blackwell Publishers

Editorial office:
Polity Press
65 Bridge Street
Cambridge CB2 1UR, UK

Marketing and production:
Blackwell Publishers
108 Cowley Road
Oxford OX4 1JF, UK

238 Main Street
Cambridge, MA 02142, USA

ISBN 0 7456 0754 3

A CIP catalogue record for this book is available
from the British Library and the Library of Congress.

Typeset in 10 on 11½ pt Sabon
by Best-set Typesetter Ltd., Hong Kong
Printed in Great Britain by Hartnolls Ltd, Bodmin, Cornwall

This book is printed on acid-free paper.

Contents

Translator's Acknowledgements

I should like to thank Ross Balzaretti, Neil Christie, Valerie Higgins and Chris Wickham who kindly answered my many enquiries about medieval Italian history, and Sally Cornish, Eve Mary Cottingham, Helen Hills, Julia Rizzoli, Martin Russell-Jones and Nigel Townson who read the translation and whose comments and criticisms were invaluable.

Introduction

This book consists of three texts which were originally published separately in Italian. All three are concerned with similar subject matter and appeared over a short time, between 1987 and 1990. However, my concern with the history of the relationship between people and their environment goes back to the 1960s, when I first became interested in the perception of the natural world in the Middle Ages and with attempts to change it. Nature was regarded as a reflection of humanity, as people recognized themselves in a landscape which was interpreted very differently depending on the social rank and occupation of observers and when and where they were writing. Since then my interests have broadened to take account of the history of attitudes to the body and of psychological aspects: passions, emotions, fears, dreams and aspirations. The presence of fear has been a central feature in my study of the medieval period and has given rise to the title of this book. What was perceived as frightening varied between different people and between different periods and places; it could be nebulous or virtually imperceptible. Over time, fear increased, as familiarity with the environment, the countryside, bodies and the animal and plant world diminished.

The break with nature has always been seen most clearly in the towns. In some periods the city stood in stark opposition to the countryside, intervening dramatically to change it. This is particularly true of the last two centuries, a period when people have become separated from physical reality. However, this has not always been the case: towns have varied enormously depending not only on time and place but, notably, on the dominant culture and social group. Moreover, the same period and the same region have seen different, even opposite, modes of behaviour and of thinking, which can conflict with each other. Despite interruptions and breaks, however, the dominant theme has always been that of a 'triumph'

over the environment. That triumph has at times had positive consequences but more often it has been characterized by far-reaching and
destructive changes, threatening not only animal and plant life and the
earth but also the human race itself. It has fostered an intellectual
dichotomy between body and mind, emotion and reason, flesh and spirit.

The contempt for the body has led to asceticism and a mortification of
the body, to bloody wars and to the slaughter of animals. Over the
centuries, religious and intellectual constraints have decreased, most
markedly in this century when all inhibitions have been jettisoned. We
are left to contemplate the ashes of a world which we have largely
destroyed, and which we continue to destroy with means more sophisticated and powerful than ever before, a process which will not come to an
end until we come to understand why we began it. In this book I have
sought to provide an answer; in particular, I have sought to help us to
understand better the impact made by human efforts on the landscape,
on the environment and the physical world in general, and on the human
body itself.

The three sections of this book reflect three stages in the development
of my views on history. It is the fruit of thirty years' study of the
economy, society and culture (in a wide sense) of the period we still today
call the Middle Ages, even though a great historian like Jacques Le Goff
has, rightly, argued that it is only from the beginning of the twentieth
century that the course of history has shifted significantly. Part I of this
book is concerned principally with the relationship with nature, part II
with the changing environment, and part III with attitudes to the body.
However, I have striven throughout, especially in part III, to avoid
imposing too rigid and uniform an interpretation on events; I have tried
to include the diversities and the contrasts, and to offer up to the reader
a feast, so to speak, which contains all the delicacies available and forgets
none. My aim has been to understand, not to justify. I have attempted to
convey the vulnerability, apprehensions, fears, aspirations, drama and
tragedy which were an integral part of the relationship with nature. I do
not judge, nor do I seek to excuse. I have long contemplated these events,
and find that they leave me deeply moved and with a sense of wonder.

PART I

When the Heavens Darken

At the height of Charlemagne's power and of Carolingian culture, when the Church, after centuries of gifts and bequests, was rich and influential, the learned monk Alcuin, familiar with classical literature, wrote elegies on the theme of the transience of every human endeavour. His poetry leaves the impression that he foresaw that everything, even that which had been created by Charlemagne and his predecessors – law and order, sound government, the defeat of the Muslims, learning – would before long vanish.

> The delights of this world fade away and ere long all will change. Everything has its own laws. Nothing is eternal, nothing is unchanging. Thus bright, life-giving day is darkened by night's shadows; the icy hand of winter fast comes to smite the fairest flower; the calm sea is tossed by the wind. The young men who once pursued deer over the fells now walk falteringly, leaning heavily on their staffs. Wretched creatures that we are, why do we cling to you so, O world, when you slip from our fingers? Ever changing, you flee swiftly and relentlessly before us.

Educated men were troubled by their awareness of the beauties of the world and the impermanence of existence. Nature was in permanent flux: summer turned to winter; young men who had hunted passionately were fated to a feeble old age; in winter the sea was lashed by storms. The words with which Alcuin ended his poem seemed to offer little solace: 'May we be ever filled with the love of God . . . He is our glory, our life and our salvation.' Awareness of the precariousness of this world and the imminence of the next could not distract even the most devout of men from this world. They continued to rejoice in it and sought to snatch some delights from all-devouring time. Alcuin celebrated the return of spring and fine weather:

Already the cuckoo has been heard high up among the branches of the trees and the ground is many-hued with the budding flowers. The vines bring forth grapes on their shoots just as our thoughts are roused by the nightingale singing in the dark trees. The sun rises high amid the constellations and, blazing forth, banishes the domain of shadows.

Winter inexorably followed summer, bad weather good, famine plenty, war peace, sickness health, death life. Nature ruled supreme and was remorseless. No technology existed which could counter it. People were swallowed up in a countryside which was still largely untamed and had vast expanses of wilderness everywhere. Life and death depended on the forces of nature, and people sought to divine her whims by examining the heavens or observing the terrifying eclipses of the sun or the moon.

1

The Domain of Shadows

Churchmen interpreted natural phenomena such as the disruption of the normal pattern of the seasons, abnormal weather, extreme cold, drought or sand which rained down inexplicably from the sky as signs of divine disfavour. For Andreas of Bergamo, unable to imagine that the disloyalty shown to the German Emperor by the Duke of Benevento should go unpunished, the bizarre phenomena which occurred in 871 and 872 were clearly at one and the same time warnings of God's anger and the instrument of divine punishment. 'Many singular events occurred before our very eyes. After the grape harvest the wine became cloudy (or, as we say, "turned") as soon as it was poured into the casks. On Easter Sunday it was as if sand had rained down everywhere, on to trees, bushes, fields and villages.'

Shortly after this a severe frost damaged the vulnerable new growth on vines and trees throughout the plains and river valleys. In August a fearsome cloud of grasshoppers came from the east and descended on to the fields of Lombardy and the Veneto, destroying the crops. Andreas quoted from the Bible to explain why the locusts flew in dense masses: 'The locusts have no king, yet go they forth all of them by bands' (Proverbs 30:27). The deaths of important figures, so educated people and chroniclers fearfully believed, could only bode ill. Andreas, for example, also believed that political disorder in Italy was linked to the death of the Emperor Louis II in 875. Strange phenomena such as solar and lunar eclipses were believed to warn of the imminent death of a king or ruler on whom people were relying for a peaceful and secure existence. According to Andreas, the death of Louis the Pious had coincided with Ascension Sunday and had been preceded by a terrifying eclipse of the sun during which it had been so dark that the stars could be seen as clearly as at night. The coincidence of the heavens darkening on the anniversary of the very day that Christ had redeemed the world and ascended to heaven convinced everyone that the end of the world had come. People were terror-stricken but eventually, to general relief, the sun slowly returned. Just as everything had returned to normal, however, strange flashes as bright as daylight suddenly appeared in the middle of the night, producing widespread panic. It was the *aurora borealis*, to contemporaries entirely mysterious. Literate people interpreted the phenomenon in terms of the Bible, preaching: 'My brothers, be prepared, for what the Lord told us in the Gospels has come to pass: "So likewise ye, when ye see these things come to pass, know ye that the kingdom of God is nigh at hand."'

Andreas ended by recounting the events which had followed the death of Louis the Pious. 'The following June the Emperor Louis died, ending his days in peace. After his death, discord broke out between the three brothers, Louis and Charles on the one side and Lothar on the other.'

Natural phenomena such as the reddish Sahara sand which occasionally fell mixed with rain and coloured the rain blood-red terrified everyone, educated and uneducated alike, as they were believed to be God's way of manipulating nature to express his anger or warn of disaster. The fantastical shapes and various, often fiery, colours of clouds at sunset were interpreted as scenes of battle and bloodshed, heralding wars for the succession or barbarian incursions. The outlines of horses and riders and the glint of weapons could be clearly discerned, and some even said they could hear the clamour of armies on the march. Paul the Deacon described how shortly before the Lombard descent on Italy in 568 fearsome crimson shapes could be seen blazing in the sky, warning of the bloody war to follow. Even battle trumpets and the thud of hooves could be heard by day and by night. The sombre picture given by clerics in their chronicles is not the whole story for it was natural for churchmen to read dire premonitions in the natural world and to see everything in millenarian terms. It is true that life was nasty and brutish, but this did not necessarily lead to alarm and despair, and all sections of society, peasants and craftsmen, nobles and rulers, went on with their business undaunted. The material that has come down to us is that which clerics, interested primarily in recording the manifestations of sin and of God's wrath, chose to record, and their interpretations are, moreover, inevitably biased. Yet even allowing for this, and for a degree of hyperbole, disasters and cases of widespread panic appear to have been common. In any case, a world in which people had no control over their environment could scarcely seem benign.

Outside the context of the Church, common pagan customs themselves reveal a combination of fear and fatalism before the forces of the natural world. During lunar eclipses peasants would encourage the moon to recover its powers by blowing horns loudly and ringing bells. They were terrified that if the moon vanished all animal and plant life, over which it presided, would come to an end. The end of the world was just as real a prospect to them, in their own way, as it was to clerics. As the great historian Marc Bloch has pointed out, the idea of the end of the world regularly surfaced whenever some particularly traumatic event magnified the everyday anxieties and apprehensions which lay permanently just beneath the surface. Church writers were therefore substantially correct when they assumed that many people were haunted by a fear of the end of the world, even if not all saw it as part of God's scheme. The figure of the Christian God in any case had much in common with the pagan gods of rivers and of other natural phenomena; all were as mysterious and changeable as the moon, itself a symbol of the instability and perils of the natural world. The death of a saint, civil strife or treachery were interpreted as punishments sent by God against his people, however innocent they might be, and such events would revive fears of the end of the world. The new Christian beliefs made slow progress, especially in rural areas, and were often only a veneer over belief in capricious and inexorable pagan gods. A large number of pagan practices, including 'helping' the moon, persisted into at least the early ninth century.

While Attalas was abbot at Bobbio (in succession to Columbanus), one of his monks burned down a pagan temple built of tree trunks on the bank of the river Staffora near Piacenza, and was beaten and thrown into the river by a band of local peasants. The narrator of these events tells us how divine intervention fortunately ensured both the monk's survival and the death of almost all his assailants, struck down by the Christian God they had refused to recognize. The episode, from the first half of the seventh century, is one of many which cast light on the long and determined campaign waged by the Church against pagan customs, both at the time and later; but they reveal, too, the stubborn persistence of these customs in rural areas. Trees, more than any other part of nature, were often regarded as sacred, the incarnation of natural forces, and an enthusiastic felling of them throughout the Middle Ages did little to diminish the reverence felt for them. It has been observed that in this period people were effectively swallowed up by nature, lost in a world where vast areas had centuries earlier reverted to wilderness, to forest, bog and undergrowth.

Throughout the Middle Ages the natural world dominated existence; people, especially in the countryside, were therefore preoccupied with the workings of nature to a degree that can today seem obsessive. Our understanding of this close relationship with the natural world is imperfect. Both educated and uneducated people were conscious of being linked inextricably to the natural world and subject to its laws, and most people, especially the poorer groups within society and those in rural areas, were profoundly aware of their environment. Every unusual event, every eclipse, comet or occurrence of the *aurora borealis*, seemed to portend some abrupt break in the regular course of events. The fear of some irreversible disaster led easily to panic. Signs seen on earth or in the sky were interpreted as warnings not to go against the natural world, while for clerics they warned in addition not to sin against God and one's neighbour.

Unfortunately the narrative sources of the early Middle Ages have been viewed almost entirely from the standpoint of political history, for the information they give on alliances, wars and treaties. A reading of them for what they indicate of the relationship with the natural world – a relationship which is in fact their principal concern – reveals them to be observant and meticulous records of everything which occurred on earth, in the waters or in the sky. It was above all in the earlier Middle Ages that all natural phenomena were interpreted as portents. This preoccupation with nature is not found in chronicles of the later Middle Ages when, in contrast, chronicles are as, or more, interested in supplying more objective descriptions of natural events and their effect on everyday life. Phenomena like eclipses and the *aurora borealis*, however, retained their power to alarm, and continued to some extent to be interpreted as warnings. Though the full history of the relationship with the natural world in the period has still to be written, it is generally accepted that in the twelfth century a rationalistic outlook began to prevail among literate people, although we know little of how far it influenced their behaviour and how far it filtered down to the uneducated. These are problems as yet unresolved: much has been written on medieval science but the history of popular mentalities has been little studied. Although the relationship with the natural world gradually evolved, many aspects remained unchanged for centuries, especially within the world of the peasants.

Nature was perceived as bounteous, the source of all sustenance. Yet intimate as the association with her was, she could not be influenced to any degree; she was mysterious, fickle and vengeful. Mysterious, for she could bring forth monstrous creatures from her womb. In the early Middle Ages some of the stories of such freaks probably had a kernel of truth, being based on elements of creatures which were real, or simply larger than life. Even more bizarre beings existed on the fringes of the known world. At the end of the eighth century, Paul the Deacon wrote that to the north of the inhabited world lay immeasurable gorges, gaping like great maws ready to swallow up everything and everyone, the impassable edge of the world. The further one moved from familiar territory, so fantastical beings multiplied and nature became even more mysterious. There were strange phenomena in these far-distant lands.

On the shores of the ocean in the far north of Germany, again according to Paul the Deacon, was a cave under a projecting rock where seven men lay frozen in sleep. Their dress revealed them to be Romans and some said they were Christians and that the day might come when God would rouse them to preach Christianity to those barbarian nations. Once someone had tried to remove the clothes from one of them, but his arms had withered. Not far from the Seven Sleepers, in a land where snow lay even in summer, lived the Scritobini, who ate only raw meat. Going westward from these shores one reached the boundless ocean and a notoriously deep whirlpool, the *maris umbilicum*, the very centre of the sea. Ships which had the misfortune to pass when the whirlpool began to seethe, which it did twice daily, were dragged down into a bottomless pit as fast as arrows speeding through the air. On these distant shores the sea rose and fell regularly while rivers flowed upstream for miles and had salty-tasting water. The Lombards were believed to have come from these far-flung lands and to have derived their redoubtable courage from familiarity with such fantastical landscapes, people and creatures.

Bizarre and fearful legends are a feature of all early medieval chronicles, a consequence of the acute observation of natural phenomena, particularly in the most grim moments of war. One night, for instance, a rampart miles long was said to have suddenly appeared in the flat eastern marches of the Carolingian empire where the defences were most hard-pressed. It was only inside their own villages that people felt secure and protected. They were deeply attached to their familiar fields and yearned for them if forced to leave, as had been the case with one of Paul the Deacon's ancestors.

In the early Middle Ages anything unusual, however much it departed from the norm, was still regarded as a product of nature. Though it might be of strange appearance, it was undisputedly part of the natural order. Later, however, any oddities of the human, animal or vegetable world came to be regarded as unnatural. The shift in thinking coincided with the gradual physical separation from the natural world as over the centuries many natural features were destroyed when the forests were cleared for cultivation. Those forests which survived the long campaign of clearance gradually came to be perceived as alien, even frightening places, and it is significant that it was there that the spirits of the dead began to be seen. In the early Middle Ages, by contrast, all strange phenomena, however beautiful or grotesque, had been seen as ultimately part of nature. Paradise itself was visualized in terms of cultivated land, a garden of delights full of brooks, flowers and trees. It was generally believed that the next world was close to this one and easily reached: on their deathbed many had a vision of heaven, filled with intoxicating music and intense perfumes, while the dead might well come back to life to describe paradise, or saints descend to earth to pay homage at the tombs of well-known martyrs – or to pray for their own souls at their own. The next world was believed to be merely an exalted version of this one, with no hard and fast dividing line between the two. In the course of time, however, the boundary would become more rigid.

Lunar and solar eclipses were for centuries seen as fateful interruptions in the pattern of nature and the universe, and were accordingly watched apprehensively, though for different reasons, by peasants and clerics alike. An unquestioning acceptance of the quirks of the natural world was characteristic of the rural mentality throughout the Middle Ages and beyond; elements of it survived well into modern times. Even literate people, trying as they might to explain strange phenomena in terms of the will of God, were influenced by the notion that natural events could inexorably sway destiny. It is difficult to distinguish between the two mental worlds, that of the peasant and that of the educated, and to unravel the different strands. This fatalism, an aspect of the medieval mentality which has its roots far back in time, was as entrenched a part of the medieval world picture as the millenarianism which throve in rural areas and which interpreted every inexplicable phenomenon in the sky or on the earth as an omen.

The ancient origins of such fatalism meant that it was the feature of the medieval outlook which took longest to die. By the late Middle Ages, however, chronicles showed far less interest in such portents and devoted considerably more space to disastrous weather and to plague, food shortages and famine. A more pragmatic, utilitarian way of thinking began to develop, if only among a few. It is especially apparent in Italian city chronicles as wealthy merchants and artisans came to dominate towns and urban pressure on the surrounding countryside increased, seeking to change it and to eliminate wild and uncultivated areas, but thereby eroding the intimate relationship with the countryside which had been characteristic of the early Middle Ages. It is no coincidence that the economic, social and political crisis of the towns in the fourteenth century coincided with a renewed, and intense, interest in omens by the chroniclers; but now, in contrast to the early Middle Ages, such omens were increasingly seen as supernatural and monstrous. To a heated imagination, the everyday could appear freakish. The chronicle of Giorgio Franchi, a priest from Berceto near Parma, recorded that in 1544

on the 22 August Maestro Gian Francesco Gabbie the barber found a snake in a field of hemp at Riole. The snake was so big that no one dared

attack it with sticks or stones but a man called Brocardo Picio shot it dead
with his arquebus and dragged it into the piazza. There it was found to be
two *braccia* long, as much as three normal snakes. It was so thick that it
was impossible to encircle it with both hands and its head was like a rock.

Monsters had been believed to exist in the early Middle Ages too but
they had not inspired the same terror. The ancient legend of the warriors
with dogs' heads, the cynocephali, of which Paul the Deacon wrote
towards the end of the eighth century, did not produce the same panic as
the ferocious wolves, monstrously large or with docked tails or other
exaggerated features, which fill the pages of Italian chronicles, particularly from the years around 1300; a classic example is the wolf of
Gubbio, made famous by St Francis's intervention. And yet these wolves
which so alarmed people were real animals, whereas the cynocephali
were mythical creatures which were frightening not because of their
strangeness but only because they might be as savage as dogs, or more so.
These fantastical wolves were a consequence of the changing conception
of the natural world, especially of the forests and the animals which
inhabited them, which easily gave rise to such imagined creatures. Increasingly forests and animals were felt to be alien and potentially close
to, if not actually in, the world of the supernatural.

In addition, ideas about the soul, the dead and the next world were
changing. Whereas death had earlier been regarded as entirely natural,
the influence of the Church had fostered disturbing and uncomfortable
beliefs. Such an abhorrence of death is reflected in the 'dance of death'
theme, where rotting corpses with exaggeratedly long worms crawling in
their bellies cavorted grotesquely. It first appeared in the late Middle
Ages and had an influence on descriptions and representations of death
throughout Europe for centuries. It was the increasing alienation from
the natural world and its laws which made death, the most ineluctable
law, unwelcome, and which resulted in a new perception of death as a
frightening, even unnatural, break. We do not know to what extent these
changes permeated different social groups and the literate and illiterate
and how much their impact varied over different regions, but no one can
have been unaffected.

Over the centuries the particular triggers of fear and panic changed
but certain crucial features persisted, albeit with diminished power,
particularly in the social groups least influenced by written, high culture.
Here new ideas clashed with ancient beliefs, often resulting in a jumble of
misunderstood notions. For example, time-honoured and innocent
practices which had never had any connection with the supernatural
were thought to be tainted with witchcraft; the influence of the Church
meant that the hand of the devil was seen even in old fertility rites, such

as those of the Benandanti in Friuli in the seventeenth century, which
were entirely innocent of witchcraft. Not all ancient customs had survived however. Pagan practices based on the shedding of human blood,
which still existed in the early Middle Ages, gradually succumbed to the
campaign waged by the Church and eventually, with the growing sense
of separateness from the natural world and the decline in the need to
placate its terrible laws, became redundant. As the ability to manipulate
the environment increased over the centuries, so attitudes shifted, both
on a conscious and an unconscious level.

Often these shifts are revealed in the passages in the sources which
have traditionally been regarded as irrelevant and trivial, but which can
yet reveal ways of thinking lost to us and which can seem strange and
fantastical. Such supposedly minor details and stories, like the return
home of Paul the Deacon's ancestor, which I shall discuss, have been
regarded as incidental and have been subordinated to what are regarded
as the mainstream issues – migrations, wars, social and economic
problems – and to 'great men' – kings, emperors and popes. Without
political and economic and social history, and of course cultural history,
the history of mentalities would be merely anecdote, but the details
which are available to cast light on the medieval world picture lend
vividness and individual interest to the general picture offered by more
traditional history. Merely to indicate the scale and significance of the
sources which exist would require a much longer book than this.

2

Nature

Sorge non lunge alle cristiane tende,
tra solitarie valli, alta foresta
foltissima di piante antiche orrende
. . .
né v'entra peregrin, se non smarrito,
ma lunge passa, e la dimostra a dito.

(From Godfrey's camp a grove a little way,
Amid the valleys deep, grows out of sight,
Thick with old trees, whose horrid arms display
An ugly shade, like everlasting night
. . .
Nor traveller nor pilgrim there to enter
(So awful seems that forest old) dare venture.)

> Torquato Tasso, *Gerusalemme liberata*,
> Canto XIII, lines 9–11, 23–4
> (Edward Fairfax translation, 1600)

Although I shall draw on the form of the countryside of the Middle Ages as an expression of contemporary mentalities, I do not subscribe wholeheartedly to the theories of the *Kulturgeschichte* (or *Siedlungsgeschichte*) school, popular at the end of the nineteenth century and the beginning of the twentieth, which sought to understand past social relations through the study of patterns of land tenure. Their approach now appears dated: in particular their association of ethnic groups with particular patterns of land tenure was too rigid, and they did not adequately account for the influence, at times dramatic, of individual economic and demographic factors. Moreover, they did not allow for the existence of different ways of life alongside each other in the same geographical area. In reality, a neat typology of scattered or nuclear settlements, enclosed or unenclosed fields, and other supposedly constant rural phenomena cannot ever have existed; at most there are recurring, temporary, patterns. The enduring value of *Kulturgeschichte* probably lies in its identification of individual settlement types and, above all, in the fact that it was the first to do this.

To move away from the *Kulturgeschichte* model then, the main feature of the countryside and a strong factor in moulding perceptions was the presence in western Europe throughout the early Middle Ages of vast reaches of wilderness. All economic activity was inextricably bound up with these areas. There was a general diffidence towards nature, a diffidence which could extend to a deep fear of tampering in any way with the natural order. Such wilderness characterized the landscape, considerably so in many places; only after the eleventh century did the balance begin to tilt towards clearance and cultivation and even then most wild areas saw little dramatic change. All classes of society depended, in different ways, on the wilderness and the resources it offered. Hunting in the forests, potentially available to all, was mainly the preserve of the aristocracy. As the part played by freemen in political life decreased, so the aristocracy gradually succeeded in ensuring exclusive rights to the ownership and use of the forests. Non-nobles could still hunt large animals such as boar and deer there until the twelfth century, but then the aristocracy began to be much more jealous of their rights and to keep the large quarry for themselves. This was a particular problem in areas where rough land had been drastically reduced by clearances. Even though we know little of the details of this development and of how it varied over different areas, there is strong evidence that north of the Alps, where the nobility was much more numerous and powerful than in Italy, hunting was an especially important part of aristocratic life. By contrast, in Italy throughout this period the power of the nobles was kept in check by the towns, with their strong bourgeoisie, and the status of the nobles was undermined, if necessary by bringing in outside powers as a counterweight.

The passage quoted from Tasso's *Gerusalemme liberata* at the beginning of this chapter is the prelude to his description of the scene in the forest where the sorcerer Ismen summons the forces of evil. Tasso deliberately exaggerates the sinister aspect of the forest. Such descriptions of vast empty forests, impenetrable and gloomy even by day, unvisited except by hunters, the home of wild beasts, abound in the literature of the period. Quite different were the woods crossed by paths, where sheep and pigs were taken to graze and where shepherds and woodcutters lived and peasants went to gather mushrooms, berries and nuts and to collect wild honey from hollow trees. This was still a relatively untouched landscape and populated by dangerous animals, but it was regarded as familiar and largely tamed territory.

Some areas of forest remained untouched because particular circumstances made intervention difficult: stagnant pools, an absence of useful fruit or nut-bearing trees, steep slopes, or sheer remoteness. In such places there was evidently a distinct boundary where the wood traversed by paths gave way to untracked forest whose dense undergrowth blocked passage to both people and animals. This is clear from the laws made in the late fourteenth century for Mirandola, on the low-lying plain between Modena and the river Po, which forbade the setting of any snare or trap in the part of the woods where domestic animals were grazed. Pigs, sheep and goats, sensing danger where the paths petered out, would not venture into untracked forest. Even hunting was difficult in these areas since horses and hounds found the undergrowth impenetrable and progress could be made only by cutting it back.

Forests which were especially dense, large or remote were regarded with mistrust and were often called *solitudines*, lonely places entered only by the occasional undaunted hermit, brigand or bandit, or intrepid hunter. Most people kept well away, partly from the fear of falling victim to these outlaws. The Po plain was covered with such forest, especially along the Po river and its major tributaries. Towards the sea the forest became ever more extensive, ending in great lagoons and cane-brakes. Such vast untouched forests, waterlogged and interminable, were common north of the Alps, and above all in central Europe; the successive pagan peoples descending on Europe from the east all halted in such *solitudines* before launching their attacks south and west. It was not until the early tenth century, with the eastward advance of Germanic settlers and the eventual settlement and conversion to Christianity in these areas of the former 'barbarians', that the region began to have a degree of civilization.

The second kind of forest, the sort that was familiar and regularly visited, was widespread. In the early Middle Ages land once intensively settled and cultivated everywhere, from the wide lower valleys of the Alps and the Apennines to the foothills and plains close to the towns, continued to revert to forest, marsh and moor. Even the towns, inside their crumbling walls, became overgrown and generally had an increasingly rural aspect as cultivated land dwindled into insignificance in comparison with the great areas of wilderness. Towns and villages were swallowed up by the advancing wilderness, and their ruins, choked by vegetation, were to be found everywhere until eventually monks began to reuse them as building material for their churches and monasteries, as did St Columbanus in France and Italy. When Columbanus reached Italy he learned of a ruined church at Bobbio in the broad valley of the river Trebbia 'in the *solitudo* of the Apennine countryside' and decided to rebuild it. The monastery he founded there was to become one of the

most celebrated of Europe. Evidently even areas of relatively low alti-
tude, like Bobbio, were deserted and overgrown *solitudines*.

At the beginning of the seventh century, then, the wild forest was
ubiquitous, only slowly to be transformed into tracked and tamed forest.
Most forests were of the first, wild type, forbidding places which were
visited only by shepherds with their flocks and herds or by hunters. In his
journey south through France to Italy St Columbanus would have trav-
elled through an empty landscape of wooded mountains and lowlands
with scattered ruins, inhabited by fierce animals such as the pack of
wolves which approached him in the *solitudines* of Burgundy. Another
wolf, according to Paul the Deacon, led his great-grandfather through the
forests of the Alps to his native Friuli after his escape from captivity
among the Avars. As early as the fifth century Sidonius Apollinaris,
Bishop of Clermont, the ancient capital of the Auvergne, was writing that
there were dioceses and parishes in the region without a single priest to
tend souls.

> Everywhere we find churches where the roofs have fallen in and the doors
> are broken and have come off their hinges while the entrances are choked
> by thorns and briars. There are animals inside, wandering in the aisles and
> grazing right up to the altar, where grass is growing. All around is neglect,
> in the town as in the country, and the office is said increasingly seldom.

Churchmen, being educated, felt the burden of such desolation all the
more because they were aware that the world had not always been so.
Their natural sobriety turned easily to alarm at the first sign of anything
awry in nature, such as an eclipse or a famine. In the sixth century,
according to Gregory of Tours, 'at the beginning of the month of
October the sun darkened until more than three-quarters of it was
hidden . . . The star with a tail in the form of a sword, called a comet,
remained overhead for a year and in the sky there were fires and other
fearful sights.'

The sixth century was a grim period, especially in Italy, where the
Gothic wars between the Ostrogoths and the Byzantines continued for
years, devastating the countryside as perhaps never before. Shortly before
the Lombard invasion, plague had arrived from the east, an outbreak
comparable only to the Black Death of 1348 which affected most of
central southern Europe. According to the contemporary account of
Gregory of Tours, the arrival of plague in Clermont was preceded by an
omen: in a disconcerting event, those present at a service in the cathedral
were terrified when a lark suddenly darted into the building and sped
past all the candles, extinguishing them as it skimmed past. So many died
in the subsequent plague that there were no coffins left and the corpses

had to be buried in mass graves. The symptoms of plague were suppurating sores similar to snake bites in the groin and armpit. Victims died in agony after a few days, while the pain and terror drove many out of their minds. The horrors of this ghastly experience were long remembered: as late as the end of the eighth century Paul the Deacon was still able to give a detailed account of it in his *History of the Langobards*, describing how whole towns and villages had been virtually wiped out. In Italy the north, in particular the western central region, was especially hard-hit. The telltale black marks and swellings in the groin and elsewhere on the body so terrified people that they began to see them everywhere, on walls, on clothes, on doors and gates. The response to the calamity, as to every untoward event at the time, was fear and trepidation: on their deathbed delirious victims would suffer delusions, hearing battle trumpets and seeing a mêlée of men and horses. The streets were deserted and wild animals came into the town, where nothing was to be seen except long lines of corpses. No shepherd's whistle was to be heard in the pastures, the unharvested corn stood high and the unpicked grapes lay gleaming on the vines. It was, Paul said, as if the world had returned to its immense original silence, when nothing, animal or human, yet lived.

Even allowing for exaggeration and generalization, and for the fact that some places may not have suffered so greatly, for the inhabitants of Italy, who had already suffered for years as a result of the Gothic wars, this plague must have been the final blow. In such circumstances, conquest of the Italian peninsula was easy for Alboin, the leader of the Lombards. Paul observed that the plague and a terrible famine had previously decimated the population; people can have been in no state to put up any resistance to an invading force.

This was not the last of the plague. It continued to return at intervals to different parts of Italy, possibly for more than a hundred years, though never again with such devastating consequences. Paul noted that in 680, when an eclipse of the sun immediately preceded a lunar eclipse and the heavens darkened, there was a new outbreak of bubonic plague in Pavia, the capital of the kingdom of Italy. Plague raged for three months through the summer, claiming numerous victims and wreaking havoc as far as Rome. According to Paul the inhabitants of Pavia fled to the hills, and grass and bushes sprang up in the deserted streets and squares as the city was turned into a ghost town. It was believed by the few who remained that at night a good angel and a bad angel walked through the empty streets. Terror-stricken, people would listen out for the thud of the spear with which the bad angel, at the bidding of the good angel, struck their door. They counted the number of blows because each betokened a death in the house at daybreak. People prayed for an end to the plague but were told by a certain man – perhaps a priest – that it would end only when they dedicated an altar to St Sebastian in the church of San Pietro in Vincola. Paul described how, once the relics of St Sebastian had been brought from Rome and the altar erected, the plague came to an end.

Shortly afterwards, cruelty, the supernatural and, perhaps, memories of the horrors of the plague are all found, in a blend typical of the period, in another episode in Paul's history. It suggests the dark world of kings and courtiers, a shadowy world of suspicion and violence and a dread of the unknown. The Lombard King Cunipert had decided to murder two men who had plotted against him, Aldo and Grauso. While the king and his accomplice, the master of the horse, were discussing plans in one of the chambers of the royal palace, they were disturbed by a large fly. When it landed on a windowsill Cunipert struck at it with his knife, but succeeded only in cutting off one of its legs. Meanwhile Aldo and Grauso, who knew nothing of the plot, were drawing near to the palace. They were approached by a lame man with a stump for one leg, who told them what the king intended; they accordingly sought sanctuary in a church. Learning of this, Cunipert believed that the master of the horse had betrayed him. However, once it had become clear that the man had never left the palace, the king had Aldo and Grauso questioned, asking them why they had taken refuge in the church. On hearing their reply, that they had been warned of the plot, Cunipert promised not to punish them for their treachery and asked who had revealed his plans. When they told him of the one-legged man who had warned them of the trap, the king realized that the fly had been an evil spirit. He was so frightened that he pardoned the two men.

In pardoning them, Cunipert was perhaps swayed by memories of Alahis, his rival, who had been killed in the battle for the crown and mutilated by Cunipert's own men. They had cut off his head and legs and beaten his body to pulp. Cunipert later built a monastery on the site of this victory. His motives seem to have been mixed: penance, perhaps, in part, but also gratitude for a victory which, as Paul tells us, was gained 'with God's help'.

The impression of the powerful given by chronicles is one of cruelty and a brutal use of force coexisting with fear and remorse. People seem to have been easily thrown into confusion and alarm by unusual or disturbing events. As for the mass of people, we know little of their responses. The fight for survival in an unforgiving environment which had everywhere reverted to nature left little scope for civilized niceties. In the mid-seventh century the Edict of Rothari was obliged to discuss the problem of the violent brawls which would break out between shepherds in the great forests. It was all too easy accidentally to lead flocks and herds on to someone else's land; the result was often fisticuffs. The concept of private property was hazy, especially in areas of wilderness, felt to be bestowed by nature for the use of all. Boundaries were marked by signs cut into trees or by large stones or boulders, either already there or shifted to a particular spot. It was tempting, though risky, to move boundaries by marking new trees or by moving the stones, or even to obliterate them by chopping down the trees. This was a capital offence if done by a *servus*, a serf.

Until the very end of the seventh century the area of land cultivated must have been insignificant compared to the vast tracts which were still wild. This was true even of areas close to towns and villages, where rough land was first cultivated, especially after the ninth century. Even after the great extension of cultivation, however, there were many exceptions to the general pattern. The marshes immediately surrounding the town of Modena, for example, remained undrained for centuries, and low-lying land in general was difficult to drain and cultivate because of the countless deep pools. The high plateaux, with too little rainfall to support more than a few sheep, and the forests of the highest mountain ridges remained untouched until recent years. At the beginning of the Middle Ages wilderness was the norm, and trees, bushes and undergrowth everywhere encroached on and smothered the ruins of long-deserted towns and villages. Where cities had once flourished, there was now endless forest and marsh. Travellers through the forest would come across ruins of abandoned towns looming up before them in the silence, populated now only by wild beasts. As we have seen, the long journey of St Columbanus and his companions was punctuated by encounters with ruins, which they used to build monasteries, thereby bringing back life to long-deserted areas. However, the monastic foundations of the sixth and seventh centuries were insignificant compared to the extent and size of Roman towns and villages. Such monasteries, and the communities which grew up around them, were largely dependent on a silvo-pastoral economy, and these first efforts at colonization were swallowed up by the endless forest and marsh.

Though the economy of the sixth and seventh centuries was primitive and unsophisticated, the drastic reduction in population meant that there were sufficient resources for all. Food could be gained from hunting, fishing, stock-raising and gathering wild fruits, berries and nuts, as well as from what limited agriculture was practised. However, people were at the mercy of this environment, vulnerable to natural forces and to extremes of climate. A warm spring meant early blossom and buds, which might then succumb to late frosts or drought. Until agriculture developed, in the ninth century, the silvo-pastoral economy meant that it was impossible to store sufficient food to guard entirely against malnutrition and famine, or against the epidemics which often followed and which took a heavy toll of a population which was already debilitated.

War was a further scourge, claiming many victims. Disorder was endemic, brawls, robbery and murder everyday. Fear dominated whenever social order collapsed. We cannot make even a rough guess at the frequency of violent events but they are mentioned too often in chronicles not to reflect reality, while the laconic manner in which they are described suggests a weary acceptance. Only the most dramatic events are noted, and the descriptions lack the shocked tone and minute detail of later medieval chronicles, by writers who were evidently less accustomed to such brutality. The grim trio of war, famine and disease appear so often in chronicles that they appear to be regarded as the normal course of events; the impression left is that the recording of such events is merely a tedious duty. But anguish is often apparent in the terror and delirious hallucinations described in the chronicles which is all too real. Stoicism in the face of a harsh environment did not prevent people from feeling distress and apprehension. Paul the Deacon described the period when Pope Gregory the Great wrote his *Dialogues*:

> In this year, plague, with swellings in the groin, again ravaged Ravenna, Grado and Istria, as it had thirty years earlier. Agilulf made peace with the Avars but Childebert declared war on his cousin, Hilperic's son. In the war between them as many as 30,000 men fell. A bitterly cold winter followed, the worst in living memory. In the land of the Briones, blood fell from the clouds and flowed into the rivers.

The *Dialogues* are quite different from Gregory's other writings. Gregory's aim in them was to show the tenacity of the Christian faith and of the will to survive, even in times of crisis, and so behind the many figures who appear in the *Dialogues* the general poverty and precariousness of life is apparent. As Gregory describes it, the life of churchmen was little different from that of peasants; everyone found it a hard struggle to survive. All yearned for another world, glimpsed in dreams and visions, but unattainable. Gregory often describes scenes of everyday rural life, which are all the more credible as evidence because they are recounted not for their own sake but as background detail in the accounts of miracles: the smoke rising from sheaves of corn set on fire after they had been cut by Probus, Bishop of Rieti, who prayed to God for help to save his supply of grain for the coming year; the priest Sanctolus, building a chapel in Umbria, without any bread to give the workmen; the hermit who lived in the forests of Samnium with only a few beehives; Isaac, a monk who lived in poverty in the mountains near Spoleto 'in the earliest times of the Goths' – soon disciples came to Isaac and tried to persuade him to accept the generous donations which were offered to him, but he refused, insisting on common poverty. Gregory gives a picture of them all, bent over, digging the soil.

Against the grim backdrop of wars, palace intrigue and every kind of violence, work in the countryside was never-ending. Ditches had to be dug around fields and villages to protect them from flooding, houses built, farms established. Tracks had to be made through the great forests and boundaries marked by letters cut into the biggest trees or by stones or boulders manoeuvred into place. Pigs and sheep had to be watched over in the plains and on the hills. The struggle to survive, to combat the ubiquitous wilderness, was unceasing. During the slow recovery after the collapse of the ancient world, there were gradual efforts to re-establish a degree of control over nature. In the wilderness the statues of pagan gods were silent witnesses of this renewal, until in time both they and the forest around them vanished.

Sometimes the sources make explicit mention of this process; at other times it has to be gleaned from chronicles, as only clerics were literate and their main interest naturally was in the activities of monks and priests. Between the sixth and the eighth centuries there can have been little difference between the monk or priest and the peasant; a rich and powerful Church, with splendidly clad ecclesiastics and richly caparisoned horses, scarcely yet existed. At Bobbio it was the monks themselves who ploughed the fields for sowing, who cut down trees, enclosed vineyards and worked the mills. Wearing a gauntlet in order to wield an axe or spade, St Columbanus would have looked no different from any woodcutter or peasant. The monastic rule of the time clearly envisaged physical labour since it advised a diet sufficient to be able to work in the fields; even wine was permitted in moderation. The extreme asceticism of eastern contemplative monasticism was as inappropriate to their way of life as was the isolation of the hermits who continued to live alone in the caves and forests of western Europe, and who were regarded with wary admiration by the monks toiling in monastery fields.

In the heart of the ancient, empty forests, countless small bands of monks led a life no different from that of the peasants who ventured into the forests to clear land for cultivation. Little by little, their combined efforts made inroads into, and eventually erased, the great forests which had covered almost all of Europe in the early Middle Ages. It was an attack on many fronts, though the result was often a tamed, tracked forest where animals could be grazed, rather than extensive clearances with stretches of cultivated land. This early medieval economy, termed silvo-pastoral by historians, would mark the face of Europe for centuries, as the resources and attraction of the forest were many. Nobles and peasants hunted there and saints and hermits, seeking out the most impenetrable parts or the highest summits, found solitude for prayer and revelation.

The development of agriculture, slow as it was, meant that an ever larger population could be supported. It also had political repercussions, ensuring wealth and power for a small group of people, a group which over time became even smaller. This was a phenomenon especially of Italy after the Carolingian conquest. Outside Italy a strong aristocracy had already emerged. Although in general the aristocracy was keen to preserve the wild areas, this task fell, especially in Italy, to the higher nobility.

3

Death

In his poetry the great monk Alcuin was intensely aware of the evanescence of the physical world and of the speed at which everything moved towards its final dissolution. Alcuin's concern with the end of the world was no mere literary conceit; in a world where deaths outnumbered births he wrote elegiacally on the precariousness of life, on the constant presence of death. High infant mortality, war, disease, and malnutrition and famine resulting from bad weather and ruined harvests all made for a low expectation of life. Few adults had a father still alive: in documents recording land deals (sale, exchange or rent) in which parties are specified by their father's name, references to the 'son of the late . . .' are common ('Pietro del fu Andrea', 'Paolo di Antonio di buona memoria'). The deaths of nobles in battle, or the death of the children of noble or royal houses at an early age from disease or during famine and epidemic, are a recurring feature in chronicles.

We are far from understanding the impact of this constant association with death; we know nothing of the suffering, remorse and terror of those who died and those who watched them die. All we can say is that death undoubtedly inspired a degree of awe and its presence could be daunting. Even in this period it was difficult to accept. Very little is known of how reactions to it varied between different groups within society. When a powerful figure died, it was common for chroniclers to note that his death coincided with some natural disaster, while the gifts given by ordinary people to churches and monasteries suggest that they, too, were anxious to help ensure eternal salvation for themselves and for their families. Death, like natural disaster, was a fact of life. For the aristocracy, for whom war and killing were a way of life, death was always a very immediate possibility, though wars were of course not on the scale of those of the twentieth century.

'The presence of death'

Christ and Abbot Gunbold. Evangelistary of the second quarter of the eleventh century, reproduced courtesy of Landesbibliothek, Stuttgart, photograph: Hirmer Fotoarchiv, Munich.

Precise estimates of population are impossible but in general, although some areas still supported fairly high populations, population density was low, and many areas were deserted or virtually so. Inventories of the great estates mention large areas of forest, moor and marsh and only a comparatively small amount of cultivated land, while the area within city walls was largely taken up by fields and vineyards. The living were outnumbered by the dead; in time cemeteries must have reached a size and importance almost impossible to imagine. It was a world of dead people, a fact which helps explain the sombre outlook of clerics, help-lessly watching as life was extinguished before their eyes. It also explains the huge number of donations to the Church, prompted by the fear of death and by the desire to ensure prayers for the hosts who lay buried in and around the churches awaiting the Last Judgment. A well-known historian has described this early medieval world as one of young people. Indeed it was, but it was even more a world of the dead. This is apparent from private documents, and especially from petitions from communities to rulers, dating mostly from the tenth century, the period infamous as a result of the Hungarian raids, but also found later. These usually list the names of everyone in the community and, as has been noted, those mentioned as heads of families seldom have a father still alive.

The number of churches grew, especially after the eighth century, as a result of the conversion to Christianity of increasingly large numbers of people. Superficial as such conversions often were, they meant that more churches and cemeteries were required to bury the dead. In the tenth and eleventh centuries there might be as many as several hundred churches and monasteries within the area of a modern diocese. Most of them were private foundations presided over by a member of the original founder's family, and frequently with very few members, although religious houses established by members of the higher or middle aristocracy often became major foundations with large communities of monks or nuns. Such houses might have to set a maximum number of members so as to avoid too much pressure on the resources of the monastery.

In the tenth century, when early medieval civilization was at its highest point, Italy had an extraordinarily high number not only of monasteries and nunneries but also of churches without any association with a religious house, that is, *pievi* (rural baptismal churches) and cathedrals. *Pievi* might have as many as a dozen priests, excluding minor clerics, and in a single diocese there would normally be twenty or more such churches. Cathedrals had between twenty and sixty priests as well as lower clergy, and monasteries of royal or aristocratic foundation had still more members. The high number of clerics ensured constant prayers for the souls of the dead and for those who had prudently made provision when they were alive. Quantity was what mattered here; more than anything else it was the sheer number of prayers which counted for salvation. It is impossible to estimate how many clerics there were, but they clearly made up a significant proportion of the population.

It was an age which knew death well, when death had not yet acquired the unnatural, even horrifying, associations which would come once the population had grown and births began to outnumber deaths. In the early Middle Ages death was regarded with respect and, perhaps, a degree of apprehension, as the moment of the passing to the next world. Though there was dismay at the deaths of powerful rulers or saints, who seemed to offer some protection in a hostile world, even in their cases dying was regarded as part of nature, like the solar or lunar eclipses which chronicles associated with such deaths. Everyone, including the educated, was thrown into consternation by such deaths, just as they were by natural phenomena, believing them to be punishments for sin or premonitions of disaster. In the year 840, marked by conflict between the Emperor and his sons, and between his sons, chroniclers were alarmed by the death of Louis the Pious. They recorded it as coinciding with terrifying eclipses which were interpreted as a warning for anyone who threatened to undermine the unity of the empire.

The lives of saints, monks and other clerics demonstrate how they lived in permanent readiness for death, while even those more attached to this world met death with equanimity when it came, fearful only of whether they would attain paradise. A common theme is the saint who falls ill and eagerly anticipates death and eternal bliss, only to be thwarted by God and to recover. These accounts of model deaths are of course intended to be edifying, but the complete absence of any fear of death itself is none the less telling. Clearly everyone accepted the near certainty of death at what would now be an early age. Few lived beyond the age of sixty: records of legal cases show that it was hard to find anyone to give evidence about events which had occurred when most of those involved had been children.

There were no lists of births, and we can only speculate whether ecclesiastical or administrative reasons lay behind this. Dates of death are often found, however, in the lists circulated between monasteries and churches of deceased men and women whose souls are to be prayed for. Similarly, the *libri memoriali* circulated between religious houses – lists of those still alive who wanted prayers in anticipation of their death to help ensure their salvation – are concerned with the dead, not the living. Chronicles also usually give the date of death of important figures, but dates of birth are rarely found either there or in documents. The inference is that life was less important than death. Certainly people appear to have made little effort to cling to life, while the meagre livelihood available to most made survival into old age unlikely. There was a vicious circle where the frequency and precocity of death meant that life was little valued, and where a scant regard for life and health in turn made death more likely.

The reasons why life was cheap were many, and included psychological, institutional and economic factors. It was not that people were indifferent to their own needs, but they could attend to them only as far as the limited material resources of the time would allow. Likewise, people were unable to conceive of any reaction to disease or natural disasters other than fatalistic submission. The birth-rate was high: in peasant families three or four children often survived to maturity, and so, given the high rate of mortality, many more must have been born. In the ninth and tenth centuries, in families of higher social standing, where we often have partial or complete lists of family members, it was common for there to be four, five, six or even more surviving siblings. The number is explained by the higher standard of living enjoyed by such families, with more and better food and clothes (though an excessive consumption of meat and wine often counteracted these benefits). In the second half of the eighth century Paul the Deacon described the wife of Pemmo, the powerful Duke of Friuli who had ruled at the beginning of the century:

> Pemmo had as wife a woman called Ratberga. Because she was of peasant appearance she repeatedly begged her husband to send her away and to find a wife more suitable for so great a leader. But Pemmo was a wise man and replied that her modesty, honesty and character were more important to him than physical beauty. He had three sons by her, Rachis, Ratcait and Astulf, all valiant in battle, whose birth raised the humility of their mother to high honour.

Pride in sons, especially brave ones, and a preference for strength and fertility in women rather than beauty, are recurring features of early medieval chronicles. In the tenth century, Liutprand of Cremona described King Hugh's concubines in his *Antapodosis*. Although Liutprand's misogyny is transparent, he nevertheless had grudging praise for women if they proved good childbearers.

> Hugh had a number of concubines, but for three especially he entertained an ardent and most disgraceful passion. The first was called Pezola, a woman of the lowest servile origins, by whom he had a son named Boso, appointed by him after Wido's death as bishop of the church of Piacenza. The second was Roza, daughter of the Walpert whom we have mentioned above as having been beheaded, who bore him a daughter remarkable for

her beauty. The third was a Roman named Stephania, who had by him
Tedbald, afterwards made archdeacon of Milan with the proviso that on
the archbishop's death he should be his successor. (trans. F. A. Wright)

The Carolingian annals stress the fact that Charlemagne lived to the
age of seventy, a rare achievement; in fact he outlived most of his
children. The high mortality encouraged people to have numerous children and encouraged widowers to marry for a second or third time if, like
Charlemagne, they lived longer than average. This helps explain why
concubines were common, a phenomenon which cannot be explained by
the coarseness of prevailing social customs alone. Having more children
increased the chances that the family and its power would survive. In a
world where life was nasty, brutish and short and conflict endemic it was
natural to seek to ensure the survival of the family by producing a high
number of children.

The high mortality and the great numbers buried in or near churches
gave the dead an overwhelming presence and made them seem very real.
They were envisaged as constantly active, as advising, warning and
chastising, to be found even in battle or fiercely protecting church and
monastery property. With no systematic procedure for canonization, vast
hosts of saints and those who had died 'in the odour of sanctity' were
believed to exist; it was natural that they should return to this world. The
boundary between the two worlds, that of the living and that of the dead,
was hazy and people believed that it was easy to pass between the two.
On their sickbed, people might pass into the next world and witness the
horrors of hell or the delights of heaven, returning to this life the wiser
for what they had seen. Even people who were definitely dead would
return to earth to pray for their soul at their own tomb or at that of a
popular saint. With no clear demarcation line between the two worlds,
the ability to come and go as God decreed seemed a natural consequence
of the fragility of life. In time, though, under the influence of the Church,
the image of death gradually changed and the dead who returned to this
world came to be seen as threatening and fearsome.

By the ninth and tenth centuries churches and monasteries had acquired great wealth, which was often appropriated or violently seized;
the patron saint of a church tended to be a stern guardian, vigilantly
watching over ecclesiastical property and frequently as violent in its
defence as the powerful nobles who terrorized and stole from the Church
and from peasants. Quite apart from the role of saints in defending
church possessions, it is apparent that they were increasingly a force to be
reckoned with, touchy and sensitive to slights and competing with one
other as patrons and healers or as guardians in battle. The author of the
chronicle of the Novalesca, the famous and wealthy monastery in Pied-

mont, described how one day the sacristan saw the candles in the church keep relighting even though he had extinguished them after divine office. The candles continued to rekindle themselves however many times he snuffed them out, and the sacristan was baffled and terrified by the supernatural and disturbing presence this betrayed. Only when it was remembered that two saints had been accidentally omitted from the office for that day, and when a mass had been celebrated for them, would the candles stay extinguished. Once the saints had been appeased they disturbed no longer.

The relics of St Martin similarly produced inexplicable happenings when they were removed from Tours for safety during the Viking raids. Miracles occurred in the church where they had been taken and when they were returned to Tours the entire journey was marked by miracles. Accounts of similar journeys survive and it is evident that the passage or arrival of relics, especially those of a famous saint like St Martin, patron saint of France, would produce both fear and reverence. On another occasion, according to the Novalesa chronicle, St Peter and St Paul were supposed to have commanded two demons to go to the house of a nobleman who had seized valuables from the monastery. They burst in on him as he was dining and gave him such a beating that he went mad; he never recovered and died without the last rites. Such instances of personal intervention by saints are common, though violence was not always involved and the saints are never actually themselves responsible for shedding blood. In the incident from the Novalesa chronicle, for instance, St Peter and St Paul conducted the beating using the demons as agents and even substituted sticks for the swords which the demons were originally carrying. It appears that when they had decided on death as a punishment, saints would never themselves inflict it.

Normally, however, the mere sight of such alarming apparitions, during sleep or at any time of day or night, was enough to alarm and deter a delinquent noble, to convey a message to a pious Christian, or to guide back to the right path a good man who had strayed. The more important the saint, in terms both of status in heaven and of the number of churches and monasteries dedicated to him or her, the more often the saint appeared. This is the case with St Benedict, the founder of monasticism in western Europe: the chronicle of the monastery of the Novalesa describes his appearance there one night. Saints often chose churches or monasteries dedicated to them to make their appearances. Violence and bloodshed was left to lesser shades or to convenient demons, although the most lethal of weapons were available to be used. The same chronicle of the Novalesa recorded that a powerful but recalcitrant lord who was in the habit of seizing monastic property dreamed that he was being violently beaten about the head with a heavy axe by the ghost of a dead priest from the monastery. He woke with a violent headache, fell ill, and died.

It is no coincidence that such spirited action from the dead, both from saints and from lay people, is found especially in the tenth and eleventh centuries. It echoes the values of the emerging aristocracy, trained in warfare and accustomed to using violence to enforce its will. Central government was weak compared to the Carolingian period; then the power of local lords had still to some extent been circumscribed by the network of royal administration, and the great feudal dynasties had yet to be established. But in time the Church, too, came to have its own military elite, consisting of powerful saints and their agents, an army which was not content simply to defend its own possessions but, like the nobles, was willing to resort to violence to augment them. As early as the Carolingian period, laws urged churchmen not to intimidate the laity into leaving property to the Church by threatening them with the wrath of God. Peasants and members of noble clans alike, fearful of an unpleasant fate after death or even of what awaited them in life if they refused, would give up all their worldly goods to churches and monasteries dedicated to particularly redoubtable saints, leaving themselves only a scant livelihood. Plagues would come to an end only when churches were dedicated to well-known saints, and similarly after a hard-won victory it was prudent to dedicate a church to a saint. Paul the Deacon described how, probably in 700, 'at this time King Cunipert, much loved by his people, left this earthly life after ruling over the Lombards for twelve years. He had had a monastery built near Coronate, on the site where he had met Alahis in battle, and he dedicated it to St Gregory the Martyr.'

4

Beauty

In Canto XIX of *Purgatory* Dante dreams of 'a woman, stammering of speech and squint-eyed, crooked on her feet, with crippled hands and sallow hue'. As he looks at her, colour creeps into her wan face and she is transformed under his entranced gaze 'as the sun revives cold limbs benumbed by the night', until she becomes beautiful, colour spreading into her features so that she inspires feelings of love in men. She begins to sing and tells him that she is a siren. Dante is drawn strongly to her, but Beatrice, 'holy and alert', appears and Virgil rips off the siren's garments to reveal her belly, from which emanates such a stench that Dante wakes with a start.

Clerical writers had always censured physical beauty in general and were especially disapproving of female beauty; the theme of women who at first enchant but who then become hideously ugly or who disgust in some other way has its roots in this tradition. Much earlier, Liutprand of Cremona, describing a strikingly beautiful concubine of King Hugh of Italy, felt obliged to remind his readers that those gazing on such beauty should recall the commonplace that all flesh was destined to decay. A little earlier, too, St Odo, the great abbot of Cluny, in one of his principal works, had warned against succumbing to beauty:

> Physical beauty is but skin-deep. And if we could see what lurks underneath the skin – just as, so Boethius tells us, the lynx is able to see deep into objects – the very sight of women would disgust us. What we perceive as their beauty is in truth mucus, blood, phlegm and gall. If we reflect on what lies inside our throats, our noses and our bellies, we know that only filth lies there. And since we cannot abide to touch mucus and excrement even with our fingertips, why then should we ever desire to embrace a sack of excrement?

For Odo, then, the skin was only a covering for slimy secretions, disgusting fluids and excrement. Since what appeared to be beauty was merely a flimsy veil covering these loathsome and nauseating substances, no one, he argued, should wish to have anything to do with women, even the most beautiful. This theme recurs in Odo's life of St Gerald of Aurillac, a classic piece of hagiography. He describes how the saint was tempted only once by the lures of the flesh: overcome by the beauty of the daughter of one of his men, he found himself quite besotted with her. 'Incautiously he let his gaze linger on the delicate tones of her complexion and began to take delight in it. O, why did he not straightaway seek to picture to himself what lay hidden under her skin! For it is from this alone that the skin derives its colouring.'

According to Odo, what attracted Gerald was in reality, in a definition similar to that already quoted, merely a mass of repulsive substances. This specious beauty so captivated Gerald that he arranged with the girl's mother to come to the house at night. But, by God's grace, on entering the house he had an experience similar to that of Dante: the real nature of woman was revealed to him and on the very brink of sin the virtuous Gerald was saved. The girl had been standing in front of the fire which had been lit at dusk to warm the house on the chilly winter evening. As Gerald approached her, he saw her change against the ruddy firelight. He looked on in horror as her beauty vanished and, in a hideous metamorphosis, she became repulsive. He rushed out, leapt on to his horse and rode headlong through the bitterly cold night until dawn to punish himself for his wicked intentions.

Though Gerald never forgot that terrible ride, God clearly did not regard it as sufficient punishment. Gerald was afflicted with a long period of blindness, a fitting punishment for his inability to see the shameful and abhorrent matter which lay beneath women's soft and delicate skin. Only God's grace, which Gerald had continued to pray for even at the height of his passion, had prevented him from succumbing to lust. Odo described how, unlike the great majority who constantly yielded to temptation, Gerald had come through his adolescent years unsullied by 'the shipwreck of purity'. The comments are revealing of Odo's own attitude and of attitudes in general to women, female beauty and sexual attraction. Indeed Odo goes on to describe how Gerald, determined to remain a virgin, refused ever to marry, rejecting even the sister of the Duke of Aquitaine, a powerful man and his close friend.

In an age when most people would have borne the marks of unremitting outdoor physical work in a primitive and harsh environment, beauty, whether real or imagined, must have been conspicuous. This probably accounts for the attraction of refined features, such as Gerald's delicate neck, specifically mentioned by Odo and an unexpected feature in one with a powerful physique from hunting and military exercises. A soft white complexion was regarded highly, as can later be seen clearly in paintings; it would have contrasted with the ruddy and weatherbeaten skin of people who spent their lives out of doors at the mercy of the elements. Though we know of these preferences only from the writings of the educated, it seems likely that those who lived out of doors, engaged in military exercises and hunting or working in the fields, would have shared this ideal. People probably had a keen eye for physical difference, and the much-prized delicate fair complexion was far removed from the everyday reality of weathered skin.

Strong passions allied with crude sexuality are frequently, and graphically, described in contemporary chronicles. In the mid-tenth century Liutprand, future Bishop of Cremona, wrote of lascivious women and lecherous men, apparently well satisfied to have uncovered and recorded their sins. Men and women in love do not appear in his pages, only lust and wantonness. The downfall of the wife of Berengar I was the passion she conceived for a short hairy priest with abnormally large genitals. She was discovered, partly because she had made little effort to keep the affair quiet. Some centuries earlier Paul the Deacon told how Romilda, the recently widowed wife of the valiant Gisulf, Duke of Friuli, was overcome by a fateful passion as she looked down from the walls of Cividale on the virile leader of the Avars, wheeling and turning on his horse. Solely in order to sleep with him she opened the gates of the city to him, thus betraying the remnants of Gisulf's renowned army. To return to the tenth century, as the men of the King of Italy were about to castrate a man belonging to the enemy near Spoleto, his Byzantine wife cried out that no worse fate could befall her. Contemporary chronicles abound in similar stories which, since they come from every part of Europe and from the entire early medieval period, must reflect a general mentality.

The very crudeness and brutality of so much sexual behaviour triggered an opposite reaction in the form of a desire for an evanescent, intangible beauty. Some even spurned real physical beauty itself, preferring to surrender their imagination to visions of lights and sounds and perfumes of unearthly beauty. Jonas of Bobbio described cases of nuns in the seventh century who had passed briefly to paradise while lying ill; when they came back to life, they told of the radiant light of paradise, and they continued to yearn for it as long as they lived out the earthly span allotted them. In his *Dialogues* Pope Gregory the Great described similar occurrences among monks at about the same time. Paradise was frequently imagined as a garden with trees and shrubs, flowers and glinting white stones, the antithesis of the ubiquitous semi-wild country of the time. The gross physical reality of this earthly world was contrasted with an exquisitely fragile and insubstantial beauty, and even, as in the descriptions of heaven as consisting of light, with the next world, regarded as the only true and lasting one.

Between these two extremes lay the ideals of human beauty, oscillating between pale translucent skin and slender limbs, and vigour and physical strength. Although we have little idea of how widespread these visions of the other world were, they serve to emphasize the barbarity and brutalism of the physical world. It can be no coincidence that the contrast between such graphic, often grotesque, stories of physical love and the escapist mystical visions of lights, heavenly music and indescribably sweet smells was at its greatest in the early Middle Ages. When a saint's body was exhumed, the air would be deliciously perfumed, and on their deathbeds saintly men and women would see angelic figures all around, while those present would hear music and smell sweet perfumes. Often when such a man or woman died there would be a dazzling light in the sky, indicating that their soul was rising to heaven.

Over physical beauty, as over the entire physical world, lay the shadow of death. Educated men, attuned to the brevity of life in a world where few reached old age, were more aware of this; the great mass of people were probably more prone to regard death as part of the normal course of events, of the cycle of nature. In their treatises and sermons, priests and monks emphasized the imminence of death in order to impress on their listeners the nearness of the fearful Day of Judgment when they would appear before God. All were aware of the ubiquity of birth and death, of physical weakness and the extreme vulnerability to age and to the inescapable ravages of disease or sickness. Throughout the period, if they found themselves compelled to mention physical beauty in their chronicles or lives of saints, clerics would write that 'she was beautiful, given that all flesh is fated to rot.' Yet these passages have none of the grisly and horrific associations which death was to acquire in the later Middle Ages. Death was still viewed as a comrade, even if inconvenient at times; only later did it become an unwelcome and hostile intruder.

5

Hunting

In the *Vita Odonis*, his life of St Odo of Cluny, John of Rome recalled Odo's memories of his military education. He described how, as a boy, the future monk had been taught how to fight and hunt until God, 'who shows the way of salvation even to those who are reluctant', deflected Odo from this rigorous schedule. Earlier, in his own life of St Gerald of Aurillac, Odo had dwelled on the same subjects of hunting and fighting, recounting how as a boy Gerald was taught 'to hunt with Molossian hounds, to use a bow, and to fly falcons and hawks, launching them into the air with one skilful toss of his arm'. However, 'by God's salvation', Gerald fell ill and could not continue his activities, just as had been the case with Odo himself, who had been afflicted by a persistent headache for three years.

In the tenth century military training and hunting were of equal importance for the scions of the aristocracy, and they came, especially after the twelfth century, to be the prerogative of the nobility and a mark of their status and inalienable rights. The rights of others were increasingly restricted: they were only allowed to hunt smaller animals, and if they were permitted to hunt larger quarry, as in some places was the case, the lord could claim the head and other desirable parts of any animals caught. Odo's nostalgia for his own youth and for his prowess in these trials of strength, from which only divine grace had turned him, is ill-concealed. In his *Collationes*, however, he strongly condemned hunting:

If we wish to avoid the cruelty of Cain, we must live a life of prayer and must shun any activity which distracts us from this, avoiding wrong-doers. Indeed the man of whom the Gospels speak, who was rescued by the Good Samaritan, would not have been beset by robbers had he not gone out from Jerusalem, which here represents the contemplation of peace . . . Thus it is written that 'Jacob was a plain man, living in tents.' Esau, on the other hand, who was not beloved of God, was a man who loved the chase.

For Odo, to hunt was to indulge in a violent activity which distracted one from thought and was the antithesis of the stillness necessary for meditation on God. Despite his censure, he clearly retained affection for a way of life which exalted the expression of physical strength in hunting. While Odo sought to reform the monasteries, both secular and regular clergy devoted much time and energy to hunting, an integral part of their way of life and increasingly regarded as the prerogative of the aristocracy, both lay and clerical. That churchmen were engaged in hunting early on is apparent from Carolingian legislation which prohibited abbots and abbesses from keeping hounds in their religious houses and outlawed hunting for clerics – though, like the laws forbidding the expropriation of land from the weakest, such laws were probably ignored.

Frankish lords created hunting forests on hitherto open land; in Italy the hunting forests owned by the Este and Gonzaga families survived into very recent times. Though hunting could be a valuable source of food, its significance lay chiefly in its cultural role. This was particularly so for the aristocracy, which in the late Middle Ages was determined to preserve forests for hunting, if necessary by depriving peasants of land needed for corn and vines. Since peasants, needing new land to supply food, were engaged in clearing the forests from the eleventh and twelfth centuries onwards, there may well have been resentment of such hunting forests, dominated by the aristocracy and symbolizing, along with the castles and massive dovecotes, aristocratic privilege. It is in the period of the early Middle Ages that the roots of the later obsession of royalty and the aristocracy with hunting lie, and it persisted for centuries. Saint-Simon several times refers to Louis XIV's passion for hunting: 'The King was devoted to the outdoor life . . . He would go out for only three reasons: to hunt deer with his packs of hounds at least once a week, and frequently more often, at Marly or at Fontainebleau . . .'

The rituals and the annual rhythm of hunting were established in the early Middle Ages. Hunting took place above all in autumn and might continue for several months. Evidence abounds that kings and the Emperor, preferring the country and the open air to the town, would spend a considerable amount of time on their great estates, or *curtes*. The same was true of the aristocracy. This preference, a feature of the entire period, first appears in the early Middle Ages. Royal diplomas issued in the autumn months frequently bear the name of some favourite hunting spot; it is thus possible to use them to establish the regular annual hunting season and, where sufficient documents survive, to estimate its duration, often of several months. Diplomas issued by the Emperor Louis II of Italy in 874 show that he was at Corteolona, on the Po plain near Pavia, on 1 September, on 9, 13 and 15 October and on 1 November; on 8 December he was at a place as yet unidentified, but which is definitely not a town. Louis would often stay in one of his hunting lodges on a vast estate near present-day Alessandria, a place which is referred to as *Orba* and which can perhaps be identified with the modern Capriata d'Orba. Evidently it had also been a favourite spot of the Lombard kings: Paul the Deacon describes two incidents which took place in the forest of the *curtis* Orba when Cunipert was king (688–700), and he records how Liutprand as king (713–44) later hunted there: 'Liutprand was hunting in the forest called *Urbe* when one of the men in his party, trying to hit a deer, accidentally shot and injured one of the king's nephews, Aufus, his sister's son.'

Here we find a further dimension, death or injury as the unintended consequence of hunting. Fatal injuries were frequent. In the autumn of 898 Lambert, King of Italy and Emperor, met his death in this same forest when he hit his head on a branch while galloping in pursuit of a boar, though there were rumours that it had in reality been murder. In a macabre short story, one of his last, Guy de Maupassant tells how in the eighteenth century a nobleman from Normandy died in the same way. The story, 'Le loup', part of the *Clair de Lune* collection, describes the furious hunting of a huge wolf by two noble brothers, both experienced huntsmen, during an autumn night in 1764. The chase begins when they notice the dead leaves of a large bush rustle, revealing the dark outline of the beast. They pursue it at full gallop, crashing through branches and undergrowth in a headlong chase, blind and deaf to all else, until one of them cracks his head on a thick branch and is killed. As his brother lifts his body on to his horse to carry him home, he catches sight of the wolf again and renews the chase. Finally, in a deep and rocky moonlit gulley, he confronts the wolf in a horrifying fight and strangles it.

In his introduction Maupassant tells us that the story had been told on 3 November, on the day of St Hubert (the patron saint of hunters), and in fact the story appeared on 14 November 1882 in the periodical *Le Gaulois*. The violence and the sense of mystery and legend found in it recall *The Legend of St Julian the Hospitaller* by Gustave Flaubert, Maupassant's master, published five years earlier. However, Maupassant's tale owes more to the world of the rural aristocracy of Normandy, heirs to an ancient way of life, and to Maupassant's constant interest, deriving from local familiarity and perhaps even from his own family tradition, in atavistic themes of terror and violence.

In 1052 Boniface of Canossa, the most powerful figure in northern Italy, died while hunting in one of his great forests on the Po plain. Rumour spread that he had been killed by poisoned arrows. Yet again the forest had been the scene of violent death.

6

Violence

Throughout the Middle Ages all social relations were characterized by violence and aggression, a fact that is familiar to us. It was not just military exercises, growing out of the needs of defensive and offensive war, which were marked by a high degree of brutality. But although we know that violence and cruelty were widespread during the period, it is hard to form a true picture of their nature and extent. Studies of the sources for the period have concentrated on what they reveal of other areas, of economic, social, political, ecclesiastical and cultural history, and there has been much less analysis from the perspective of violence. The studies which do exist are unsystematic and anecdotal. Institutional and social historians have concentrated largely on analyses of landholding and political power as reflecting the relations between different social groups. Historians of the feudal aristocracy, for example, have largely ignored the widespread use of violence or have tended to diminish it, preferring to concentrate on other aspects of the nobility such as their ecclesiastical patronage or their role in defence and war. Elsewhere violence has been discussed only in terms of the exercise of power at an institutional level, with much stress on the use of exile as a means of dealing with political opponents in the Italian city-republics from the twelfth century. The social and psychological implications of the prevalence of violence between individuals have been little explored.

The historian ought not to use violent events merely for dramatic effect. Rather, a measured consideration of the evidence for the practice of violence and an understanding of its background are the necessary foundations for a history of violence. The study of violence in the past can also help us to understand the outbreaks of violence which occur even today. However, a narrow 'history of violence' which failed to refer to the general historical context would be inadequate and distorted; it would run the risk of over-emphasizing a single aspect of a period and of implying that the past can be understood through that aspect alone. Violence needs instead to be seen in its social and economic context, and the situation which gives rise to it understood. Yet despite these misgivings about past studies, and reservations about the work still to be done, it is nevertheless possible – and desirable – to suggest some possible approaches.

That violence was common in all social groups emerges both from the so-called barbarian law-codes and from the Edict of Rothari, as well as from other contemporary sources. In the early Middle Ages violence was not yet the prerogative of the aristocracy, which in any case hardly yet existed and was insignificant where it did. Violence was practised by all towards all, though the tendency for violence to be inflicted on those lower in the social scale by those above them was already apparent, with freemen attacking *servi* (serfs), for instance. However, there is also ample evidence for aggression between freemen, or between *servi*. The largest section of the Edict of Rothari is that concerned with criminal law. A wide range of violent crimes appears: murder, woundings (both slight and serious and using a great variety of weapons), assaults of every kind.

The bulk of the laws concern assaults on *servi* but there are almost as many concerning disputes between freemen. The number and variety of crimes and the heavy penalties laid down are evidence that violence was endemic. The severity of punishment for anyone entering the enclosure around a house without warning, for instance, suggests that there was a constant state of alert, a situation which must have fostered a sense of insecurity. Every dwelling, vineyard or field, both in the town and in the countryside, was enclosed against malefactors and wild animals. The prevalence of danger – a consequence of the breakdown in social relations and of the hazards found in a countryside which had been wild for hundreds of years – helps explain the numerous references to protective fences and hedges in the sources, and suggests that it came to be perceived as normal to live in a permanent state of apprehension.

Occasionally, in times of crisis, this sense of apprehension would go beyond what was regarded as normal and there would be widespread fear and alarm, even terror. We have very little idea of what was regarded as abnormal, although if we did we could better understand contemporary fears. War, fatal disease, injury and death were so common that they appear not to have caused particular consternation. The impression left by a reading of contemporary chronicles is that people found inexplicable happenings in the sky much more alarming than wars or disastrous weather. Natural phenomena such as solar or lunar eclipses, comets and shooting stars, or hallucinations, the products of a heated imagination, resulted equally in panic. People would see the outlines of unearthly riders on horseback in crimson sunset clouds, or blood fall from the sky (in reality the red Sahara sand mentioned before, blown in by the sirocco and falling mixed with rain).

Chronicles and saints' lives from the early Middle Ages are full of episodes of the most extreme brutality. The writers appear little perturbed by them, although the overwhelming impression they leave is of a world of barely contained passions ready to explode at any moment. Violence seems to have been a possible outcome of every situation, of every encounter. Yet there were also dissenting voices. Not only did the Church deplore the use of violence and many monks and priests reject it entirely, devoting themselves to a life of peace, but there were strong countervailing forces even among those not subject to canon law. It can be no coincidence that throughout the Middle Ages prudence, moderation and temperance were regarded as necessary virtues for the aristocracy. These cannot have existed solely in the minds of those who wrote about them: writers were of course eager to attribute good qualities to their subjects so as to provide examples of model lives, but they were none the less frequently familiar with the characters and lives of those they wrote about.

The widespread use of violence can be inferred from the many and varied crimes which are mentioned in legislation, as well as from the punishments prescribed there: equally harsh and crude, they ranged from the amputation of limbs to death, and were often to be carried out in public. Narrative sources, especially those which deplore the shedding of blood, whether as a result of crime or as punishment, are valuable since they considerably enlarge our knowledge of the range and gravity of violent crime. Saints' lives are particularly rich from this point of view: stories of the intervention of saints to prevent violence, or of their reluctance or refusal to carry out or be otherwise responsible for harsh punishments, suggest just how commonplace violence was. Where such people were in a position of secular power or held public office, writers would often dwell on their refusal to oppress the weak.

In the lives of saints we come upon people who are wrongly accused but who are promptly blinded, peasants at work in the fields who are attacked and beaten by a noble's retainers, or people found guilty of a crime but who find that they are punished much more severely than the laws prescribe. The laws themselves, as we have seen, were draconian. Odo of Cluny praised Gerald of Aurillac for having allowed convicted men who were awaiting harsh punishment to escape from prison. While boldness and courage in battle were universally regarded as praiseworthy qualities in leaders, clemency and a refusal to sanction bloodshed were esteemed equally highly, at least among churchmen. In his history, Paul the Deacon describes how many Lombard kings would pardon traitors and those convicted of violence, and he regards such clemency as reflecting the magnanimity and self-restraint towards malefactors to be expected from those in high positions. Tellingly, he wrote of King Liutprand that 'he was mighty in battle and merciful to the guilty.'

The early eighth century was marked by extreme violence, and the horrors did not diminish over time, although it appears that the frequency of violence decreased, save for occasional outbursts. With the emergence of the aristocracy, violence came to be particularly associated with them, even to become their prerogative. Although the use of force continued to be a feature of all sections of society, power and the ownership of weapons became limited to a small group, the aristocracy, which was thus well able to harass those weaker than themselves. Whereas it is clear from Lombard legislation that at that time the main problem was ill-treatment of *servi* by freemen, Carolingian royal legislation is concerned chiefly with the problem of the oppression of freemen by the aristocracy, by this time increasing in power and establishing itself as the ruling class, even in Italy.

Violence as the prerogative of high social status has to be seen in the context of the profound changes, economic, social and even ecclesiastical, which were occurring as a result of the emergence of the great landholding aristocracy in Italy and elsewhere. Just as land became concentrated in the great feudal estates, the *curtes*, so those who controlled the land increasingly had a monopoly on positions of authority within government and the Church. This could be exploited, along with the power that came with wealth, to acquire vassals. With the increasing power and prestige of the aristocracy within society, violence underwent a similar process, becoming associated with the aristocracy. Moreover, particularly from the tenth century, the main preoccupation of the aristocracy was the profession of arms: the Church defined them as *ordo pugnatorum*, the order of soldiers.

The Church warned the nobility against quarrelling among themselves and against using violence against the defenceless, urging them instead to champion the weak, uphold law and order and defend and expand Christendom. The concept of chivalry and the establishment of the crusading orders were further efforts to mitigate the consequences of the combative attitude of the aristocracy. Both were responses, successful in varying degrees, to the grave problems produced by the existence of a class dedicated to warfare within societies where governments lacked the authority and power to restrain them.

In his *Ecclesiastical History*, written shortly after 700, Bede told how King Sigbert of the East Angles, a once redoubtable warrior who had retired to a monastery to live out his days in the peace of the cloister, received some unwelcome visitors. They begged him to lead the army into battle once more, as he had done in former days. Sigbert refused, but they would not give up, reminding him of the perilous state of his country, which was facing a crucial battle against Mercia. Eventually, regardless of his protests, they dragged him out of the monastery. They hoped that his presence would give heart to the soldiers, but Sigbert spurned lance and sword and refused to carry more than a stick. In the ensuing terrible battle many fell, including the former king himself.

At the height of the feudal era, a similar reluctance to kill is seen in the violent battle between Berengar I of Italy and Rudolf II of Burgundy at Fiorenzuola, between Parma and Piacenza, in July 923. After Berengar was defeated, his men were pursued and massacred as they fled until finally Count Gariard, who together with a certain Boniface led Rudolf's army, shouted out to his men to put an end to the slaughter. He ordered them to reverse their lances and to use only the blunt end so as not to injure the fleeing men too severely. Some decades earlier, St Gerald of Aurillac had pursued the same policy, invariably ordering his men to use the handles of their lances. Odo of Cluny, from whose life of Gerald this detail comes, relates that God approved and Gerald was just as successful in battle.

Whether true or not (and some of the anecdotes sound highly conjectural), such stories reveal the deep revulsion felt by many from bloodshed and the indiscriminate and oppressive use of force, a use which was the natural consequence of the aristocracy's enthusiasm for war and killing, and of their refusal to be deterred even by the worst suffering. Nobles did not hesitate to inflict the most severe agonies. After Aripert, one of the last Lombard kings, gained the kingdom of Italy, he had the eyes of a rival's son gouged out and the ears and noses of the man's wife and daughter cut off. Liutprand, the younger son, was spared only because he was still a child – and, Paul the Deacon writes, of such unprepossessing appearance that no one could have foreseen that he would later be celebrated in battle and acclaimed king. These episodes are typical of many which darken the pages of the chronicles but which seem to have been regarded as part of the normal course of events. Those we have described are paltry when compared to some of the other instances of the gross use of violence, described in appalled tones by horrified chroniclers.

Lombard history is frequently marked by elemental emotions – burning passions, lust for power and revenge, intense hatred and jealousy – and by crude, primitive responses, apparent both in courage in battle and in savage brutality. Some decades after the Lombard conquest of Italy, the Avars under their leader, the khagan, attacked Friuli. It was the most vulnerable of the marches regions of Italy and always bore the brunt of invasions from the east. The leader of the Lombards, Gisulf, fell in battle, leaving his widow Romilda and what remained of his army to prepare to defend Cividale, the most important town in the area. As Romilda looked down from the city walls on the young and proud khagan astride his horse and surrounded by his men, she was filled with passion for him. As we have seen, she was so overcome by lust that she sent a message that she would let the Avars into the city on condition that the khagan would afterwards marry her. The khagan agreed and Cividale thus fell into the hands of the Avars. They sacked the city and carried off the entire population to their great encampment on the other side of the Alps, which they called 'campus sacer'. There it was decided to kill all the men and to keep the women and children as slaves. All Gisulf's sons managed to escape, including the two youngest, destined for slavery. One of these last, Grimoald, who later ruled the duchy of Benevento, gave early proof of his bravery. As he was being carried back to captivity after his first escape bid had failed, he managed to stab his captor with his dagger and to push him off his horse. Paul the Deacon described the joy of his brothers when Grimoald finally caught up with them and told them of his exploits.

After the Lombard men had been killed, the women were raped. Only Gisulf's two daughters escaped this fate: they had ingeniously thought to put pieces of raw meat between their breasts which as they rotted gave out such a stench that no one would touch the women and they were sold as slaves. Their mother Romilda, who was waiting for the khagan to carry out his promise of marriage, found that a horrific consummation awaited her. Paul describes how the khagan did, in a sense, keep his promise to marry her. She was repeatedly raped by twelve Avar men through the night until at dawn the khagan had her impaled on a sharp stake driven into the ground in the middle of the encampment, telling her that this was the husband that she deserved.

Perhaps wishing to provide a distraction from such horrors, Paul then digressed from these ghastly events to describe his own family history. His affection for his people, his family and his home contrasts sharply with the grim tale of Romilda. According to family tradition, five of his own forebears had been among the Lombard children carried off by the Avars. One of them was Lopichis, his great-grandfather, who grew up among the Avars. On reaching adulthood, however, he found that the pull of his homeland was too strong and decided to return. He took some bread and his bow and arrows and set off through the forests of the Alps for Italy. During his journey a wolf came to guide him through these strange and empty lands and stayed by his side until, exhausted and starving, Lopichis decided to kill it for food. He took aim but the wolf ran off and disappeared. Lopichis collapsed to the ground and was all but ready to give up. Yet it was his destiny to reach Italy. He fell asleep and in his dream a man appeared to him and said, 'Arise! Have courage! Go in the direction your feet are pointing as you lie. There is Italy.' He set off again and eventually reached a house where an old woman lived. She looked after him and fed him, a little at a time so as not to put too great a strain on his weakened body. When he finally reached his native village, he found his family's old house with its walls still intact, though the roof had fallen in. He wearily hung his bow and quiver on a sapling growing among the brambles and thorns inside the remaining walls, and began his new life. He had a son called Arichis, and Arichis a son called Warnefrid. Warnefrid's sons were Paul himself and Arichis his brother, evidently named after his grandfather.

After this digression, an unexpected respite from the relentless succession of grim events, Paul returned to his narrative of terrible deeds. The Slavs, he tells us, paid regular tribute to the brothers Taso and Cacco, who were sons of the valiant Gisulf and ruled as dukes of Friuli. Their peaceful rule came to a violent end when Gregory, a Byzantine patrician governor, promised Taso that he would adopt him as his own son. The two brothers therefore went to visit him at Oderzo where Gregory was to shave Taso's beard, the ritual which would symbolize the adoption. But no sooner had the brothers and their retinue entered the town than they realized that the gates had been shut behind them and that the traitorous Gregory intended to murder them both. They could only bid each other farewell and fight to the last in a desperate defence through the streets until both fell. Gregory kept his word, to his own satisfaction at least: he had Taso's head brought to him and shaved it, thereby fulfilling his promise to adopt him as his own son.

7

War

All through the Middle Ages churchmen condemned bloodshed, regarding it as justifiable only for the defence or expansion of the True Church, for the protection of the weak or for the preservation of the state. How energetically they defended its use varied according to where and when they were writing and their intellectual background. All the same, a reading of treatises, homilies and saints' lives reveals that their writers found the use of force, which obviously often resulted in bloodshed, repugnant. This distaste, however, derived more from a moral stance than from any deep-seated conviction. Writers make ritual denunciations of violence, but when they describe events or outline the lives and deeds of valiant laymen they frequently reveal an acceptance, generally implicit but occasionally explicit, of the use of force and of death in battle. Studies of the Church and of the secular aristocracy have laid too much stress on a separation of the two worlds, on distinct roles and ways of life. Monks often came from noble families; they lived in an age of warfare, and although in earlier centuries all freemen had fought in battle, the aristocracy came to dominate the business of war. Their preconceived ideas, then, were more firmly ingrained and stubbornly persistent than the creed of non-violence they were supposed to profess, and which they might well find difficult to accept.

Liutprand of Cremona, who was writing in the mid-tenth century, was moralistic and misogynous. The works of the future Bishop of Cremona are both learned and gossipy, and typical in that whenever he wants to give a passage verve and colour he does so entirely in terms of military glory. An example is his account of the death of Anscar, Marquis of Spoleto. Liutprand, who clearly preferred the hothead Anscar to his wily and cautious half-brother Berengar of Ivrea, later King of Italy, describes how King Hugh had decided to have Anscar assassinated, despite the ties of blood between them. After a battle in which he was heavily outnumbered by the king's forces, Anscar was left with a broken lance and faced death. By this stage he was opposed by an enemy captain, one of his own vassals, who had betrayed him and who was now taking advantage of his vulnerability to press him hard. Anscar spurred his horse on against him and thrust the stump of his lance into the man's mouth with such force that it came out at the back of his head, dripping with blood. Then he seized his sword and single-handedly killed a great number of the enemy until he was surrounded. His horse slipped backwards into a deep hollow, crushing him as both perished in a hail of arrows and spears.

This event is only a small part of a much longer description of the battle as a whole. Liutprand clearly enjoyed bringing the battle vividly to life through a painstaking and realistic account. He reserved his criticism for the numerical superiority of the enemy forces, the trap set up by the king, the treachery of Anscar's vassal and, at the end, the shameful way in which Hugh and Berengar gloated over Anscar's valiant death.

Again, Liutprand gave a detailed account of the battle which raged at Fiorenzuola in July 923 and which led to the downfall of Berengar I. He dwelled on the heavy slaughter on both sides, and the only suggestion of pity or regret in his account is his note that at the end of the battle one of the leaders ordered his men to cease the bloodshed as Berengar's routed army fled the battlefield. Liutprand went on to describe the murder of Berengar, stabbed in the back and slain in front of a church in Verona, his blood pouring out on to a stone in front of the church door; he tells us how the bloodstains could not be scrubbed out and were still visible even in his day. The crimson stains were, he noted, a sign of the heinousness of a deed carried out by such duplicitous means.

A little earlier, Odo, the second abbot of the monastery of Cluny, reflected on war in his *Collationes* and in his *Life* of St Gerald of Aurillac. Clearly Odo disliked acts of gross violence. In the *Collationes* he describes how nobles are granted their swords by God so that they can maintain the social order, and he expresses the hope that one day they will be able to return them to God unused. In his *Life* of Gerald he makes great play of the fact that Gerald never injured anyone and that when battle was unavoidable he would even go so far as to order his men to fight using the handles of their reversed lances, as we have seen. This was wishful thinking, a pious hope entirely impractical beyond the monastery walls and unthinkable in a society which constantly required violence in self-defence. It is telling that in later versions of the *Life* this detail is omitted, along with nearly all the other references which sought to portray a layman who had sought to live by the values of the cloister.

The notion that war and military training were the preserve of a limited circle, the aristocracy, is already apparent in writers of the tenth century. Even military action and battle are described in terms of individual acts of bravery by members of the aristocracy. The *Gesta Berengarii*, for example, refers to the bravery of the *Supponidi*, the name given in the sources to several interrelated aristocratic families all called *Suppo*. This close association of valour with the aristocracy is found frequently in chronicles, a literary reflection of the profound changes occurring in European society between the eighth and the tenth centuries as the task of defence gradually came to be restricted to a professional military class. At the same time, many people found themselves more and more excluded from any role in government. As early as the ninth century, freemen, both small and medium landholders, found not only that they were no longer called on to fight in defence, but also that they were losing various rights and obligations within society, such as those of attending trials and of building bridges and roads.

The pace of change varied enormously between different areas (change came much faster in France than in Italy, for example) but the way was open for a society increasingly dominated by the aristocracy. This domination had economic, cultural and religious ramifications. The economic effect of the power of the aristocracy was clear. Those who presided over courts or held other public office in return for military services for the king quickly learned how to exploit their position to acquire wealth; the activity was endlessly denounced by Carolingian laws. On the cultural level, though the full elaboration of the theory of the three orders (of those who fought, those who prayed and those who worked) was yet to come, the changes in society began to be reflected in the sources. In the ninth century, annals, chronicles and histories still described military activity in terms of entire peoples or their armies; individuals were referred to only in their capacity of leaders of great hosts. Descriptions of single combat are occasional and peripheral, and even here the intention, whether explicit or implicit, is generally to point up the valour of the people in general or of a particular lineage group (*fara*), not of individuals.

Paul the Deacon, writing in the second half of the eighth century, after the Lombard kingdom had fallen to the Carolingians, gives us such an account. He describes how Gisulf, nephew of King Alboin, would not agree to take responsibility for the defence of Friuli, the border area desperately in need of men experienced in battle, unless he was given those *farae* with a reputation for courage. The King gave him the men he wanted, as well as the sturdy horses which were indispensable for the region's defence. With the *farae*, Gisulf fought long and hard to defend Friuli against the Avar and Slav raids, but eventually fell with his *farae* in battle, which led to the sacking of the town of Cividale. Paul the Deacon evidently believed that strength and courage were inherited and were associated with particular *farae*. At the beginning of his description of Rothari, perhaps the bravest of all the Lombard kings, he wrote: 'After Arioald had ruled over the Lombards for twelve years, he died. Rothari, *of the tribe* [genus] *of Arodus*, then became king of the Lombards' (emphasis added).

The emphasis on the role of the leader and the idea that courage and strength were inherited and were to be found in a limited circle is thus seen in Italy among the Lombards, and elsewhere even earlier. Over time warfare came to be the prerogative and profession of certain families, understood in the widest sense. There were many reasons for this: the pressing need for a sophisticated military training in order to counter the peoples invading from the east, with their highly developed methods of fighting; the growth of central administration, which required office-holders from families loyal to the king and probably related to him; the desire to install trustworthy vassals in the border areas of the expanding Carolingian empire; the increasing influence of the great feudal estates; and, finally, the new personal relationships which resulted from the development of feudalism. Behind all these lay the need for defence and for a strong army. As a result, a military class evolved out of the previously undifferentiated host. The identification of the aristocracy with warfare would long persist. In Marcel Proust's *Cities of the Plain* the notion of an aristocracy valiant in war was still very much alive for the Baron de Charlus, who declared that:

> I know it is not good form to speak of the merits of one's own family. But it is well known that our people were always to the fore in the hour of danger. Our battle-cry, after we abandoned that of the Dukes of Brabant, was *Passavant*! So that it is not unjust on the whole that this right to be everywhere the first, which we had established for so many centuries in war, should afterwards have been granted to us at Court. And, egad, it was always acknowledged there. (trans. C. K. Scott Moncrieff and Terence Kilmartin)

Paul the Deacon, himself a Lombard, described his people as invariably fighting with courage and valour, in victory as in defeat. For him the bravery of Taso and Cacco in the attack in Oderzo described above was typical. His history has as a backdrop a popular and widespread heroism, although towards the end individual military leaders play an ever greater role until, at the very end of his history, when an elite has emerged, they have become virtually the sole focus of attention. The idea of the valour of an entire people survives the establishment of a feudal system and the conquest of Italy by the Franks, but Paul comes to emphasize the military prowess of the aristocracy. Though elements of the Lombard custom of freemen all fighting together continued, the role of the military leader steadily increased until armies came to be made up of the retinues of a few horsemen led by a local lord or, perhaps, a count, duke or king. For a while the descendants, albeit much reduced in number, of the Lombard free-born warriors continued to join the retinues of the most prestigious knights. Yet it is clearly the achievements of the Lombard people as a whole which are closest to Paul's heart, as well as the legends of their past, which told of how they had migrated from the frozen wastes of Scandinavia across Europe all the way to Italy. Paul describes Authari, perhaps the greatest of all the Lombard kings: on reaching the straits which separate the southernmost point of Italy from Sicily, he struck a column which emerged from the sea with his spear and declared that, 'The land of the Lombards will reach even unto here!'

Extraordinary stories were associated with the Lombards who had marched the breadth of the great central plains of Europe, and they were indeed skilled in warfare as few others and long undefeated. Exceptional individuals appear even at the beginning of Paul's *History*. For instance, Lamissio, the second king of the Lombards, had been found as an infant floating in a pond together with the bodies of his six brothers and sisters by King Agelmund after the children had all been abandoned by their mother. As Agelmund poked with his spear among the mass of little bodies he saw a tiny hand reach out and grab hold of it. He adopted the child and gave him a name derived from *lama*, the Lombard word for a pond. When Agelmund was murdered by the Bulgars, Lamissio succeeded him and avenged his adoptive father by defeating the Bulgars. It was said too that he had defeated the fearsome Amazons.

For the Lombards death was preferable to any taint of cowardice and they did not flinch from it if it was to be the proof of their valour. And valour in battle frequently meant death. An event recorded by Paul the Deacon evidently lived long in the collective memory as a striking example of the stubborn determination to fight to the last, even at the cost of defeat and massacre. After Lombard rule had been established in Italy for several decades and only the borders needed to be defended, Ferdulf, a brave but arrogant man, ruled the duchy of Friuli, under continual threat from Slav raids. The Slavs had attacked some shepherds but had escaped before the captain of the local garrison could reach them. The captain's name was Argait, a name which invited mockery as in the Lombard language *arga* meant coward. Duke Ferdulf played on the man's name to taunt him, 'When will you succeed in doing some brave deed, you who are named Arga?' His target, who was far from cowardly, answered that he would show him which of the two was the coward. His opportunity came when a raiding party of Slavs stopped to rest on top of a precipitous outcrop. Ferdulf and Argait were down below with their men. While Ferdulf was looking for the easiest way up to attack the Slavs, Argait spurred his horse up the steepest slope, challenging the

Duke to follow him if he dared so that they could find out who was the coward. Duke Ferdulf followed, along with all their men. It was a massacre: the Avars did not even have to use their swords but rolled stones down on to the Lombards and knocked them from their horses as they struggled up the slope. Nearly all the Lombard party were killed, including Duke Ferdulf and his target, Argait.

The pages of Paul's *History* are full of such feats, both of groups and of individuals. They are intended to demonstrate the greatness of Paul's people though they also suggest nostalgic remembrance, since Paul was writing after the conquest of the Lombard kingdom by Charlemagne, an event which he chose to pass over. Paul evidently preferred not to write of the faint-heartedness, treachery and weak leadership which must have made the Frankish victory possible. Valour in battle was for him everything. When listing the virtues of Liutprand, regarded as the wisest and the most Christian of Lombard kings, he stressed straightaway that he was 'most valorous in battle'. As evidence Paul recounted a particular incident, all the more surprising as our knowledge of Liutprand suggests that he was not especially strong. The king knew that two of his soldiers were planning to kill him, and so one day he let them follow him deep into a thick forest, then suddenly drew his sword and challenged them to fight. Terrified, they threw themselves before him and begged for mercy.

In both laymen and clerics, a warlike spirit, more than any other quality, was regarded as defining manhood. Even when men renounced the world to become monks, their struggles with the devil and temptation are described in terms of combat. The most popular saints were those who had been soldiers and there are many instances of their returning to earth to fight as they had loved to do when alive. Their ambitions after death were presumed to be the same as before: to command armies, terrify the enemy, wield spear and sword and ride into battle. Paul told of a strange meeting shortly after the Lombard conquest of Italy. While Duke Ariulf of Spoleto, a brave and valiant man but a pagan, was engaged in fierce battle against Byzantine forces, he found himself in a tight corner. A soldier whom he did not recognize came to his aid and was fearless in his defence. After the battle, which he won, Ariulf asked his men which of them had fought most courageously, but was told that none had fought better than he. He went away puzzled, convinced that someone else had indeed fought much better. On reaching Spoleto he saw a large building and asked who lived there. He was told it was a Christian church and that it contained the relics of the bishop and martyr St Savino, a saint customarily invoked by Christians when going into battle. Ariulf scoffed, asking how a dead man could be of any help in combat, but went in all the same to inspect the building. As he looked at the frescos on the walls he was suddenly brought up short; in a picture of St

Savino he recognized the face of the brave soldier who had saved his life.

Paul observed that it was only Ariulf's paganism that made it hard for him to believe that a long-dead man could have come to his aid; had he been Christian he would have found it entirely credible. We can see this in a similar incident much later, after most of the Lombards had been converted to Christianity. One glimpse of the Archangel Michael in the advancing enemy lines was enough to terrify the otherwise courageous usurper Alahis, since he had earlier sworn an oath by the Archangel. His men told him that he was seeing things and was being hysterical, but in vain; Alahis lost his nerve and was killed in the ensuing battle. As we have seen, his body was horribly mutilated, with his head and legs cut off and his torso reduced to a shapeless mass. In an earlier battle Alahis had killed a deacon, mistaking him for Cunipert (the king had lent the deacon his armour). On discovering his mistake he had exclaimed, 'In this battle I have succeeded only in killing a cleric. I therefore swear that if God grants me another victory I shall fill up a well with clerics' balls!'

8

The Nobility

In the Middle Ages people were considered not as individuals but in broader terms, as part of society; they were viewed in the context of their family, their clan or even, especially in the early Middle Ages, as a member of a whole nation. This is evident from the titles of early medieval histories – *History of the Franks, History of the Lombards, History of the Saxons, Ecclesiastical History of the English People.* Paul the Deacon's outline of the history of the Lombards, his own people, is a celebratory epic which praises their courage in battle, generosity and vigour but also passionately deplores their faults. At one point in his chronicle Paul gives the history of his own family as far back as his great-grandfather, a remarkable achievement given the dearth of written documents, but evidence too of the stress on lineage; it shows the tendency to relate personal characteristics, both good and bad, to the past and to see them as inherited characteristics. Earlier in his history, Paul had noted that when the Lombards came to Italy under Alboin the most courageous lineage groups, or *farae*, had settled in Friuli, his own homeland. Paul's family was therefore descended from one of these superior *farae* and would have inherited its tradition of valour.

True nobility was considered to consist of courage, strength and valour in battle, qualities which were believed to be inherited. The origins of the hereditary aristocracy lie here. This belief in the significance of heredity lasted for a long time: in the fourteenth century, the labourers and small craftsmen in Florence who revolted against the government were called 'the nameless people' and 'people born yesterday'; they were contrasted with those whose wealth and power were regarded as legitimated by possession over many generations. It was at this time that leading families, convinced that true nobility required origins lost in antiquity, began to claim that their families could be traced back to the

Romans. By contrast, the constant wars and insecurity of existence in the early Middle Ages meant that a clan or even a whole people could all too easily lose its ascendency, and leading families were therefore constantly changing. Since nobility was synonymous with liberty, even slaves could aspire to it: the Lombard king Lamissio promised slaves their freedom if they acquitted themselves well in battle. The Carolingian kings did not hesitate to remove even the highest from office if they proved unworthy of it. Within the Carolingian empire after the eighth century, only members of the royal family, and not all of them, could be assured of inheriting land and power. For everyone else the general and dramatic instability of institutions and of the economy, and the precariousness of life itself, which meant that families often died out, made it difficult for individual families to establish themselves and militated against the development of an aristocracy. Later, however, and especially after the twelfth century, the mere fact of being born into a noble family became sufficient to confer high status.

In early medieval lives of saints who lived between the fifth and seventh centuries, the attributes of sanctity are wisdom, generosity, self-restraint, abstemiousness and, frequently, a withdrawal from the world to live as a hermit; whereas after the tenth century the writers of the lives of those regarded as holier and closer to God felt obliged to stress in addition their noble birth. Abbot John of Metz, writing the life of the great tenth-century Benedictine reformer John of Gorze, found himself in an awkward position since John did not come from a noble family. Despite his earnest endeavours to show that John's parents were moderately wealthy, it is abundantly clear that the family was far from affluent. No longer were freedom and a degree of prosperity enough to claim nobility. The increasing emphasis on the aristocracy thus affected every aspect of society, even sanctity. A pious, even saintly, ancestor whose life had been spent in devoutly attending mass, in good works and in prayer came to be indispensable in aristocratic families. Saintliness, like nobility, was regarded as a quality which ran in families. Odo, biographer of St Gerald of Aurillac, describes how Gerald's noble father would periodically sleep apart from his wife, an act which foreshadowed his son's chastity throughout his life. Odo seems as gratified by the father's virtuous habit as he was by the saint's illustrious forebears, related to the royal family, whom he lists.

Towards the end of the thirteenth century St Louis of France, according to his biographer Jean de Joinville, rebuked a master at the Sorbonne for wearing clothes which were too grand for his humble origins. Joinville felt obliged to comment on this, urging others not to follow the king's example as his sharp words had been hurtful. Evidently Joinville, himself noble, disapproved of such breaches of courtesy and of the strict aristocratic code of behaviour. In time this code became formalized and institutionalized into rigid etiquette. In the eighteenth century Saint-Simon, another well-known biographer of a famous king, devoted an enormous amount of space to an account of the ancestry and genealogy of the French aristocracy and their respect for etiquette. Even more conscious of the past is the Baron Palamède de Charlus in Proust's *The Guermantes Way*, the third part of *À la recherche du temps perdu*. He is smugly convinced that his family, the Guermantes, is the most aristocratic and ancient in France and boasts constantly of its nobility and titles, its prerogatives and privileges. The principal concern of de Charlus is to show how his ancestors were always the first into battle in times of danger; centuries earlier such boldness had been the original reason for the privileges of the Guermantes.

None the less, in the novel the best example of this, the most ancient and genuine aspect of aristocratic privilege, is to be found not in the Baron de Charlus but in his nephew Robert de Saint-Loup, who as a young officer sacrifices himself on the battlefield to protect his retreating men. After a life as a *bon viveur* with democratic leanings, a life characterized by intelligence and openness, only in dying does Saint-Loup find his true self. For the narrator Saint-Loup's courage in death suddenly reveals aspects of his character which he had not noticed or had simply not appreciated: the way in which, even when walking across a drawing-room, he had seemed to be restraining an impulse to charge; the evening when he had slapped the face of an impertinent journalist; the simplicity and strength of his love. Only after Saint-Loup's death, writes the narrator, did he fully realize the firm set of his solid head and the steady gaze of his blue eyes. Saint-Loup's life had only outwardly contrasted with the nobility of his death, and the capital 'G' on the hangings in the church at his funeral showed that in death he had preserved the tradition of the house of Guermantes.

Although Proust's portrayal of Saint-Loup's death draws on his own view of the Middle Ages, it reflects the persistence in France – where the feudal nobility had first emerged – of the association of loyalty and courage with the aristocracy. There are many similarities between Proust's *À la recherche du temps perdu* and Marc Bloch's *Strange Defeat*: both reveal a deep attachment to the French tradition of valour among the aristocracy and the officer class; both exalt the courage shown in battle by peasants and simple workmen; both despise the bourgeoisie as cowards.

One thousand years earlier, the army of King Berengar I of Italy was engaged in a fierce battle with the supporters of Rudolf of Burgundy, who was attempting to usurp the throne. Berengar's men were overwhelmed, but at a certain point, as we have seen, one of the joint leaders of Rudolf's army ordered his men to stop the slaughter and to strike the enemy only with the handles of their lances. The Italian chronicler of this grim battle, one of the bloodiest of the period, wrote that many aristocratic families were decimated and that in Italy as a whole the aristocracy lost many members in the massacre. Courage and mercy, even if often accompanied by bloodthirsty ferocity, constantly marked aristocratic behaviour.

9

The Priesthood

The Middle Ages, especially in the feudal centuries, was the age of the Church, of priests and monks. Monasteries dedicated to the worship of God and the relief of the poor were to be found almost everywhere. From the smallest to the largest, they dominated the countryside for hundreds of years, as characteristic a feature as the ubiquitous *castelli*, forts and city walls. Daunted by the prospect of the next world and oppressed by the fear of hell and eternal punishment, people were impressionable. They sought burial in the shelter of churches or religious houses, having left lands and possessions to them in return for the assurance of intercession after their death. In this way church property grew over the years and this in turn allowed the number of clerics to rise. The cumulative effect of all these donations, which ranged from the small plots of land bequeathed by yeomen to the great estates given by the aristocracy and the monarchy, was that in time church lands came to be second only to those of the monarchy.

By the second half of the ninth century the monastery of St Columbanus at Bobbio, near Piacenza, owned dozens of large estates, or *curtes*. Parts of these *curtes* were cultivated directly by the monastery, using landless *servi*, while the rest was rented out to individual tenants on the understanding that they gave a certain number of days of labour services to the monastery. At this time Bobbio had more than six hundred such tenants, or *coloni*, and the monastery of Santa Giulia in Brescia about a thousand. Other Italian religious houses had similarly high numbers of tenants. Further south, monasteries had equally extensive possessions: notable examples are San Salvatore near Monte Amiata and Sant'Antimo near Siena, Santa Maria in Farfa, north of Rome, and San Vincenzo al Volturno in the Apennines south of Rome. These were merely the most prominent of dozens of monasteries in Italy, nearly all of royal foundation and at the height of their power and wealth in the tenth century.

Churches associated with bishops, by contrast, tended to be less wealthy. The cathedral of Modena, for example, was continually embroiled in property disputes with the neighbouring monastery of Nonantola, a royal foundation. The bulk of church land was owned by the most celebrated monasteries and most prestigious cathedrals, which also had the monopoly on learning. However, countless smaller religious houses offering food and shelter to the poor and to travellers were to be found everywhere, from the Alps and Apennines down to the malaria-ridden lagoons by the coast. North of the Alps there was a similar abundance of religious houses. In France the monastery of Corbie was renowned, in German-speaking lands those of Fulda, Reichenau, St Gall and Prüm.

The larger monasteries had communities of several hundred, all occupied with the heavy demands of the daily office and with praying for peace, for the Empire and the individual kingdoms, and for the Christian faith. Masses were sung on the anniversaries of the deaths of important figures, and food was provided daily for hundreds of poor people. In local churches and in minor religious houses everywhere in the villages and countryside, prayers went up for men and women, long forgotten, whose salvation had once been assured by the gift of a field, a strip of woodland or a vineyard to a religious house.

Though pagan practices and beliefs long persisted in the peasant world, Christianity gradually came to prevail. People often drew on elements of pagan and Christian practice and would believe both in the ancient nature worship and in the tenets of Christianity, a strange confusion of ideas about which we know little. Lombard and Carolingian laws had to forbid the pagan rituals which derived from such worship of nature. Particular trees, springs or boulders were regarded as sacred and were venerated; peasants would meet around them to perform time-honoured rites. Many churchmen shared this peasant apprehension about the natural world and trembled if the moon was thrown into shadow, if a comet could be seen in the sky for nights on end, or if a necromancer warned of imminent disaster. Thunder and lightning or hailstorms were believed to be signs of divine wrath, whether that of the pagan gods or of the God of the Christians. War or disease made people more fearful and then frightening tales would spread, of stones which fell from the sky during hailstorms, of bolts of lightning sent as a punishment, which set all the villages in a particular area on fire, of blood raining down, of images in the sky at sunset when swords and spears or phantom armies of horsemen riding into the distance were seen.

Given this atmosphere, where pagan and Christian beliefs alike fostered apprehension, it is easy to understand why whoever represented divine powers on earth, whether Christian priest or pagan holy man, should be respected and venerated. Similarly, the constant presence of disease and sickness made death feared and induced people to seek the intercession of the clergy by donating or bequeathing their possessions and land. With growing wealth, the way of life and even the dress of churchmen (and especially of the higher clergy) increasingly mirrored those of the aristocracy. The Carolingian rulers constantly had to prohibit abbots and abbesses, bishops and the clergy in general from hunting. Odo of Cluny, as we have seen, wrote that God disapproved of Esau because he was a hunter, since hunting distracts the mind and arouses uncontrollable instincts. The Church, simple and unostentatious in its early years, became hugely wealthy, with imposing and powerful cathedrals and abbeys. Richly clad bishops and abbots prized their horses and hounds and enjoyed great feasts, leading a life no different from that of the aristocratic families from which they often came.

At the same time, all classes of society reacted strongly to such ostentation and opulence among those who were supposed to live an exemplary life. Discontent among peasants in rural areas manifested itself in rebellion, discontent among the powerful in religious crisis. Nobles would give up their worldly position and all their wealth to enter monasteries, like the two aristocrats who joined the monastery of Novalesca in Piedmont and were given responsibility for the monastery pigs. During the grim tenth century, the century of iron, many retreated from the world. One such was the Count Palatine Sanso who gave up the highest office in the kingdom of Italy, second only to the king, for the obscurity of a monastery and a life of humility and penitence as a monk. Often one particular event appears to have been all that was needed to make people abruptly reject their former life: the sight of the suffering of others, a warning dream, a period of illness. John of Gorze, for example, was so impressed by the manifest faith of a woman he met who wore a hairshirt beneath her clothes and never complained that he too was inspired to mortify his body.

The constant military exercises and hunting which were central to the education of the sons of the aristocracy were exhausting and stressful. Those of a reflective turn of mind frequently rejected this single-minded devotion to physical pursuits. St Odo of Cluny, as he later told a follower, was for three years tormented by headaches which he believed had been caused by military practice and hunting. He decided to give up his career as a knight at the court of William the Good, Duke of Aquitaine, and became in turn a cathedral canon, a hermit and finally a monk. None the less, it was with pleasure tinged with sadness that shortly before his death he recalled his strength as a young man and his exploits with arms and on horseback and in the chase: 'Everyone said I was handsome and strong but now you look upon an ugly old man.' Hearing that his friend Fulk the Good, the powerful Count of Rheims, was considering retiring from the world, he urged him to follow him into the monastery to fight God's battles there. Fulk ultimately decided against this, on the grounds that he could have more influence for the good as a layman.

Many aristocrats chose to continue to live as laymen, following Christ's teachings and using their position to benefit the poor and those clerics they approved of. In the mid-tenth century one such was Gerald, the influential Count of Aurillac in the Auvergne. In Odo of Cluny's life of Gerald we read how he, too, had been afflicted for a long time by infirmity, temporarily struck blind as punishment for a grave sin. After nearly yielding to lust, as we have seen, Gerald had wanted to punish himself for his ardour and rode all through a cold winter's night to extinguish the last flames of his desire. Yet this was not enough: God punished him with a long period of blindness. When he regained his sight he led an unblemished and saintly life. He had his head tonsured and during the day would cover it up with a cap until at night he could at last dedicate himself entirely to God, living as a monk though still in the world. The fact that Gerald did not renounce his position, and continued to exercise his authority as count during a period of serious troubles when, as Odo wrote, 'the kingdom was thrown into disorder because of the overweening behaviour of the nobles' meant that he could protect his subjects from maltreatment by other powerful lords.

The increasing importance of the aristocracy had two contrasting results: on the one hand, some lords constantly devised new ways of ensuring that people were dependent on them and of appropriating their land, by force if necessary; on the other hand, many gave up their position to enter monasteries or chose to live as monks while still laymen. A realization of the everyday use of violence and a rejection of it were often behind inner turmoil and spiritual crisis. These crises were frequently also an element in the insistence on a return to the simplicity of earlier centuries and the movement for monastic reform. Both violence and saintliness could be found in the higher clergy and the aristocracy for not all those in power exploited their position. A sense of restraint and justice could often be found, and many in authority did in fact seek to exercise power in accordance with it, or even renounced their positions.

10

Spiritual Crises

Throughout the entire period there are frequent instances of personal crises and abrupt breaks with the past. Studies to date have concerned members of the aristocracy and, for the later Middle Ages, also of the merchant class. However, only isolated cases have been examined and in the absence of systematic work on the phenomenon it is difficult to assess how common such crises were. Here, as in so many other areas, the emergence of the aristocracy had considerable effect. Early medieval sources record such crises among the very poor, or at least the lower strata of society, as well as among the powerful, but over time the examples described come to be limited almost exclusively to high-ranking men and women. They need to be seen as the product of a society which was increasingly dominated by the values of the emerging aristocracy, and have to be used with care as they give only a partial picture. At the same time, however, they mirror the changes in society. As the social structure became more rigid and social mobility decreased, the growing labour-service obligations of those at the lower end of the social scale must have been a major impediment to choosing a monastic life.

As far as the aristocracy is concerned, although reasons for renouncing the world and withdrawing to monasteries varied over time and between different parts of Europe, revulsion at the use of violence frequently lay behind such decisions. The path from knight to cleric to monk was well-worn and is one frequently encountered in the lives of holy men. Descriptions of such spiritual conversions can be found in nearly all narrative sources, though they are especially common in saints' lives and in cathedral or monastery chronicles. From the late ninth and tenth centuries, as combat and violence became increasingly central to the way of life of the aristocracy, many rejected their past and were drawn to a life they regarded, if not as perfect, then at any rate as superior to the one they had been leading. Often the decision to make a new life, usually marked by entering a monastery, would come at the close of a life spent fighting, as was the case with Ratchis, the Lombard king, and with many others whose lives had been dominated by war. This lends support to the idea that such conversions, a feature of the entire medieval period, represented a reaction against the military preoccupations of the aristocracy.

Instances of the repudiation of the military life can be found throughout the Middle Ages and well into the early modern period, St Ignatius Loyola being the most conspicuous example. Individuals varied greatly in their responses to the dilemma. Another famous instance is Louis the Pious who throughout his life succeeded in combining his royal duties with a level of spiritual activity worthy of the most conscientious cleric, an example continued in the thirteenth century by St Louis of France. For some it was sufficient to spend some time in a monastery every now and again, perhaps in one associated with their family, while others would enter a monastery with the intention of remaining there for the rest of their lives, only perhaps to find themselves recalled to their worldly duties in an emergency for the sake of their people. Many found that their spiritual needs could be assuaged by the foundation of monasteries and the consequent assurance that monks were constantly at prayer and occupied with the daily office; they derived vicarious satisfaction from the knowledge that monks were carrying out what they themselves had not the time or the urge to do. Nevertheless there remained many who made irrevocable breaks with the past and contentedly lived out the rest of their lives in monasteries with no regrets.

Such periods of transition in individuals often coincided with a period of sickness. It is very probable that in many cases such illnesses had a psychosomatic origin or were in fact depression or nervous breakdowns. In addition, the enforced inactivity associated with illness often compelled introspection and a review of one's life and thus could be the catalyst for change. The spiritual crises of St Odo of Cluny, St Francis and St Ignatius Loyola were all preceded by a period of illness. Since illness could also be seen as purification, a step on the path of spiritual development, the lives of saintly men and women were frequently marked by intervals of sickness, each worse than the last. In the eleventh century Alpert of Metz wrote in his *De diversitate temporum* of the Count Ansfrid, a former knight who had become a bishop and then, on being suddenly struck blind, entered a monastery. While count, Ansfrid had devoted himself as far as his secular responsibilities allowed to a fervent life of prayer. Alpert recorded that he had been so conscientious in attending divine office that 'heedless people mocked him and went around saying that he was living like a monk.' After he had become a

bishop he was struck blind, but his affliction encouraged him yet higher
up the path of spiritual perfection, convincing him that it was his duty to
become a monk.

> Through God's mercy, when he could no longer see and the desires of the
> eyes had been extinguished, thus shutting the portals to sin, his face
> retained the same dignity of expression it had borne when he was a bishop.
> His blindness meant that, no longer afflicted by the desires of the senses, he
> could contemplate God and meditate with the fullest concentration. Dur-
> ing his blindness he came to realize, almost with terror, that compared to
> God the flowers of this world are but ordure . . . He put aside his fine
> clothes for the Benedictine habit, a habit which I would call not poor, but
> rather of the angels.

Dramatic volte-faces were often preceded by the sudden onset of
psychological crises, which could often be of long duration. Contemporaries seldom speak directly of them, especially if they concerned people
who were not prominent and whose lives caused no reverberations. An
exception is the *Dialogues* of Gregory the Great, which has many examples of people of humble origins who sought refuge from the world by
embracing monasticism. Over time the writers of saints' lives became
increasingly imbued with the values of the aristocracy, while the changes
in the structure of society meant that the people about whom they wrote
tended to come from the higher end of the social order. This was a
reflection of the shift after the ninth century, when institutions changed
radically with the development of an aristocratic elite which came to
have a monopoly of high civil, military and ecclesiastical office. Just as
the aristocracy dominated the political structure and the Church, so in
the context of spiritual crises and withdrawal from the world we read
only of nobles. Contemporary writers of chronicles, treatises or saints'
lives seldom mention conversions of people outside the aristocracy.

It was quite common for lay people with a modicum of learning to
reject violence and to lead a life whose daily pattern was virtually that of
a monk. This was perhaps the case with the aristocratic and powerful
father of St Odo of Cluny. According to the *Vita* of Odo he knew the
scriptures well and led a moderately austere life, to the extent that at
mealtimes in his presence one had either to listen to edifying readings or
to discuss religious or moral topics. The author of the *Vita* evidently
intended to criticize those who led less exemplary lives. This had been the
intent of Odo himself in his *Collationes* and in his life of St Gerald of
Aurillac. In the latter he sought to provide models of behaviour: Gerald
is represented as eschewing all the faults we find denounced in the
Carolingian royal laws. To understand the kind of behaviour Odo had in
mind, and was criticizing, we need only consider the section of the laws

which sought to ensure that nobles did not arrive to preside over court sittings drunk. Those nobles who led virtuous lives were evidently the exception; the activities repeatedly censured in the legislation suggest what most were usually engaged in. We know little, at least for the present, of what the differing impact was of these two opposite ways of life, but nearly all contemporary sources indicate that violence and the use of force were normal and cruelty commonplace. In this context the sobriquet 'the Good' – Gerald the Good, William the Good, Duke of Aquitaine, Fulk the Good, Count of Rheims – is revealing. This custom of naming virtuous kings or nobles 'the Good' persisted until well after the Middle Ages; goodness was evidently sufficiently unexpected for it to be remarked upon as a contrast to the prevailing pattern.

Moderation or, as the Benedictines called it, *discretio* was a quality rarely apparent in the lives of aristocrats and kings: in the thirteenth century St Louis of France constantly felt the need to urge it on those around him, especially his councillors. His biographer Jean de Joinville, royal seneschal for Champagne, described how the king would frequently chide him.

The king used to mix his wine with water, the quantity depending on the strength of the wine. Once, in Cyprus, he asked me why I never diluted my wine. I answered that my doctors had assured me that I had a large head and cold stomach and that therefore it was impossible for me to become drunk. But the king replied that the doctors were misleading me and unless I acquired the habit of diluting my wine while I was still young I would suffer from gout, stomach pains and general ill-health in old age. He added that if I drank wine when I was old I would be drunk every night, which in an old person would be deeply shameful.

Centuries before St Louis was praised for it, the written lives of lay nobles emphasized the virtue of moderation. Despite the shift away from monasticism and its values towards an acceptance that a spiritual life could be led also in the secular world, moderation in all things was still highly regarded. Joinville wrote of St Louis:

He was so temperate in his habits that I never heard him order a particular menu in advance, as so many lords do. Instead he was content with whatever food his cook prepared and with the amount that was served up to him. He was judicious in his speech: never did I hear him speak ill of anyone, nor did he swear *par le diable*, as is heard every day throughout the kingdom, a habit which, I believe, is displeasing to God . . . He would say that one should exercise restraint in dress and should bear arms in moderation, avoiding all extremes, so that wise people of one's own age do not consider it excessive, nor the young inadequate . . . He would hear mass every day, first a low mass for the dead, then the office for the day, as well as the particular mass for that day, if appropriate. After his meal he would go to bed and rest and when he had slept he would afterwards hear the mass for the dead in his own room with one of his chaplains. In the evening he would hear vespers and then compline . . .

PART II

The Living Rock: The City and Nature in the Middle Ages

'It was as if the world had returned to its very first days, when all was silence and no human voice or shepherd's whistle was yet heard in the countryside.' In his *History of the Langobards* Paul the Deacon gave a picture of the empty countryside after the terrible plague which ravaged central and southern Europe in the mid-sixth century, the nadir in the slow but steady decline of the ancient world in the West. Once-great cities were empty shells, and villages survived barely at subsistence level. Everywhere forest encroached and marsh and moor advanced, surrounding and eventually obliterating towns and villages which had existed for hundreds of years. Where for centuries order had been imposed on the environment, and stone buildings erected in despite of nature, now nature ruled again. Settlements fell into ruin and their walls and houses became overgrown. Cities shrank until they were eventually abandoned, and thriving villages contracted to a handful of dwellings. The great Roman roads were broken up by tree roots and plants and, with the collapse of the aqueducts, water supplies failed. In the cities the baths, theatres and basilicas, all sacked and looted during the barbarian attacks, now served solely as strongholds or makeshift shelters, even as hiding-places.

In the fifth century Sidonius Apollinaris, Bishop of Clermont in the Auvergne, was clearly bewildered by what he saw: 'Everywhere we find churches whose roofs have fallen in and whose doors are broken and have come off their hinges. The entrances are choked by thorns and briars. There are animals inside, wandering through the aisles right up to the altars, where grass grows. All around is neglect...' Many other accounts echo this tone of bitter melancholy. This tone cannot be as-cribed simply to the naturally sombre outlook of churchmen; there is abundant evidence that people clung on laboriously to a precarious existence and that these descriptions do not exaggerate.

Ruins were to be found everywhere, but where their dark outlines loomed up in the empty expanses of country they inspired especial fear. There were tales of strange noises, of dazzling flashes of light at night. The ancient stones were regarded as sacred because they contained the burial-places of martyrs or the bones of Christians slaughtered by the barbarians. At one and the same time they repelled and fascinated, and were felt to be alive and to be insistently demanding attention. Monks sought out ruined churches to restore and reconsecrate, pacifying the uneasy souls of the martyrs they had originally been dedicated to. For centuries those martyrs had lain beneath turf trodden only by passing shepherds with their flocks, as at Brescello, near Reggio Emilia, where the tomb of Genesius, the first bishop, lay all but hidden in the ruins of a Roman town which had been destroyed by fire at the beginning of the seventh century.

After the year 1000 the remains of the city were reused in a great surge of building. The stones of the ruined Roman buildings received a second lease of life in houses, palaces and public buildings and as paving for streets, while in the countryside new villages and estates rose, all built of Roman stone. The underlying cause of these great and widespread changes in the rural and urban landscape was the steady rise in population; and in turn the increased food supplies resulting from the changes allowed the population to grow, accelerating the gradual and painful repopulation of the West. The rebirth of the towns made for a strong civic pride which found expression in the construction of ever higher cathedrals. Cities waxed great on trade and the new wealth derived from commerce was flaunted in sumptuous clothes and splendid feasting.

In Italy towns had never completely disappeared but had survived even the darkest moments of the early Middle Ages, with some maintaining local influence. After the year 1000 they once again became significant centres of power, determined to control the surrounding countryside. For the cities the remaining uncultivated land was a challenge, to be transformed so as to increase productivity: land was cleared for crops and vines, canals were cut, marshes drained, rivers embanked and forts and agricultural colonies were established. The reasons for this increasing urban pressure on the countryside and for the ever growing demands on both peasants and city artisans were many: the need to guarantee food supplies; civic pride; a sense of superiority over the country and its peasant inhabitants and a desire to distinguish the city from the countryside; rivalries between neighbouring towns; and the exigencies of war.

In Italy the period when the cities were at the height of their power was marked by devastating floods and by violent popular revolts. Not only had the towns put too much pressure on the natural environment, but they had also created dangerously deep social divisions. This, the darker aspect of the city, is one almost invariably overlooked or tolerated, because the conviction that civilization is synonymous with the city has ancient roots and has always prevailed.

11

Dead Cities

In the life of St Columbanus we read that, towards the end of the sixth century, Columbanus was travelling through a forest in what is now France when he came across a dozen wolves. According to the author of the life, he remained motionless as the wolves came up and nuzzled his clothes, and since he had faith in God and was not afraid, they went away without harming him. Such encounters with wild animals must have been frequent in the early Middle Ages, when animals were a common sight, roaming through countryside which had long since reverted to wilderness. Dense forest stretched for mile upon mile, interrupted only occasionally by the stark ruins of towns and villages destroyed during the barbarian invasions or abandoned after long decline. The population had declined virtually everywhere, not only on the formerly populated uplands but also on the plains, once intensively farmed. Vast areas were covered by tangled vegetation and overgrown ruins.

Probably in 612, St Columbanus founded the monastery at Bobbio in the Apennines above Piacenza, which after his death was to be dedicated to him as well. Though Bobbio is only 270 metres above sealevel, by the time of Columbanus the area was abandoned and desolate, its slopes covered by forests and ruins. Columbanus had earlier founded another monastery on the site of a Roman town at Luxeuil in France, where the statues of the pagan temples were still standing in the depths of the forest, frozen in silence. Dense forest had sprung up all around the abandoned ruins and only wild animals roamed there. The site in Normandy where St Wandrille built the monastery of Fontenelle, probably in 649, was equally neglected. According to the ninth-century text which describes the monastery's foundation the area was choked with scrub and brambles and waterlogged.

These monasteries, and others like them, brought inhabitants and agriculture back to areas which had been long abandoned. Both Fontenelle and Bobbio also became renowned centres of learning; in this they and other monasteries took over the central role which had earlier belonged to the towns. During the Roman empire towns had stimulated the development of their hinterlands, encouraging agriculture and functioning as centres for trade and crafts as well as for political, ecclesiastical and cultural activity. In the early Middle Ages this economic and cultural role shifted to the monasteries, many of which were more influential than the surviving towns. Monasteries were to be found above all in rural areas; in a sense they had grown out of the countryside and remained intimately connected to it. This adoption of the role of the town by the monasteries was a characteristic mainly of France and Germany, where towns tended to grow up around monasteries. In Italy, by contrast, towns continued to have an economic and administrative role, though their importance was greatly diminished. Monasteries there were often situated inside towns or immediately outside the walls.

All the same, everywhere towns had decayed and had lost their central position. The ancient world had created a highly sophisticated and essentially urban civilization: the Romans, like the Etruscans before them, had been city builders and the vast and complex network of their towns had had a profound influence on the landscape. No part of the countryside was unaffected by the city as roads linked all urban centres, large and small. Roman cities had often been of a considerable size, centres for administration, religion and learning, commerce and production as well as a forum for the exchange of ideas. They gave vitality to the surrounding territory, animating it, as it were, and imposing a degree of uniformity and a sense of unity. Although agriculture was the most important part of the Roman economy, and the majority of people lived in the country, the production and sale of everyday and luxury goods was important.

Over time, however, the vast reaches of the Roman empire everywhere atrophied. Many towns slowly but inexorably faded away, and economic and social life died as communities became isolated from one another. Central power collapsed and learning declined. The trend was apparent well before the barbarian invasions, which only hastened it. Even agriculture collapsed, and forest, moor and fen began to invade areas which had been cultivated for centuries as city walls and buildings crumbled and squares and open spaces began to be colonized by grass and saplings. Urban populations decreased dramatically and many towns vanished altogether. By the sixth century vast tracts of country had become wilderness, increasingly desolate and interrupted only by the ruins of churches, towns and villages. Ravaged by decay and war and by invaders eager for booty, these ruins stood awaiting reconsecration or reuse, a task often accomplished by monks, as we shall see. Travellers found the ruins daunting. Sinister and threatening, the abode of evil spirits, they would loom up out of the wasteland or unexpectedly block the path through the forest.

They were the dead cities, the remains of the ancient pagan civilization which Christianity had come to redeem, where the bones of Christians massacred by barbarians and the tombs of martyrs awaited rediscovery and veneration. Strange noises, spine-chilling silences and eerie gleams at night indicated the presence of these martyrs. Occasionally they could be glimpsed, but more usually they stayed hidden below ground or in the undergrowth. In the early Middle Ages these Christian dead seemed to be everywhere, gliding around the ruins of abandoned towns or churches. They could make phantoms appear, bring about strange happenings or even leave physical traces of their passing. The world around became an extraordinary blend of natural and supernatural, coloured with unaccustomed hues, and the earthly world was felt to be very close to the next. Paradise, for instance, was envisaged as a garden of delights, in a projection of this world on to the next. In the eleventh century the chronicler of the monastery of Novalesa in the Val di Susa near Turin noted that a donation of estates to the monastery had included the site of a Roman town where a number of Christians had been martyred. According to tradition, so many had been slaughtered and so much blood shed that the stones of a river running through the land had oozed blood at the moment when it was given to the monastery. The martyrs' blood was believed to have remained in the ground, hallowing the spot for ever and destining it for monastic ownership.

Four hundred years earlier, in about 612, St Columbanus arrived at the court of Agilulf, the Lombard king of Italy. When a member of the court told Columbanus that 'in the fastnesses of the Apennines' not far from Piacenza stood a ruined church dedicated to St Peter and associated with miracles he decided to take his companions there to restore it. The monastery which he founded there was that of Bobbio, soon to become famous. Columbanus had already been drawn by ruins in France during his long journey south from Ireland. He had decided to found a monastery at Luxeuil on the ruins of the abandoned and overgrown Roman town.

There were many reasons why, in their search for a suitable site, monks should be attracted to abandoned churches or, failing this, to the ruins of towns and villages: ready availability of stone, the knowledge that the site had been able to support a community in the past, and the presence of natural beauty which, as they knew well from the Bible, was indicative of a place conducive to spiritual life. Yet the presence of long-dead martyrs must have been a compelling reason, and among such abandoned ruins it was easy to suppose that Christians had been slaughtered in barbarian raids and thus become saints and martyrs. Like Columbanus, monks enquired where ruined churches and towns might be found or simply chanced upon them, no hard task in a landscape which until the eleventh century was a confused mass of forest and empty scrub dotted with ruined buildings half hidden beneath the undergrowth and visited only by the occasional shepherd. In such a landscape, typical of much of central southern Europe, many found that the presence of the dead made the ruined churches and villages fearful and daunting.

Towards the end of the tenth century Adalbert-Atto, founder of the house of Canossa, decided to erect defences for a new settlement on the river Po near Parma. The settlement, Brescello, lay close to a Roman town and former episcopal seat which Byzantine forces had sacked and burnt in 603 so as not to leave one of the strongest fortresses on the Po in Lombard control. The outlines of the overgrown ruins could still be seen, and were found menacing by the local people. The *Chronicle of St Genesius* tells how Adalbert-Atto had ordered the ruins to be quarried for building material. A shepherd boy reached into a deep hole in the ground but found that his arm was trapped. Hearing his desperate screams, like those of one possessed, people came running and prayed to St Genesius, believed to be the first bishop of the city. Once the saint had been duly placated the boy was able to free his arm from the rubble.

The episode has the ring of a cautionary tale for those who fail to respect ancient ruins which contain a saint's tomb, and a whole series of events in fact demonstrates how the stones of these derelict buildings were felt still to be a living, potent force. The area was sparsely populated and at night the spirits of the dead were said to be abroad. One evening the parents of the over-adventurous boy were woken by sweet music and looked out of the door to see a procession of clerics, chanting and carrying lighted candles, dressed all in white and led by a tall figure who towered above them, the saint himself. The procession continued across the fields and receded into the heavens, becoming ever smaller until there were mere pinpricks of light far away among the stars.

Shortly before, St Genesius had appeared in a dream to a man in Milan who was suffering from leprosy and promised him that he would be cured if he made a pilgrimage to his tomb. The man made the long journey to Brescello where, after a series of strange occurrences, the saint's tomb was rediscovered, wedged in a solid wall. As a team of workmen toiled in vain to uncover it, it became apparent that Genesius was reluctant to allow his tomb to be easily excavated. One of the workmen, exasperated by the lack of results, struck the tomb with his pickaxe and promptly fell down dead, punished for his presumption. Only humble prayer and contrition could resolve this last problem.

All these episodes come from the chronicle of a monk from the later monastery of St Genesius in Brescello. He obviously had a vested interest in supplying detailed evidence for the miracle-working powers of the saint's relics. He noted, for example, that the dramatic rise of the house of Canossa could be dated from a penitential pilgrimage to Genesius' tomb by Adalbert-Atto and his wife. Such an emphasis on the power inherent in relics is a standard element of saints' lives and accounts of the rediscovery of tombs and of relics, but it is clear that these long-dead martyrs did inspire real fear in a large part of the population. Much early medieval source material – foundations of churches and monasteries and gifts and bequests to them – derives from attempts to placate the dead.

From the seventh century onwards, the stones of the abandoned Roman towns were gradually salvaged and reused, primarily to build monasteries and churches but also to give new life to villages and towns. From the tenth century, as we shall see, under the pressure of continual invasions ruins were ransacked to build fortifications and defences as well as walls to protect towns, which had survived in relatively high numbers in Italy. Yet ruins were still a common sight throughout the countryside, and change on a large scale came only with the economic expansion in the centuries after the year 1000, when a dense network of roads, canals, fields and buildings began to alter the landscape dramatically. Existing towns expanded and new ones, large and small, emerged, using the ruins of the old as building material. This was the final chapter in the history of the ancient dead cities. By the late Middle Ages ruins had vanished from the countryside of western Europe and were no longer there to strike awe and dread into the hearts of travellers.

12

Fortress Cities

The death of Charles the Fat in 888 marked the final disintegration of Charlemagne's empire. The unity of the empire had been steadily undermined since Charles the Bald and Louis the German had defeated Lothar their brother at the bloody battle of Fontenoy in 841, and since the treaty of Verdun two years later, which had confirmed the division of the empire. Europe lacked a strong central power. The empire had collapsed and the new French, German and Italian monarchies which had developed out of it were still weak and struggling to assert themselves, particularly in Italy. It was just then, at the close of the ninth century, with Christendom at its most vulnerable, that attacks were unleashed from all sides: Vikings from the north, Arabs from the south, Hungarians from the east. Under an onslaught similar to the barbarian invasions of the late Roman empire (and often in fact called 'the second wave' of invasions), Europe fell into chaos. In 909 the bishops of the ecclesiastical province of Rheims, meeting at Trosly, declared that: 'We see the Lord give vent to the full measure of his wrath. Before us are but deserted cities, monasteries razed to the ground or burned down, abandoned and neglected fields . . . Everywhere the strong oppress the weak and men are as the fish of the sea which devour one another indiscriminately.'

Terror, which for centuries had been seen in sporadic outbursts, was now widespread and intense. As had been the case during the earlier barbarian invasions, the constant threat of attack made for political and social change and affected the landscape itself. Everywhere villages built defences and towns put their walls in order, while many new fortresses were erected. The face of western Europe changed as it took on an embattled air which was to mark it for centuries.

The Hungarians, originally from Asia, reached the area of present-day Hungary in 896; their first attacks on Friuli, the marches region of Italy which always bore the brunt of invasions, appear to have occurred only two years later, in 898. Over the next two years the invaders poured down into northern Italy, especially the Po plain, sacking towns, villages, farmsteads and abbeys and slaughtering their inhabitants. In September 899, on the river Brenta near Venice, they annihilated an army drawn from all over Italy and led by Berengar I. Berengar had been undisputed king of Italy since 898, and yet this defeat was caused mainly by the lack of unity in his army. Though the inhabitants of Italy might have only one king, their loyalties were profoundly divided and they had no common ground. After this victory the Hungarian attacks and sackings intensified. The spoils were rich. The great abbey of Nonantola was burned down and the nearby town of Reggio Emilia sacked and its bishop murdered. Out of all the towns in the western Po plain, it appears that only Modena was able to hold out against attack. Piacenza, a crossing point on the Po, suffered so many assaults over the following years that centuries later it was generally believed that the entire city had been burned down during a Hungarian raid.

Grim tales, inflated by fear, sprang up or had a new lease of life. It was said that the Hungarians had faces of monsters, that their cruelty was unbounded. It was at this time that the legend of the great bronze gates which Alexander the Great had supposedly erected near the Caspian Sea to hold back the barbarian hordes of Asia spread for a second time, as the Hungarians were believed to have somehow succeeded in breaking them down. Another legend grew up, of a great rampart which Charlemagne had earlier built to contain the Avars. Such tales, which sprang from the widespread sense of helplessness against the Hungarians, had recourse to invincible historical figures like Alexander and Charlemagne to try to account for the present impossibility of defence. Not until the victory of Otto I at Lechfeld in 955 was western European cavalry able to defeat the highly mobile Hungarian horsemen, and until then the only sure defence was to take refuge inside a walled town or within palisades. The Hungarian raids on Italy came to an end only towards the mid-tenth century, and ceased soon after in the rest of Europe as the Hungarians became established in what is now Hungary and were gradually converted to Christianity.

This withdrawal behind walls resulted in extreme political fragmentation. This, the most characteristic feature of the tenth century, persisted until at least the thirteenth century and the reassertion by the towns of their authority over the surrounding rural area. During the invasions of the tenth century people gravitated towards fortified places and would cultivate only land close to them. Thus towns increasingly became refuges and focal points for the surrounding area, and their size and importance grew. Their role was still limited, however, as they were primarily fortresses, surrounded by moats and ramparts, and did not as yet function as administrative centres for large areas.

The period saw not only attacks from outside Christendom but also raids from permanent bases within Italy and France themselves. Around 890, an Arab pirate galley anchored on the Mediterranean coast of France, near the present site of Saint-Tropez. The pirates set themselves up in caves in the middle of dense woodland on a nearby headland called Frassinet and would sally forth to raid French and Piedmontese villages. At about the same time, another band of Arab corsairs established themselves at the mouth of the river Garigliano in Campania and used this base to plunder central and southern Italy. As with the Hungarians, sinister and alarming legends grew up around the Arabs. In popular imagination the impenetrable Frassinet lair took on supernatural qualities. It was said that the Arabs had made the forest impassable and that there were trees and bushes with strange sharp thorns on which people risked being impaled. Fear of man and fear of God, inextricably mixed as always, meant that such raids were thought to be a punishment from God for sin. The Arabs of Garigliano were driven out only in 915, and it took some eighty years, until 970, to dislodge those of Frassinet.

The final group of invaders was the Vikings, from Scandinavia. Their first raids on France date from the end of the eighth century, while Charlemagne still ruled, and continued until Normandy was given to them as a fief in 911, when their attacks almost entirely ceased. Like the Hungarians in Italy, they relied on speed and surprise for success. Much of their strength lay in their fast, easily manoeuvred longships, of which Marc Bloch has written:

> Seldom longer than twenty metres, they could be propelled by either oar or sail. Generally each could carry forty to fifty men, doubtless packed closely. Their shallow draught of slightly more than a metre was a great advantage on leaving the open sea for estuaries, and even more so on rivers. Like the Arabs, the Vikings regarded the sea as a highway leading to plunder.

Whereas in Italy towns had normally been able to defend themselves against the attacks of the Hungarians, in France they fell victim to the raiders. Even major cities were vulnerable: in 845 Paris itself was stormed, though later, in 886, under the leadership of Odo, Count of Paris, it succeeded in repelling the Vikings. As a result of this victory Odo was proclaimed King of France. He was the first of the Capetian dynasty, though the dynasty was not to be firmly established until a century later. In France it was at this time that kingship regained its prestige and mystique, whereas in Italy the idea of loyalty to a single ruler had ceased to be attractive. In March 924 the citizens of Pavia, the capital of the kingdom of Italy, led by their bishop, defended the city against the Hungarians for themselves. Berengar I, king and emperor, was occupied elsewhere, and only a month later was assassinated by one of his own vassals. His rival, Rudolf II of Burgundy, who had defeated him in July 923, was also absent, far away in Burgundy. The contrast between Pavia and Paris is illuminating: in France the feudal aristocracy took charge of defence; in Italy it was the citizens themselves, led by their bishop, who did so. Towns, initially important solely for military reasons, became steadily more prominent as administrative centres.

The principal contenders for the Italian crown had originally been Berengar I of Friuli, Guy, Marquis of Spoleto, and Lambert, Guy's son. Guy's death in 894 and Lambert's death four years later, killed while hunting in the forest of Marengo near Alessandria, left Berengar the principal claimant. He easily defeated other claimants such as Hugh of Arles, Marquis of Provence, and Louis the Blind, King of Provence, and he was crowned Emperor by Pope John X in 915. However, Italian magnates such as the Marquis of Tuscany undermined his authority and he was loathed by many of the bishops. Local powers were too embroiled in their own interests to be prepared to support a central authority, and in any case they saw little need for, and felt little loyalty to, such an institution. The lack of loyalty when Berengar I was eventually assassinated in 924 by one of his own vassals, who had led the plot against him, is indicative of the weakness of the crown. In the plot against the king the previous year, the aristocracy had supported the claims of Rudolf II of Burgundy. According to Liutprand of Cremona, a near contemporary of these events, the issue split the country. 'And so half the kingdom supported Rudolf and half Berengar. A bitter civil war was imminent.' When Berengar was defeated in the terrible battle of Fiorenzuola on the Via Emilia near Piacenza on 21 July 923, casualties on both sides, particularly among the aristocracy, were much higher than had been seen in Italy for a long time. News of the battle reverberated far beyond Italy, and the French chronicler Flodoard wrote of a total of 1,500 dead.

Fiorenzuola devastated the Italian aristocracy. Many towns must have lost their lords, further weakening central administration and enabling local forces, especially the bishops, to increase their power. The city, precisely because of the growing stature and prestige of bishops, extended its influence over large areas. Central authority was undermined on all sides as the autonomy of cities, towns and rural strongholds all increased. After the assassination of Berengar I in 924 while Rudolf was absent in Burgundy, Italy collapsed into anarchy. Rudolf returned to Italy but the Italians once again, as Liutprand wrote, 'hurled themselves against one another'. Rudolf was deposed and the crown was offered to Hugh of Arles, who ruled between 926 and 945. Hugh made his sickly son, Lothar II, co-king and when he died in 948 Lothar ruled. But Lothar's rule was only nominal; the real ruler was Berengar II of Ivrea. On Lothar's death in 950, his widow Adelaide was imprisoned by Berengar, but she escaped and sought the protection of Adalbert-Atto of Canossa. In 951 Otto of Saxony, King of Germany, invaded Italy and became King of Italy. He married Adelaide, made Berengar his vassal and was crowned Emperor by Pope John XII in 962.

Berengar II attempted a revolt, but he was defeated and imprisoned. The kingdom of Italy and the imperial crown belonged thereafter to German dynasties. At the same time local powers, particularly the bishops and the towns but also the noble clans, themselves frequently based in the towns, continued to assert their power. The tenth century saw powerful and influential women: Marozia in Rome, Berta of Tuscany in Lucca, Ermengarda in Ivrea and Adelaide, married first to Lothar II and then to Otto I.

The first indications of the great urban revival of the eleventh and twelfth centuries were evident as early as the tenth century. Especially in Italy, where powerful bishops and great feudal dynasties held power, the city began to assert itself against the countryside; it was here that the clash was sharpest between the emerging, specifically urban, artisan, merchant and banking classes and the old-established rural aristocracy.

13

The Myth of the City

Up here there is too much Asia. It is not without significance that the place is full of Muscovite and Mongolian types. These people – do not put yourself in tune with them, do not be infected with their ideas . . . cling to everything which to you is by nature and tradition holy, as a son of the godlike West, a son of civilisation: and, for example, time . . . Take our great cities, the centres and foci of civilization, the crucibles of thought! (Thomas Mann, *The Magic Mountain*, trans. H. T. Lowe-Porter)

These words are spoken by Ludovico Settembrini to Hans Castorp, the engineer from Hamburg, in the silent snow-covered countryside near the sanatorium where both are patients. Settembrini is remonstrating with Castorp, who has expressed a cavalier disregard for time, a disregard which Settembrini relates to his fascination with the East. In the novel the West and its cities are represented as a world where time and space are precious commodities, to be used purposefully and not squandered, whereas the East, with its endless steppes, is the realm of the infinite.

The enduring myth of the city has ancient origins; the city has always been seen as synonymous with the civilization of the West and it continued to cast its spell even when the ideal failed to correspond to the actual physical appearance of the city. Over a thousand years earlier, around the year 800, the city of Verona was celebrated in a poem.

In Italy, near Venice, lies a great and prosperous city, much celebrated, which, as Isidore tells us, has been called Verona since ancient times. The city, built as a square, is protected by thick walls and surrounded by forty-eight gleaming towers. Eight of the towers, soaring, overtop the rest. Inside the city there is a vast and deep labyrinth in the form of a circle. He who once ventures in cannot escape unless he has a lantern or a ball of thread. There is a great square, paved throughout . . . Consider how evil men who

were ignorant of God's law and who worshipped ancient idols fashioned of
wood and stone could yet build so well . . .

Shortly before, Milan was described in a poem as 'queen of cities and
the mother of our country'. The qualities which the writers of these
panegyrics chose to emphasize are magnificence – city walls, paved
streets and squares, stone towers glinting in the sunlight, imposing
buildings – and sanctity – churches with the relics of celebrated martyrs.
Yet eighth-century Verona and Milan hardly resembled these descriptions, which should rather be understood as an evocation of past glories
and a dream of what might be. Centuries were to pass before the cities
matched these eulogies.

All the same, the idea of the city still continued to exercise its fascination, though civic pride and the determination to build impressive
cathedrals led some towns to overreach themselves and as a result to
suffer economic decline and near-ruin. An example is Beauvais in
northern France. By the thirteenth century it was wealthy from its
Europe-wide trade in woollen cloth. Its population increased so much
that another circuit of walls had to be built, and among the towns under
the French monarchy it was second only to Paris. Its bishop, enthusiastically backed by the cathedral chapter and by the citizens, was determined to build a new cathedral for the town, which was to be the highest
in Christendom. Work began in 1247 but in 1284, before it was finished,
the great vaulting collapsed. It was largely rebuilt, but at enormous cost
in labour and money. The cathedral, still unfinished, today dwarfs the
low houses, towering over the small town. The stubborn determination
to build so magnificent a cathedral was undoubtedly a major factor
behind Beauvais's economic decline: the population level stagnated, cloth
production decreased and the town never enjoyed the prosperity of the
nearby Flemish cities.

In the rolling countryside of northern France towards the coast, travellers suddenly see rise before them the great cathedrals which loom
above the market towns of the region. In *The Guermantes Way* Proust
compared the cathedral of Laon, dominating the empty countryside
around, to a colossal Noah's Ark, and that of Beauvais to a huge black-
winged bird:

> The sky was still empty at those points where later were to rise Notre-
> Dame of Paris and Notre-Dame of Chartres; a time when on the summit of
> the hill of Laon the nave of its cathedral had not yet been poised like the
> Ark of the Deluge on the summit of Mount Ararat, overcrowded with
> Patriarchs and Judges anxiously leaning from its windows to see if the
> wrath of God has yet subsided, carrying with it specimens of the plants that
> will multiply on the earth, brimming over with animals which have even

climbed out through the tower, between which oxen grazing calmly on the roof look down over the plains of Champagne; when the traveller who left Beauvais at the close of day did not yet see, following him and turning with his road, the black ribbed wings of the cathedral spread out against the golden screen of the western sky. (trans. C. A. Scott Moncrieff and Terence Kilmartin)

To go back in time, the monk and chronicler Rudolf Glaber from Burgundy, writing in the first half of the eleventh century, marvelled at the changes he saw all around:

Almost everywhere, but in Italy and in France in particular, churches were rebuilt. Nearly all of them were well built and in good condition, scarcely requiring restoration, yet it seemed that all Christians were vying with each other to build churches more magnificent than the rest. It was as though the world were trying to shake off all things ancient and to clad itself with a resplendent white mantle of churches.

In the eleventh century and before, there was also change, if less dramatic, in the countryside. Everywhere the great forests receded and the wilderness contracted as land came under the plough and the number of villages multiplied. Above all, towns increased in number and size and gradually pushed into the background the old landscape of abbeys, castles and villages. Even the defensive towers, once a feature of the countryside, began to be seen in the towns wherever an entrenched urban aristocracy had emerged, as in Italy.

As in antiquity, the reality of the city once again lived up to its myth. The desire to make the city splendid was at its strongest during this period. Just as in antiquity amphitheatres, theatres and baths had been the expression of civic pride, so now cathedrals were built or existing ones added to. The topmost point of the choir of Beauvais cathedral stands forty-eight metres high and the later cathedral of San Petronio in Bologna is only slightly lower. In the twelfth century scenes of peasant or craft work from the transformed countryside – ploughing, harvesting, viniculture – were depicted on cathedral fronts. The faces of the figures lost the angularity and starkness of earlier Romanesque church sculpture and its heirs, such as that in San Zeno Maggiore in Verona, the abbey of Nonantola near Modena, San Nicola in Bari, Saint-Pierre in Angoulême and the cathedral at Hildesheim. These were all added to in the twelfth century, while at the same time new cathedrals were being built in the Gothic style, graceful and soaring. As early as 1140 Abbot Suger presided over the start of building of the great abbey church of Saint-Denis near Paris, built in the Gothic style, and in one of his writings he declared that: 'The work which radiates above all others is that which serves to illuminate the mind. Light should elevate our minds to the entrance to the True Light, to its portals – in short, to Christ.'

The passage irresistibly calls to mind the new Gothic architecture, with its tall narrow arches, high windows suffused with light, and the vertical thrust of its arcades. Italy has nothing as overwhelming as the great Gothic cathedrals which dominate the small towns of northern France and the surrounding countryside. In northern and central Italy towns were larger and had higher populations, as well as numerous churches, monasteries and convents and imposing civic buildings. The cathedral would generally be situated at the centre of the city but it was usually comparatively small and all but hidden by the other buildings clustered around it.

Italian towns, with their large merchant class as well as the aristocracy, had a very different social composition from towns north of the Alps. Towards the end of the thirteenth century Salimbene of Parma recorded that at that time the city authorities in Bologna were passing stringent legislation against nobles resident in the town to prevent them from abusing their power. If a noble injured any member of the *popolo* (craftsmen and tradesmen above a certain social level), his land inside the city was to be confiscated and his palaces razed to the ground until not a stone remained. Salimbene observed that by the time he was writing, the nobles, alarmed by these measures, had gone to live on their estates in the country, as was the custom in France. Those who remained in the town, the non-nobles, were termed *borghesi*, as in France.

Nevertheless, in Italy there was never a drastic division between city and country. Cities, with their large merchant population, and the countryside, dominated by the great abbeys and the nobility, where villages huddled in the shadow of castles and abbeys, continued to share common features. Villages might have urban elements, while even in the later Middle Ages towns retained distinctly rural characteristics. The only exceptions were remote areas in the Po plain or in the mountains, where the feudal lords ruled virtually unchallenged.

14

The Changing Countryside

Though there is much about the way of life in the Middle Ages which is strange and even alien to us, certain familiar figures stand out. We can empathize with the peasant behind the plough, with the merchant eager to travel and equally at home anywhere in Europe, with the arrogant nobleman whose generosity and passion for war are recounted in contemporary chronicles. The writings of the time offer glimpses of the profoundly and unremittingly rural way of life, the backdrop to all the events they describe. Settlements, surrounded by fields and vineyards, were swallowed up by the endless expanses of forest, although the great tracts of empty land offered unprecedented opportunities. Despite the dangers of these wild areas, and threats from tyrannical nobles, they made for a sense of wide horizons and an exceptional feeling of freedom. The low productivity of the large estates meant that the aristocracy and the great monasteries required a disproportionate amount of labour: in the ninth century, for example, some thirty families were seemingly necessary to maintain each of the sixty monks of the French monastery of Saint-Bertin in the condition to which he was accustomed. The economic system was vulnerable if it could not prevent the silent opposition of peasants and stop them from making contact with the outside world. Above all, it was at risk from peasants migrating to seek freedom and their own land.

Despite suggestions that it is a historical myth, such peasant mobility did genuinely exist. Gradually but steadily such people pushed back the frontier of forest and wilderness. Though peasants were poor and relatively powerless, it was more than economic need alone which impelled them to embark on what has been called 'the great economic adventure of the twelfth century'; they were inspired by the same spirit of adventure that later spurred merchants to ride the roads of Europe. Traditionally

'Changes in the countryside'

The cultivation becomes more intense. June. Stained glass, English fifteenth century, reproduced © The Board of Trustees of the Victoria and Albert Museum, London.

the phenomenon has been portrayed as a triumphant advance, where the interests of peasants eager for freedom and land coincided with those of lords keen for new subjects and increased territory, resulting in the 'free towns', settlements established inside wide breaches in the forest. The desire for freedom is seen as the main impetus behind the changes: that these new communities were jealous of their liberties is inferred from the fact that their statutes were proudly modelled on those of the towns, and from their relationships with their overlords, which were marked by greater openness and flexibility. According to this interpretation, change in the countryside came about only with the revival of the towns in Italy and northern Europe in the twelfth century, a result of the new civic outlook of the merchant class and a further symptom of the dominant role of the bourgeoisie in the renewal in western Europe.

Though the general outlines of this interpretation are valid, it needs revision. Further study of the clearances has robbed them of some of the glamour traditionally attached to them. The dramatic story beloved of earlier generations of historians, of an epic struggle against an implacable forest, has been replaced by detailed and sober accounts of a slow but inexorable extension of land already under cultivation around established villages as scrubland and thickets were cleared. This, the simplest and most common type of clearance, accounted for some five-sixths of all new cultivated land. It has been noted of medieval Picardy, for example, that 'rather than tackle virgin forest peasants preferred to extend land already under cultivation by clearing untilled areas, and rather than contend with oak forest they would remove undergrowth.' There is no doubt, though, that some clearances were indeed carried out by peasants desperate to escape poverty and prepared to go to the most remote and desolate areas to do battle with forest and marsh. Even if the tradition that it was peasants themselves who always initiated clearance is mistaken, and colonization was not necessarily the heroic undertaking that has traditionally been portrayed, their determination and efforts cannot be denied.

> Although we know the names of those who decided on the land to be cleared and of those who afterwards had the land worked, it is obvious that, with the exception of a few monks whose rule insisted on physical work, none of those named in the sources ever laid hand on an axe or plough. All of them – the canons of Saint-Quentin, the citizens of Arras, the lord of Vignacourt – left the work to more expert hands. The royal official at Dargies, the nobleman at Coullemelle and the citizens from Abbeville, are most unlikely to have participated personally in the clearances, even though they claim to have done so. This is an area about which we are in the dark as unfortunately the documents tell us virtually nothing about those who actually felled the trees and cleared the ground for cultivation. Even where it is possible that monks were indeed involved in the work, there is evidence that gangs of peasants were also recruited. The forty-two men who were employed by the monastery of Saint-Nicolas-de-Arrouaise at Ligescourt in 1190 to clear land must have been laymen. Moreover, the sheer scale and speed of many of the clearances rules out the possibility of a few monks alone being responsible. It was peasants who wielded the axe and later the plough, people like the *rustici* who are mentioned in an agreement of 1183 made by the monastery at Corbie about the village of Bus.

In this passage the clearances regain some of their epic quality. They are indeed the dominant feature of medieval economic history. As clearance progressed, there was constant tension between land in cultivation and land still wild. The boundary between them was fluid. Usually the wilderness was pushed back but there is evidence that at other times it advanced, and cultivated areas were abandoned. The eleventh century marked the watershed, when the balance shifted from a primarily silvo-pastoral economy to one dominated by agriculture, the result of centuries of toil by determined peasants and their lords with only primitive tools and technology. The economy of the late Middle Ages differed fundamentally from that of the early Middle Ages, and once agriculture had begun to be a dominant element the process was to continue inexorably up to the modern period.

Clearances and the triumph of agriculture affected everyone, peasants, nobles and merchants alike. The forests of the Po plain came under attack from all sides. The ring of fast-expanding cities around the edge of the plain needed arable land for their expanding populations and to banish the all too frequent spectre of shortage and famine. It was here, in northern and central Italy, that the countryside was most affected by the city. Prompted by the need for defence against neighbouring cities and by the growth of trade, the cities promoted clearances, constructed roads and canals and established agricultural colonies and military outposts. Large areas none the less proved too great a challenge, especially in the forests and moors of the mountains and in the more impenetrable marshes and waterlogged forest of the plains, which were to remain uncleared as late as the nineteenth century.

In the late Middle Ages, clearance of uncultivated land was most marked around towns and it was here that wild areas were completely eradicated or declined sharply, so much so that strict regulations had to be made to safeguard the remaining forests. Wood was an essential material, needed not only for cooking and heating but also for building and for agricultural implements and utensils of all kinds as well as for furniture, tools for tanning leather, barrels and containers, ships, boats and oars. The pressure was so great that it frequently became necessary to dig a moat around woodland, leaving just one entrance, which could be closed off with a heavy chain.

The struggle to impose order on nature and to control it resulted in a backlash. The attempts to increase production by endlessly bringing new land into cultivation imposed too great a strain on the ecological balance and ultimately upset it. Nature itself rebelled. Once tree cover had been lost, rainwater could no longer soak away and instead went to swell the rivers, with the result that floods, especially of the Po, began to affect wider areas. From the thirteenth century disastrous floods are a recurrent feature of chronicles. They formed great lakes, ever more extensive and ever closer to the cities. One chronicle describes how in the middle of the thirteenth century the rivers of the Po plain between Parma and Reggio Emilia all flooded until their waters merged and became one immense lake which stretched as far as the eye could see.

15

The Changing City

Italy, according to a proverb, is 'terra di città', land of cities. Even in the early Middle Ages there was a great variety of types of town. In some the landowning aristocracy prevailed, while others had a high proportion of, or were even dominated by, the merchant class (or bourgeoisie), the class which would later emerge in the cities of northern France and the Low Countries. The town of Mantua, in the north of Italy, was situated in the middle of marshes and depended entirely on agriculture and stockraising. It was ruled in turn by two powerful landowning families, the Canossa and the Gonzaga. Many other cities, such as Reggio Emilia, Parma and Modena, had a similar economic base. However, gradually they moved away from dependence on agriculture to develop distinctly urban institutions, while their merchant class also steadily increased in importance. Virtually all the towns of the interior of southern Italy, by contrast, were profoundly rural, sprawling townships on hilltops, often mere clusters of hovels from which peasants walked or rode miles every day to work their land.

Towns which even in the early Middle Ages had a high proportion of artisans, coiners and merchants were Pavia, Cremona, Piacenza, Milan, Verona, Lucca, Florence, Rome, Fermo on the Adriatic, and other coastal towns. Pavia, the capital of the kingdom of Italy, had excellent communications via the rivers Po and Ticino and was one of the largest centres of trade. Its citizens were a force to be reckoned with as early as the late ninth century, when they put Arnulf of Germany to flight as he was retreating from Liguria after his first invasion of Italy. The towns of Lombardy and the Veneto would not allow him to return through their territory, and Arnulf had to make a long and punishing detour over the northern Apennines to Piedmont, heading for Ivrea and the Great St Bernard pass. It is clear that towns like Pavia, enriched by the activities of the aristocracy and merchants, jealously guarded their independence and freedom as early as the rule of the German emperors, who were equally determined to exert authority over them. The struggle between the two began with Otto I and continued into the reign of Henry II, intensified under Conrad II and Henry III, and was only finally resolved in the contest of the cities with Frederick II of Swabia in the mid-thirteenth century.

Finally, the two towns of Comacchio on the Po delta and Venice were dominated even in the early medieval centuries by a powerful merchant class; in contrast to the towns of northern France, which had a similar merchant class, these towns enjoyed effective independence and had a considerable degree of political power.

In the early Middle Ages, in Italy and elsewhere, the economic activities we would associate with towns – trade, finance and banking, crafts – had an insignificant role. What set towns apart in this period were their walls and defences, not necessarily of stone, and their great churches with miracle-working relics of revered saints. By the later Middle Ages, however, descriptions of Italian cities begin to stress in addition the wealth generated by trade and crafts and the fame and magnificence of leading families. In the fourteenth century Giovanni Villani noted in his chronicle that in his native Florence some 30,000 people worked in the manufacture and sale of woollen cloth and that in the first decades of the century the population had grown to some 90,000. According to Villani there were dozens of banking houses, lawyers, doctors and merchants and numerous traders and notaries. He described the many churches and monasteries both inside and outside the walls, the innumerable cloth workshops of the Arte della Lana (the cloth manufacturers' guild) and the hundreds of bakers' shops. Milan enjoyed a similar level of economic activity: in 1288 Bonvesin della Riva wrote that the city had more than a thousand workshops and hundreds of bakers.

North of the Alps, the economy of Paris could not match that of many Italian and Flemish towns. Even so, the thirteenth and fourteenth centuries saw a great wave of building in the city, of houses and palaces, churches and religious houses, with the result that Paris became one of the largest cities in western Europe, equalled only by Milan. The university on the left bank of the Seine flourished and new colleges were founded. The royal castle was continually modified and enlarged, while the aristocracy were eager to have residences in the city. Hugh d'Aubriot, provost of Paris, consolidated the defences on the right bank of the river and built the Bastille, the Pont-Saint-Michel and the Louvre. Towards the end of the thirteenth century there were more than three hundred different trades in the city and at the beginning of the fourteenth century more than six hundred people were employed in the various stages of the

manufacture (spinning, weaving, cutting, dyeing) and sale of woollen
cloth. There was rivalry between dyers, spinners and weavers as early as
the end of the thirteenth century, though the tensions were not as great
as those in contemporary Bologna, where the fullers rose in rebellion, or
those in Florence, where the revolt of the Ciompi, the cloth-workers,
erupted in 1378 and was not finally quashed for a considerable time.

In Italy the city was once again beginning to dominate the surrounding
area, though in this it met opposition. A clause in the thirteenth-century
statutes of Reggio Emilia required everyone of standing in the city and its
territory (coterminous with the diocese) to attend the celebrations on the
feast-day of St Prosper, patron saint of the town. City legislation covered
every aspect of social and economic life both inside and outside the town.
The Reggio Emilia statutes, for example, stated that a serf who had lived
in the town for more than ten years became free, a measure which
severely undermined the economic basis of the great country estates,
dependent on serfdom as they were.

But it was above all within the city that change occurred, and particularly in Italy, where city councils tried to insist on certain standards
and pride in both town planning and everyday life and behaviour.
Wealthier citizens were invited to possess some brightly coloured article
of clothing which would bring credit to the town. Colour was increasingly seen in clothes, in houses and furniture. The city sought to civilize
the way of life of its citizens and to moderate the coarser aspects, seeking
to end the conspicuous public displays of emotion which were normal.
For instance, legislation forbade close female relatives to accompany
funeral processions to the graveyard because, it was claimed, they wailed
and beat their breasts, or fainted and had to be supported, behaviour
which, the laws observed disapprovingly, was indecorous. The city was
to be seemly: laws decreed that derelict buildings were not to mar its
appearance and that houses and other buildings inside and outside the
walls might not be demolished in order to sell the wood and stone for
building material (a contrast with earlier centuries when much of the area
inside town walls had been occupied by the ruins of Roman and later
buildings).

Other measures, concerned in part with the outward appearance of
the city, were intended primarily to encourage trade by ensuring regular
maintenance of the roads 'to make the highways safer for merchants and,
indeed, for all travellers'. Statutes ordered roads to be gravelled, a contrast to the muddy tracks of earlier centuries. These routes, regularly
maintained, radiated out from the towns into the countryside, itself
transformed by the increase of cultivated land. The city was not to be
disfigured by unpleasant sights: the gallows had to be hidden away
inconspicuously, and goats, foul-smelling and devouring everything in

sight, had to be kept well away from the town. Indeed, the distance from
the town at which they might be kept steadily increased, while some
towns imposed a limit of one goat per family. Inside the city, squares,
arcades, streets and waterways had to be kept clean and unobstructed.
It was forbidden to throw slops out of the window, keep animals in open
spaces or under porticoes or, in particular, dump manure there. Some
statutes even ordered trees in the town to be chopped down or fruit trees
to be planted in the countryside, or specified which crops were to be
grown.

The appearance of both city and country changed. Military and economic factors encouraged the cities to establish new settlements in their
territories, while villages established rural outposts to cultivate newly
cleared land. Such change was typical above all of central northern Italy,
but throughout western Europe the land was repopulated by the hosts of
new settlements. Agriculture became more systematic and better organized and uncultivated land contracted markedly. Cities expanded to
cover ever greater areas: Florence, for example, needed three new circuits
of walls in the twelfth and thirteenth centuries. As well as commercial
and financial activity, the city was increasingly a centre for crafts, encouraging the influx of artisans and specialist workers. The city became
a crossroads for different people and customs – one of the distinctive
features of towns.

16

The Merchant Ethic

questi risurgeranno del sepulcro col pugno chiuso

(these shall rise from the grave with fist clenched tight)

Dante Alighieri, *Inferno*, Canto VII, lines 56–7

Between the eleventh and the thirteenth centuries the city saw the development on a large scale of manufacture and trade. The established aristocracy tended to stand aloof from business and a new and quite distinct merchant class emerged, whose members were dramatically different from both the early medieval and contemporary nobility, and were attracted by the unheard-of fortunes to be made in trade. Where in the early Middle Ages the Church had urged powerful nobles not to abuse their position, now it denounced the profit ethic of merchants and of those who had been converted to commerce. The period between the second half of the twelfth century and the fifteenth century saw an explosion of religious movements exalting poverty. Their followers believed that the increase in wealth was contrary to the spirit of true Christianity, and sought a return to the simplicity of the early Church. Penitence played an important part in these movements, often in extreme forms, as among the flagellants, who first appear in the mid-thirteenth century and who practised particularly harsh self-flagellation.

All the same, wealth was overwhelmingly concentrated in a few social groups, while the lower groups in society were obliged to accept bleak living conditions. The new economic ethic was unforgiving for those who failed to learn to create their own wealth. The meticulous calculations and the new emphasis on profit are reflected in tenancy agreements: the chief difference between contracts of the early Middle Ages and those of the central and late medieval centuries is the widespread introduction of fixed rents in either cash or kind. Landlords had previously set rents at an agreed proportion of the yield, which meant that after a poor harvest less rent would be due. Over time, however, as both aristocratic and merchant landlords came to fix rents at a set amount either in kind or in cash, the rent due lost all connection with the yield. As a result, after a poor harvest tenants would be forced into debt to pay the rent. The physical violence typical of the early Middle Ages, when it had been common for nobles to seize stores of food and animal fodder, had ceased, only to be replaced by inexorable contracts insisting on immediate payment of rent in full, however difficult. Overt violence had been replaced by covert ruthlessness.

The nature of the relationship between the rural and urban poor has long been debated. Some historians have argued that their common poverty and wretchedness united them; others that any solidarity was outweighed by the traditional rivalry of city and country. As far as social discontent is concerned, though it is clear that urban and rural revolts had little in common and arose from entirely separate causes, it is significant that both urban and rural revolts occurred above all in the fourteenth and fifteenth centuries. Each might have unique triggers, but the grinding poverty caused by the economic changes was a common feature. It has been observed that while in England and France the class struggle manifested itself primarily in peasant rebellions, in the Low Countries and Italy class conflict first occurred in the cities. It was the precocious development in Italy of towns and a sophisticated economy which meant that there were revolts on a large scale among wage-labourers as early as the second half of the fourteenth century, while rural disturbances on a large scale were first seen only in the early sixteenth century. By contrast, in England and France the first notable discontent and revolts were seen among peasants. To cite one history: 'Peasant revolts . . . occurred mainly in the second half of the fourteenth century as well as in the years around 1500. The best-known examples are the Jacquerie in France, of 28 May to 10 June 1358, with its centre to the north of Paris, and the Peasants' Revolt of 1381 in England, in Essex and London in May and in East Anglia in June.'

According to a French proverb, 'Jacques Bonhomme [proverbial for the peasant] has a broad back and can bear anything.' A similar German saying claimed that 'The peasant is like an ox – but he doesn't have horns' (to fight), and an Italian one that 'The peasant is like a walnut tree, the more you beat him, the better he be' (walnut trees were traditionally beaten with sticks to knock down the nuts and to break off dead branches). Such proverbs became popular in the late medieval and early modern period, a time when conditions were becoming increasingly oppressive, especially for landless labourers who worked for others, and when peasants were becoming more aware of the grimness and immutability of their condition. Far more was demanded from them than ever before. As early as the late thirteenth century, city statutes in Italy laid down the obligations, frequently onerous, of peasants. Their wretchedness – and their doubtless unprepossessing appearance – are reflected in the 'peasant satire', a literary genre which came into existence at this time in which peasants are represented as ugly deformed scoundrels. In Germany, paintings which caricature country folk, portraying them as boorish and clumsy and with twisted, deformed faces were also common: 'Paintings of rustic weddings, village fairs and dances from this period [early sixteenth century] depict festivities which have degenerated into drunkenness, brawling and lechery . . . The genre originated in Germany, where it found a ready market among city-dwellers.'

It has been claimed that resentment of and contempt for the peasantry were prompted by rising food prices but this alone does not account for the animosity. Rather, it is the attitude of the rentier who despises his rural tenants and regards them as uncivilized. It is also a result of the new relationship between landlord and peasant-tenant, in which the tenant is increasingly regarded as a mere instrument of production. In short, 'The peasant is like a walnut tree, the more you beat him, the better he be.'

The lot of peasants had always been a hard one. In earlier centuries, though tenancy agreements had been less onerous, peasant-tenants had often been subjected to robbery and violence from the aristocracy, even from their own lords. This emerges from Carolingian legislation. In 850 a law of Louis II, King of Italy and Emperor, urges that 'those with power must not use violence against neighbouring lands, oppressing the weak . . . They are in the habit of allowing their horses to graze on land belonging to others.' In the early Middle Ages people might have reacted to such harassment by escaping or by becoming outlaws, but theirs were individual responses. Organized rebellion was unknown. Revolt on a large scale – mass movements which were occasionally successful and saw their demands met – dates only from the late medieval and early modern period.

Movements like this occurred because conditions for the majority of people had worsened and because new expectations were gaining ground among the poor and dispossessed, for whom exploitation was increasingly intolerable. It was in Italy, where social tension between classes in the cities was exacerbated by the presence of both the aristocracy and the merchant class, that uprisings first broke out, frequently fostered by the constantly shifting pattern of alliances between different social groups. There had been revolts of this kind as early as the beginning of the eleventh century but uprisings occurred mainly towards the end of the period, particularly in Florence, where the lower craftsmen and wage-labourers, driven to desperation by the harsh living conditions, would take advantage of rifts among those who ruled.

The immediate cause of revolt was usually economic: low wages meant severe hardship when food prices or taxes rose, and whenever this occurred there would be mass migration of wage-labourers to Siena, Lucca, Bologna, Genoa, Milan, Naples or even to Catalonia. In 1300 the wage-labourers of Florence called themselves the *popolo di Dio* ('God's people'), a sign of their conviction that God was with them in their struggle to improve their meagre existence. The year 1378 saw the Ciompi revolution. The Ciompi were wage-labourers, mainly employed as woolcarders in the woollen industry, and lesser artisans. Their initial demand for the right to form a legally recognized guild to protect their interests had, at least to start with, very little to do with any wish to overturn the traditional order. Yet a consequence of this new relationship between employers and workers was an awareness among labourers of belonging to a group which gains no benefit from its work while its employers enjoy ever greater prosperity and comfort.

This awareness is revealed in one of Franco Sacchetti's *novelle*. A group of Florentine workmen were in the habit of going to the Duomo after work to hear the sermon. The preacher harped continually on the sin of usury and the men grew bored with sermons that had little relevance for them. One of them, a certain Romolo del Bianco, lost his temper and shouted out that none of the crowd listening could possibly be guilty of usury since they were all wage-labourers, 'poor cloth-workers who, far from lending money, beg for it'. As a result the preacher changed his tune in future sermons: he took poverty as his theme and stressed the need to submit to it patiently.

The background to the Ciompi revolt was intolerable strain and hardship, a result largely of the war between Florence and Pope Gregory XI. At the time of the revolt, the Ciompi included not only wage-labourers but also artisans such as tailors and dyers who had not been permitted to form legally recognized guilds. Faced with open revolt, the government was forced to allow the Ciompi, along with the tailors and the dyers, to organize themselves in guilds. However, the creation of these new guilds posed a challenge to the established guilds, who saw their power weakened and who therefore joined forces with the tailors and the dyers against the Ciompi. The Ciompi were defeated and their guild dissolved. A contemporary chronicler quoted one of the convicted rebels as saying: 'Our execution is wrong indeed, but if through us the world should be put to rights in any way then we shall die content.'

As a result of the social upheavals of the fourteenth century in Florence, the lower groups in society were for a time able to ensure that the legislation they wanted was passed. Later, however, the participatory republican government of Florence became an oligarchy, prior to falling under the control of a single man. The merchant class was willing to give up many of its rights in order to have a single ruling family who would assure firm government and the repression of any popular murmurings.

In the same year as the Ciompi were crushed (1378) there had been further manifestations of discontent. On Christmas Eve a crowd collected in the evening, but the uprising was immediately put down and several of its leaders executed. In order to avoid any repeat, Giorgio degli Scali proposed that the government organize a ceremony which would serve both as a symbolic and impressive exorcism of the menace of rebellion and as a warning and deterrent. A solemn procession, bearing aloft the executioner's axe and block, passed through the streets of the city, while Salvestro Medici proposed the institution of a 500-florin reward for anyone who revealed a conspiracy and betrayed the names of those involved. In January 1379 a dyer called Carota del Corso was executed after a failed uprising and two wage-labourers from Poggibonsi were hanged; in March a workman had his hand chopped off and his tongue cut out for saying that 'the government was no good' and 'wouldn't last long'. The same month saw a further unsuccessful uprising. Two of the leaders were beheaded and another had the privilege of being hanged, while the parish priest of San Lorenzo, who was to have given the signal by ringing the church bell, was put in a cage high up on the prison wall and left to die. The man who had betrayed the conspiracy was murdered the following year by his former associates 'because', as a chronicler wrote, 'he had been the cause of the wrongful death of many of his comrades'.

Unrest continued for the rest of the fourteenth century. Florence was in a state of political and social flux and a need was felt for someone who could offer a guarantee of civic order. In 1434 Cosimo de' Medici gained power, an event which marked the beginning of the Medici ascendancy.

17

The Impact of the City on the Landscape

The countryside of the early Middle Ages was dramatically different from that of today, and to understand the changes in medieval agriculture and the difficulties facing those engaged in it, we need to picture a countryside that was in large part semi-wild. Northern Italy was covered by forest and marsh which drastically impeded the development of agriculture. Tools were few and primitive and clearance painfully slow and laborious. Given the paucity and inadequacy of tools, sheer force of numbers was necessary and landlords therefore sought to ensure an ample supply of labour by imposing obligations on peasants, who thus saw their freedom gradually eroded. Nobles' estates depended on an increasingly large workforce. The great clearances and draining of the huge forests and marshes of the Po plain between the eighth and twelfth centuries were achieved through *corvées*, or labour-services, on a huge scale, though after the eleventh century the initiative for clearance increasingly passed to the towns.

To the south of the Po plain, in the northern Apennines, great forests of oak, beech and firs had sprung up and stretched virtually unbroken, although the foothills, like similar areas of low hills all over Europe, were partially cultivated. The 'Bassa', the low-lying area between the Via Emilia and the Po, was characterized by dense forest and interminable marsh, particularly as one approached the river. The banks of the rivers were ill-defined, further encouraging the already frequent floods. Huge areas which had been cultivated in Roman times had reverted almost to their original state. To the north, in Lombardy and the Veneto, the Po valley was even more marshy. Here the plain is still crossed today by the main tributaries of the Po, while a line of springs rises south of the towns which mark the northern edge of the plain. In the Middle Ages this area was waterlogged and largely untamed. The cities were accordingly obliged to look north, towards the hills, for their arable land. Milan, for example, depended on the Brianza, the fertile region north of the city, and Verona on the valleys and foothills of the Alps.

Whereas large areas of the Alpine region of Italy have seen little change since the Middle Ages, in the Apennines, up to 1,000 metres above sea-level, there used to be dense forest, consisting mainly of oaks, particularly common oaks and Turkey oaks (*Quercus robur* and *Quercus cerris*). Above 1,000 metres there were beeches and firs. As late as the fourth century AD there must have been extensive coniferous forests, perhaps as a result of a drier climate, but in the fifth century firs gradually gave way to beeches until by the sixteenth century few examples of such coniferous forest remained.

The Po plain, largely covered by oak forest, would have looked quite different from the open, fen-like expanses of today. The oaks there included numerous common oaks (*Quercus robur*) as well as sessile, or durmast, oaks (*Quercus petraea*), the tallest and strongest varieties, which can exceed thirty metres in height and one metre in diameter and can reach an age of more than five hundred years. The trees the peasants were obliged to clear between the eighth and thirteenth centuries were thus formidable obstacles, each requiring an enormous effort to fell. They would have been a valuable source of timber and of acorns (for pigs). Hardly any examples of such great oaks have survived in Italy.

Similarly, the birch spinneys which were once common along the banks of the Po have all but vanished and are now attested only by place names of medieval villages. Birches, which had flourished during the Ice Age, gradually declined, victims of the climatic change of the fifth century AD. Coniferous forests, the most ancient species of tree, have also declined over the past millennia and continue to decline, though imperceptibly, in the short term. Conifers, which first appeared in the carboniferous period some 270 million years ago, reached their greatest extent in the Jurassic age, 170 million years ago, when there were around 20,000 varieties, but today only four to six hundred varieties survive. In the early Middle Ages the Apennines and the Po plain, with their great coniferous forests and birchwoods, must have looked similar to present-day Scandinavia. They gradually lost this appearance, although stretches of such forest survived where the soil and climate were favourable. Expanses of mixed forest, and undergrowth rich in tree and plant species, continued to be dominant features in the landscape.

Near Carpi, which lies in the heart of the lower Emilian plain close to Reggio Emilia, was a large communal forest, the Gaium Regense. In 772 the two last Lombard kings, Desiderius and Adelchis, made a generous gift to the convent attached to San Salvatore (later Santa Giulia) in Brescia, giving the nuns a tract of forest of some thirty square kilometres in the vicinity of Carpi. The boundaries of the land are indicated in the document by large letters and other signs which corresponded to marks cut into the bark of the trees. Several species are specifically mentioned in the passage defining the boundaries: common oak, ash (often found in the same habitat as oak), hornbeam, field maple, wild pear and Cornelian cherry. Such a forest, with its great variety of species, was clearly an invaluable resource, supplying not only timber of a high quality for furniture and hardwood for agricultural tools, but also quantities of acorns for pigs.

In the eighth century, the period of this document, such estates were insignificant breaks in great areas of wilderness. They were small and had to be carefully enclosed to protect them against damage from wild animals and intruders. According to the document of 772 recording Desiderius's and Adelchis's donation, Migliarina, the *curtis* in the middle of the Gaium Regense, was completely surrounded by a hedge, and we know that land belonging to the village of San Giovanni in Persiceto, halfway between Bologna and Modena, was similarly enclosed.

In the early Middle Ages, oak, primarily the common oak, appears to have been the dominant species of tree on the Po plain. It flourished in the deep and damp soil near the river and was well able to resist even prolonged immersion in water. Other varieties, the Lusitanian or Portuguese oak (*Quercus faginea*), the Turkey oak (*Quercus cerris*) and the lanigerous oak (*Quercus pubescens*), grew on higher, less damp land. However, other species were also common in the Po plain and dominated some areas. In marshier soil limes seem to have ousted oaks. In the low-lying plain around Verona, as far as Mantuan territory to the west and that of Vicenza to the east, place names and later more reliable documents attest to lost limewoods of some considerable extent. As late as the tenth century the name of the site of a fortress built during the Hungarian attacks was Villa Tellidana (*tellio* = lime), although this was later superseded by the name Nogara. Villa Tellidana lay close to the river named Tellionem, now the Tione. Near Legnago, in an equally marshy area, was the ancient *pieve*, or baptismal church, of San Pietro in Tellida, which later declined in importance and lost the second part of its name. As late as 1304 the statutes of the settlement of Cerea, deep in the country, mention common oaks, Turkey oaks, ash and limes in the forest on the Po plain near Verona, where all enjoyed rights of access and use. Such forests supplied many of the needs of local communities.

The variety of different environments and microclimates in the Po plain makes it necessary to examine the vegetation of each area separately. The meagre thickets which line the banks of the rivers Po and the Ticino today are the remnants of the poplars, willows and alders which once flourished there, a type of woodland quite distinct from that des-

cribed in the San Salvatore document, which was to be found further
away from the river. The uplands were quite different again, with great
variations between regions. Friuli had unproductive stony and sandy soil,
while Piedmont, Lombardy and the Veneto had rolling hills; Emilia had
a rich alluvial soil and a plentiful water supply. Because of the abundant
spring-line a few kilometres south of Milan, marsh was (and still is)
particularly extensive in Lombardy and the Veneto. In Emilia, near
Piacenza, Parma and Reggio Emilia, the topography is marked by the
foothills of the Apennines whereas to the south of Modena the network
of streams means the land is as marshy as that in the Bassa. The enormous local variations in environment, water supply and climate mean
that we should be cautious of sweeping generalizations about forests in
the past and, as the palaeontologist Angelo Pasa pointed out some years
ago, of the pervasive 'myth of the ubiquitous oak forest'.

To the north and south of the Po the landscape changed dramatically,
especially in the areas close to the river. By the river itself there were
stony dried-up meanders and islets surrounded by, and often covered by,
water. Here only dwarf willows and tiny stunted alders could grow, as
well as poplars which did not reach any size because of the precariousness of their habitat. These were 'pioneering' species, hardy and sun-
loving, which found it possible to thrive in the stony ground and intense
light of the riverbank, though the poor habitat meant they were short-
lived and stunted. In the early Middle Ages the river itself, with its many
meanders and normally dry overflow channels, would have looked entirely different from today when it is constricted by solid embankments.
The riverbanks would have been covered almost down to the water's
edge by dense and unproductive willow and alder scrub. Willow, with its
more than three hundred varieties, is notoriously hardy and adaptable,
well able to survive the inhospitable conditions beside the river.

In a document from the 830s requiring the tenants of the monastery of
San Silvestro in Nonantola to clear the choked north bank of the Po at
Ostiglia, near Mantua, such riverine scrub, with sun-loving, hardy plants
with a short life-cycle typical of an alluvial damp habitat, is described as
silva infructuosa, unproductive woodland. Once cleared, the land was to
be used for fields, vineyards and vegetable plots. Each tenant was allotted
a narrow strip of the riverbank, only a few dozen metres wide but
extending several hundred metres back from the river. The result of the
clearances was a large rectangular area of open riverbank cleared of
unproductive vegetation, with scores of long narrow holdings stretching
back into the forest. Being long and narrow, it was easy to plough such
holdings and to drain them with only a few drainage channels.

Apart from the Ostiglia forest, evidence survives for intense clearance
throughout the lower Po plain. As we have seen, as early as 772 part of

the *Gaium Regense* was being cleared, and there was widespread clearance throughout the marshy area north of the Po around Mantua and Cremona. In the ninth century there are explicit references to clearances in the great registers of the lands belonging to the monasteries of Bobbio and of Santa Giulia of Brescia (formerly San Salvatore). Tenancy agreements, royal charters and numerous private documents all show that from the eighth century to the end of the ninth the proprietors of the great estates, the peasants and the inhabitants of the towns all sought to extend cultivation away from the Po plain up into the valleys of the Apennines and the Alps, perhaps doubling the area of arable land.

At the turn of the tenth and eleventh centuries the rate of clearance increased. Place names reveal intense activity and a host of new villages over a huge area, though the situation is made complicated by the habit of referring to minor settlements which have evidently developed within the former area of the villages as *ubi dicitur* (the place called . . .) and by the many new place names. The old Roman place names were lost and from the first decades of the tenth century names of the type *curtis Atonis* or *runcum Sigefredi* (*curtis* = estate, *runcum* = clearance), which perpetuate the efforts of individuals to establish farmsteads, recur. The Hungarian raids in the tenth century slowed down this process. The efforts of towns, villages and individuals to extend agricultural land at the expense of the wilderness were far from complete. It is true that a large part of the foothills and upland plains, except for the most infertile dry and stony areas, had been cleared, but in the Po plain and in the Apennines clearances were limited to occasional gaps in the vast expanse of marsh and forest.

18

Nature as Friend and Foe

For centuries, the conventional view of the countryside in the Middle Ages was that almost all of western Europe had reverted to wilderness at the beginning of the period and had remained wild almost everywhere up to the eleventh century. It is a view which has been strongly and increasingly challenged in recent years by historians. This emphasis on the primitive nature of the environment and landscape derived from the generally negative idea of the Middle Ages and its culture and customs which prevailed in the Enlightenment in the eighteenth century. Many historians considered that the so-called 'dark age' had tangible expression in the countryside and that significant change occurred only with the growth of the towns in the twelfth century, when more land came under cultivation and the wilderness, forest, woodland and marsh retreated. Not until then, they argue, was the countryside slowly tamed and civilized.

Yet it is quite clear that there was change well before the twelfth century, and that as early as the eighth century, as well as in the ninth, tenth and eleventh, there were clearances on a significant scale, as well as efforts to modify the environment by bringing new land into cultivation. None the less, the landscape continued to be characterized by wilderness throughout the period. The economy itself remained closely linked to the exploitation of these areas.

This was particularly the case in those areas where it was difficult to contend with the surfeit of water. Except where there were settlements of some size, no attempt was made to control the course of the waterways which meandered across the plain, dividing into innumerable channels which frequently did not even reach the sea but spread out into great marshy deltas. All over Europe there were similar river valleys, where water was a more dominant feature than dry land. Yet although exceptionally high spring and autumn floods might from time to time drown land and turn large areas into vast lakes, damage was slight compared to the devastation such floods were to cause in later centuries. In the early Middle Ages the river system was well able to absorb any excess of water in the many high-water beds and extensive marshes, and such sporadic flooding caused little damage in a world which even in normal times was dominated by water. After the twelfth century, however, cultivated land was concentrated along the riverbank and rivers were imprisoned in a single channel, contained by redoubtable embankments. These embankments, however, could be all too vulnerable. Floods began to be a serious threat to the countryside, to the economy and to those who lived in the expanding riverside settlements.

In early days settlements had generally been on higher land, in the foothills, on plateaux or in mountain valleys, well away from any serious risk of flooding. However, there had also been some colonization of the lowland plain, where villages developed on ridges of higher land which their inhabitants defended by digging canals and ditches or adapting the ruins of Roman buildings. There were several reasons for settlement in this area in the Middle Ages: the survival of some Roman settlements; the need to cultivate some land even in areas where the local economy depended principally on the resources of the wild areas; and, above all, the attraction of a livelihood from forest and fen, more appealing than toil at the plough.

Though population density along the Po and its numerous branches and in the marshes of the delta was lower than in the upland areas, villages, hamlets and isolated homesteads were by no means scarce in the Po plain. Moreover, people adapted to this semi-wild environment. Along the Po itself and in the marshes of the delta, they were as at home on the water as on land, expert at fishing and hunting, and fattening pigs in the expanses of woodland which divided the waters. Skiffs were easily manoeuvred in the maze of channels and travel by water was generally easier than on the few remaining passable roads. The most common type of settlement in the area around rivers and their tributaries was on an island, surrounded by natural or artificial waterways.

It is difficult, perhaps impossible, to appreciate fully the extent to which people lived on and from the water at the time in these areas. It is hard for us to envisage the dense network of canals and waterways that existed in the Po plain as recently as the nineteenth century, offering much the fastest and most convenient method of travel and transportation between cities and within the cities themselves. Water-mills, often on floating platforms moored to the bank, were a common sight well into the nineteenth century.

Until the eleventh century the landscape in Europe was largely wild, though the natural vegetation varied greatly from area to area. In central northern Europe and to the east, moorland, forest and marsh stretched for hundreds of miles. Large expanses were not exploited in any way and were quite untrodden; no one ventured there even to hunt or fish or for any other of the activities traditionally associated with forest and marsh. Here the first real efforts at settlement, on the edges of the great forests or in clearings deep inside, date only from the tenth century, but after this there was an advance eastwards of colonists who depended on their flocks and herds and on hunting for a livelihood. All the same, much of the forest in this region would remain empty and untracked for centuries to come.

Further south, Europe was similarly covered by forest. Here, though, the forest was criss-crossed by paths and supported a silvo-pastoral economy with goats, pigs and sheep as well as wild animals. Such 'familiar', tracked forest could be found in all areas of southern Europe except the most mountainous regions. In Italy, although there were few forests on the scale of those north of the Alps, woodland could be found everywhere from the mountains to the coast, though in contrast to the forests of the north here it was broken by towns, villages, *castelli*, abbeys, churches and hamlets. Most of the Po plain was wooded, especially along the riverbanks, near the coast and in some areas of the low-lying 'Bassa' plain. These forests, as we have seen, were made up of oak, ash, elm, maple, willow and hornbeam, with the last two predominating along the riverbank, while in some areas limes, poplars or other species dominated. There was green right up to the towns and even within them, giving them a distinctly rural aspect: with drastically diminished populations, they had dwindled in size and had fields, vineyards, orchards and vegetable plots inside their walls.

With the growth of the towns in the twelfth century and later, such 'rural' areas within the city boundaries were gradually reduced to make way for buildings and streets and squares. In Emilia, immediately to the north of the great Roman road which linked Parma, Reggio Emilia, Modena, Bologna, Imola, Faenza and Forlì, marsh and forest began to crowd in almost immediately on cultivated land. Going from Emilia towards the Po and, particularly, the Adriatic, the marsh and forest increased in density and extent until it became one great continuous marsh in which the occasional brake or reed-bed was lost. Downstream from, roughly, Mirandola the waters occupied an ever greater area, as the Po divided into numerous channels and increasingly fanned out into the great sprawl of the delta. The area of cultivated land exceeded that of wilderness only on the plains around the towns, on the hills behind them and where the mountain valleys broadened out as they descended to the plains. As well as around the cities, cultivated land was also to be found concentrated around villages, although to the north of the Via Emilia settlements were more likely to be surrounded by woodland and bog than fields.

Wolves, boar and deer lived on the Po plain as well as in the mountains. All these animals were hunted: there were wolf hunts in the Po valley as late as the sixteenth century, and in particularly grim periods wolves would venture right into the towns. In his chronicle Salimbene of Parma recorded how during the winter of 1247–8 ravenous wolves would descend at night and howl for hours on end outside the city walls, sometimes even getting into the town. Many place names bear witness today to a fear of wolves and to their enduring presence in folk memory. Similarly, place names record vanished woods and trees: Rovereto (*rovere* = oak), Saliceto (*salice* = willow), Pioppa (*pioppo* = poplar), Alberone (great tree), Cadelbosco, Boschi, Selva (*bosco, selva* = woodland) and many more.

However, the most striking feature of the Po flood-plain was not woodland but water, especially along and near the branches of the Po where the inhabitants were kept safe from floods by the existence of run-off channels, mostly natural, and the fact that villages and cultivated land were generally on higher land. The situation had not changed radically by the eleventh century, although with the untiring efforts at clearance and the steady advance of cultivated land, wild areas had diminished and water no longer dominated the environment. Even allowing for local variations in the economic pattern, with the twelfth century the balance finally swung decisively towards arable land and viniculture, a turning point throughout the entire Po plain. The environment, increasingly moulded and manipulated, changed markedly.

The impetus for change came from both country and city, although it was the cities above all, with an increasing need to ensure food supplies at the expense of the wilderness, which were responsible for the transformation. Between 1100 and 1300 the rate of change accelerated and the face of the countryside altered ever faster. The ancient great forests vanished and the marshes contracted dramatically everywhere in Italy except the eastern part of the Po plain. City statutes of the thirteenth and fourteenth centuries emphasize the general determination to transform nature both inside and outside the cities as a war without quarter was waged on the remaining wilderness. At the same time they are in themselves a document of the changes which had already occurred. The policy was to extend arable land, plant orchards, eradicate unproductive land and fell trees which did not yield edible fruit or nuts. The fourteenth-century Piacenza statutes laid down that everyone who lived anywhere outside the town had to plant four fruit trees every year. At the same time they ordered that all 'copses, trees and stumps' beside roads were to be cleared. Evidently thickets and brakes were disappearing from the sides of roads and from the landscape in general, while drainage channels were being dug alongside the roads and undergrowth eradicated.

This contraction of wild areas made for an ecological imbalance and for problems as early as the fourteenth century, particularly regarding flooding and the availability of wood. The measures taken by Reggio Emilia in 1268 to counteract the problem appear unusually precocious even in a period when drastic clearances in order to create arable land and vineyards were the norm. The city proposed the removal of all undergrowth near the city moat and in the smallholdings in outlying areas, as well as specifying that the trees to be felled were those on the eastern and southern boundaries; the inference is that the government was concerned to remove all obstructions to light and to maximize sunlight during the hours of the day when it was at its strongest. This is probably an extreme example of the zeal for clearance and therefore not typical, but it sums up the changes in the rural landscape from the twelfth century onwards which are attested in many similar measures. It is sensible to regard such legislation as an expression of the wishes of those who governed rather than of the actual situation, but the energetic clearance suggested by the policy summed up in the Reggio statutes cannot have been too far removed from the truth. In Italy, where it had always wielded power, the city was well able to intervene over a huge area of the countryside. A historian comments:

> Identical decrees are found for about a century and the same provisions recur. Sometimes they are explicit about the reasons which lie behind them: 'because trees (walnuts, willows, poplars and oaks) are causing serious damage to small-holdings and orchards'. But then there is a complete about-turn: earlier injunctions are no longer repeated, there is no more mention of trees to be cleared, and between 1439 and 1500 the government of Reggio Emilia instead passed a series of laws to protect trees and hedges. It became an offence to chop down a tree or merely to damage its bark or branches. By this time there was an effort to preserve trees and bushes in every way possible.

It was the city, then, especially in the twelfth and thirteenth centuries, which became the driving force behind the dramatic changes in the countryside. The zeal with which Reggio Emilia used legislation to encourage the cultivation of cereals and vines in every possible way appears to be unusual and to reflect local circumstances and a particular need to ensure food supplies not found elsewhere. The steady disappearance of trees from the landscape is attested in other areas as well. Areas of forest, woodland and marsh were increasingly hemmed in as ever more land

'The Italian town by the fifteenth century'

Fra Angelico, *The Deposition from the Cross*, detail. Museo di San Marco, Florence, photograph: Scala, Florence.

went under the plough. The pattern of agriculture which is seen in the Po plain today – rows of fruit trees interspersed with rows of vines, the so-called 'promiscuous cultivation' – began to appear. The countryside was transformed into fields which had to be protected. Accordingly, the legislation of towns and rural areas from the thirteenth and fourteenth centuries is increasingly concerned with ensuring adequate drainage through ever more detailed provisions for the construction and mainte-nance of a network of drainage ditches.

By this period the countryside was crossed by a considerable number of highways, whose upkeep was the responsibility of those whose land they passed through; legislation laid down precise obligations for their maintenance. More canals were dug. They were preferred for navigation since, unlike rivers, they went in a straight line, contained a small quantity of water, and were not vulnerable to flooding and drought so that they could be used throughout the year. As fields, roads and canals all required protection from flooding rivers and the backwash from the remaining marshes, there were intense efforts to construct dykes and, as far as possible, to drain marshes and reclaim land.

For ease and speed of dredging, canal and river banks were generally kept clear of undergrowth and constructions. The most pressing prob-lem, particularly in the lower Po plain of eastern Emilia, was how to control the course of rivers and streams to prevent flooding. It should be pointed out that the complexity of the river network at the time and the paucity of evidence make it difficult to form a coherent picture of the pattern of the watercourses in the Po plain in the medieval period. Attempts to channel the rivers required a huge investment of capital and resources; we have to wait for the second half of the fifteenth century and the sixteenth for the first serious attempts since Roman times to manage rivers and streams systematically and permanently through controlling their course and digging run-off channels. Almost all through the Middle Ages individuals and communities had been involved in a constant battle with the waters. Yet the waters were an insuperable adversary, both in the early period when the economy did not as yet require control of waterways, and later, when the expansion of agriculture made control of the watercourses crucial. The struggle was an unequal one and the best chance continued to be to hope for a dry spring.

In the early Middle Ages floods on a large scale had occurred. For example, the occasion was long remembered when the Adige burst its banks at the end of the sixth century, after which it appears to have permanently changed course. Floods could be just as common and disas-trous as they were to be after the twelfth century, but later they would swamp arable land whereas in earlier times the floodwater could easily run off into high-water beds or be absorbed by marshes. The most pernicious consequence of this shift from the twelfth century onwards was the cumulative effect of the tributaries pouring into the Po. They made breaches of the banks more frequent and the aftermath of flooding more serious. It was possible to protect land from the waters to a limited extent, perhaps warding off the worst blows. Rivers were by now increasingly confined by embankments and imprisoned within specified channels, while at the same time the old high-water channels were being steadily filled in and were no longer available to take excess water. This meant that rivers in flood frequently overflowed or burst their embankments, pouring over arable land, and minor watercourses changed course, wreaking havoc on cultivated land. Land laboriously reclaimed over centuries would revert to marsh and the work of years be sabotaged. The principal rivers, breaking the bounds which restrained them, would reoccupy their former flood-plains, and drainage and reclamation would have to begin anew.

To avoid the build-up of water and to allow for a smooth flow, it was necessary to ensure that instead of debouching into intermediary marshes the tributaries of the Po drained directly into the river itself. The only solution was engineering and drainage on a huge scale and control of the courses of the principal rivers. The first works date from as late as 1500 or so, when the Po plain began to take on its present appearance, and they had dramatic consequences. Yet the environment could only be manipulated so far. It is no coincidence that probably the worst floods to occur in the whole recorded history of the Po have been the deluges of the last hundred years or so, when the development of agriculture in the region has entailed the virtual elimination of the remaining marshes and high-water beds along the central section of the river.

After 1200 it became increasingly apparent that intervention on a mammoth scale was necessary for many watercourses. Floods of the Po and of its tributaries are found recorded among natural disasters with growing regularity in chronicles from the thirteenth century onwards, and writers depart from their usual sobriety to register their alarm. Obviously some city chronicles reveal more concern than others – some areas suffered less from floods than others and the subject might in any case have little interest for the writer – but it is noticeable that we find far fewer references to floods in early chronicles from the sixth to the ninth century. In part this silence can be explained by the scope of these chronicles: they usually covered a wide geographical area, whereas later ones covered a much more local area and were preoccupied with local problems of famine, plague, bad weather, breaches of riverbanks and flooding. Though this accounts in part for the silence of the early medieval chronicles, the main reason that floods were not regarded as worthy of mention was the simple reason that, unlike later, they had little impact on the economy: floodwater was generally absorbed by rough, uncultivated areas, and even if newly cultivated and vulnerable land beside the river was ruined this was accepted as the natural, inevitable course of events and caused no alarm.

The great list of the lands of the monastery of Santa Giulia near Brescia, dating from around 900, included a piece of arable land close to the Po near Piacenza: 'a plot in the vicinity of Caorso where 70 *moggi* of grain can be sown, provided that the Po does not rob us of it.' Evidence survives for numerous peasant holdings along the banks of the Po as early as the late ninth century and perhaps before, although they were surrounded by untamed countryside. As long as tenant-farmers were not dependent on arable land and viniculture, flooding did not cause any particular problem and was not regarded as a disaster. At the most, tenants might insist on the inclusion in the contract of a clause permitting the holding to be abandoned without payment of the usual fine if the land was flooded by the Po during the customary leasehold period of twenty-nine years.

Cereal production was in fact relatively insignificant within the local economy, which depended primarily on pigs, sheep and goats and on the resources of the forest. In the thirteenth century, however, floods of the Po plain began to cause alarm, even if not yet as much as they would in the early modern period, when floods were much more frequent and wreaked considerably more damage. The impact of these floods can be assessed from the descriptions given by chroniclers of the areas worst hit. One chronicler described the flood of 1230 thus: 'There was a great flood, and people had to take refuge in the trees if they wanted to escape the raging waters. This flood devastated all these places: the contados [surrounding territory] of Ferrara, of Padua, of Mantua and of Cremona and many other areas in the entire Po delta.'

Many others echoed his words. A climatic shift towards colder winters was one factor behind the floods: in the thirteenth century some winters were long remembered as being exceptionally severe, with heavy snowfalls, long periods of sub-zero temperatures and rivers frozen over, followed by food shortages and high prices. Almost all contemporary northern Italian chronicles record, in varying detail, the terrible winter of 1215–16. These accounts are typical:

> In the month of January the Po froze over and people could walk across on the ice . . . It was so cold that bread, apples and pears, and all manner of food froze solid and could not be cut or eaten until they had been warmed up and thawed out at a fire. This great freeze lasted for more than two months.

The vines were quite frozen and the ice on the Po was so thick that it was possible to ride across ... Wine froze solid and it was necessary to hack lumps off with an axe. The snow that winter was deep. Wheat cost nine imperial *solidi* a bushel and spelt [a variety of wheat] four *solidi*.

That winter there was deep snow and terrible frost. The vines withered. The Po froze and everyone went on to the ice. Women danced there and soldiers trained with the lance and peasants took wagons and carts and sledges across. The icy weather lasted for two months. At that time a bushel of wheat cost nine imperial *solidi* and a bushel of spelt four.

There were other similarly severe winters throughout the first half of the century. In 1234 'it was so severe a winter that vines and fig trees and olive trees died' and

snow and ice *fuerunt magne* [were severe] throughout the month of January, so much so that the vines and all the fruit trees died. The wild animals perished too. At night packs of wolves came into the towns and during the day many were captured and strung up in the squares. Plants were split their entire length by frost and many withered and died.

In the following year:

On 18 April, a Wednesday, a bitter wind sprang up and icy-cold snow fell. During the night there was a severe hoarfrost which shrivelled up the vines. On 24 April snow and frost came again and thus the vines were completely destroyed. The Po froze over and people could cross it on foot or on horseback.

In 1239 there was a terrifying eclipse of the sun on 3 June and in the middle of the day 'the stars shone as brightly as at night'. In 1249 the river Crostolo, which flows through Reggio Emilia, overflowed and a few months later came a terrible earthquake.

By 1247 the worsening climate, food shortages and an intensification of the war between Frederick II and the Guelph cities had all combined to make life intolerable. Salimbene of Parma gave a vivid description:

In Parma people starved. They considered themselves fortunate to have bread made from linseed flour ... Work in the fields, be it ploughing, sowing or harvesting, was impossible; the vineyards could not be tended and it was impossible to remain in the villages. This was the situation everywhere, especially in Parma, Reggio, Modena and Cremona. Only fields close to the towns could be worked and an armed guard was necessary for protection ... This was because the number of thieves and outlaws had increased out of all proportion. They would seize people as hostages and demand a ransom or steal cattle to eat or sell. If no ransom was paid for their captives they would hang them up by their hands or feet, pull out their teeth and stuff toads into their mouths to encourage speedy payment . . . They were crueller than devils. The countryside was deserted. No peasant or traveller was to be seen . . . Everywhere wild animals and birds multiplied: pheasant, partridge, quail, hares, deer, buffalo, wild boar and marauding wolves. No domestic animals remained for the wolves to prey on since the villages had been completely burned down; ravenous, they congregated in great packs outside the city moat and howled. At night they would come into the towns and devour anyone who was sleeping in the open in the porticoes or in carts, especially women and children. Sometimes they even managed to break down wooden house walls and snatch infants from their cradles . . . The number of wolves multiplied exceedingly.

Even allowing for a degree of exaggeration in these accounts and for an inflation of the negative effects – the frost which wreaks havoc among plants and fruit trees is a standard element – it is clear that as early as the thirteenth century the economy, with arable land and fruit-growing playing an ever larger part, was vulnerable to bad weather and to flooding. The transformation of the environment had reached crisis point in a world where there was intense competition between the natural and the artificial environment. Despite the taming of nature with the canalization of rivers, the drainage of marshes and the maintenance of ditches, the environment was far from being controlled. As clearances progressed and forests and marshes contracted, so the forces of nature, which had earlier been in equilibrium, were unleashed. Methods of farming required ever more land and clearance, but the more that the natural ecology was disrupted, the more drastic were the side-effects, especially flooding, which in turn required yet further intervention. As new areas were brought into cultivation, the land already under plough had to be scrupulously protected from floods and a cycle developed: the farming of new areas entailed tight control of the waterways, with the elimination of run-offs, high-water beds and marshes – and as the river network was ever more confined, yet more land was released for agriculture.

Nature posed an ever greater threat, especially in areas difficult to colonize such as the Po delta. The ecosystem, if we can use that term, was disrupted, and the more efforts were made to mitigate the impact of the clearances, the more nature continued to wreak havoc. There was a vicious circle of damage, requiring intervention, which precipitated yet more damage. Local laws were severe, and punctilious on the need for systematic efforts to maintain the waterways. The 1287 statutes of

Ferrara, for example, obliged all heads of households in the city and the *contado* to keep a spade, shovel, rake and mattock available. Lombardy faced severe problems of flooding, especially in the endless stretch of marshy land between Mantua and the original channel of the Po, along which lay the small towns of Luzzara, Gonzaga and Pegognaga, and other centres. But even further north, almost all the plain was traversed by rivers and countless smaller streams, difficult to control and maintain and impeding drainage. In addition, it became necessary to protect the delicate balance of the artificial irrigation network, of particular importance in Lombardy compared to other parts of the Po plain.

The waterways, from the twelfth century increasingly regulated and controlled or newly created, were used not only for irrigation but also for travel and transportation. It was therefore necessary to provide for the maintenance of canals (*navigli*), less affected by bad weather than rivers and so faster and more reliable. The Naviglio, the canal which links Modena to the Po, was already in existence in the late twelfth century. Water from nearby springs and from the numerous branches and marshy areas of the rivers Secchia and Panaro was used to fill it. Such a use of the natural river network and of marshes implies that a continuous check was kept on the waters flowing into the Naviglio and that the Naviglio was well able to absorb them.

With constant feuding and shifting alliances between neighbouring cities, there were also compelling military reasons for towns to take a keen interest in the control of the canals. Both the territory where a waterway began and the places it passed through were involved, as well as adjacent territories, even if they were politically separate. The commercial treaty of 1277 between the citizens of Brescia, Cremona, Modena and Ferrara laid down that the city council of Modena was to build a stone tower halfway along the Naviglio. It was also agreed that a raised road wide enough for carts was to be built along the Naviglio as 'an alternative to transportation by water in periods when the water-level drops and to enable barges to be loaded at all times'. Two further towers, to be paid for by Modena and Ferrara, were also to be built along the canal.

19

The Ravaged Countryside

During times of war between cities, whoever controlled fortresses and watchtowers on the waterways controlled movement by water. Armies would accordingly attempt to capture them in order to disrupt communications and to use them as a base for attacking each other's territory. The waterways and the fortresses built on or near them became both a pretext for and an instrument of war, particularly in one area, the Po plain, characterized above all by the overwhelming presence of water. What had been laboriously constructed was thus periodically destroyed. This was a further factor contributing to a constantly unstable, precarious environment where no one could feel secure from floods of both natural and artificial watercourses.

In 1234, during the war between Cremona and Milan, Bologna broke its truce with Cremona's ally, Modena, and Bolognese troops invaded Modenese territory on the plains to the north and in the hills to the south of the town. The fortress of Solara, the strongest point on the Naviglio (the canal between Modena and the river Po), was attacked and burned down. But this was only the beginning of the onslaught on the Naviglio and on Solara, its principal defence. After Azzo VIII d'Este was expelled from Modena in 1306, he used Ferrara as a base for his campaign against the town, obliging Modena to defend itself on that flank. The danger was greatest at Finale, also on the Naviglio, and in March that year the garrison there was increased from forty to one hundred. On 3 February 1312 Solara once again fell to Bolognese troops and when in 1325 Bolognese forces occupied much of Modenese territory they recaptured Solara along with many other forts. At the same time they breached the dyke of the nearby river Panaro so that it broke through into a new channel towards Bomporto and flooded a wide area. It was at this time that the city council of Modena agreed to dig the canal linking the Naviglio to the Panaro which still exists today.

Rivalry between neighbouring cities was endemic and any means of laying waste to each other's territory was exploited; manipulating the waters in this way was an invaluable tactic. The practice dates from this period. Although this possibility had been known for a long time, it had not been used because wars had usually been waged over large areas. With the increasing regionalization of conflict after the late twelfth century it became widespread. At the same time accounts of the deliberate destruction of fields, vineyards and orchards begin to be common in chronicles.

In 1233, war and a series of natural disasters had created a situation of extreme stress which had worn down the rural population of the Po plain. The constant plundering of the countryside by armies, on top of natural calamities, was more than people could tolerate. They rebelled. In May great crowds of countryfolk massed in the squares of the cities, responsible for the devastation of the countryside, to demand peace. The movement is known as the 'Great Hallelujah' after the rallying cry of 'Hallelujah' used by those involved in their processions, certain that God was with them. The strength of popular feeling was evidently great, enough to oblige the leaders of the warring factions of the Po plain to lay down their arms, albeit for only a few months. Ezzelino da Romano and his opponents publicly exchanged the kiss of peace on the plain of Pagnara by the river Adige near Verona before crowds stretching, according to the chronicles, as far as the eye could see. But by September the violent course of history had begun anew.

The destruction of old fortresses and the construction of new ones on the waterways long continued, as did the breaking down of embankments to bring about the flooding of surrounding land. In 1362 Bernabò Visconti of Milan was master of the strongholds of Crevalcore, Castelfranco, Piumazzo and Crespellano, from which he launched his attacks on Bolognese and Modenese territory. In May that year his troops took Solara and he ordered twin forts to be built on opposite banks of the Naviglio. A chronicler recorded that 'there was talk of building another one as well' but that the captain of the soldiers had to return to Lombardy where revolts had broken out.

From the fourteenth century onwards war, severe weather and an inadequate drainage system constantly worsened the state of the land. In addition, depopulation in much of the uplands resulting from the economic crisis meant that maintenance of the upper reaches of watercourses was neglected, with the result that the rivers flowing into the plain carried more water and flowed more swiftly than before, causing considerable damage. In the fifteenth and sixteenth centuries floods were both more frequent and more damaging, so much so that reclamation on a vast scale became unavoidable, especially in the Ferrarese, where conditions, particularly in the second half of the fifteenth century, must have been intolerable. In the second half of the seventeenth century an observer reported that in Ferrara 'the air is heavy from the countless miasmas which rise up on every hand.' Blocking leaks in the dykes of the Ferrarese was a laborious, endless task. Even the earth required could not be found locally in sufficient quantities and importing it on rafts and barges was expensive. Moreover, 'there are too many timber stanchions along the banks that need repairing.' The situation worsened over time, as the delta became almost entirely desolate, unproductive and malaria-ridden, though its inhabitants obstinately remained.

In some parts of the Ferrarese the situation was marginally less bleak, but floods of the Po were a recurring feature of the area. They increasingly threatened an economy now dominated by arable farming, since an entire harvest could be ruined by floods. Even pasture and rough land were badly affected by floods. Not only did the Po flood more frequently than before, but at the same time there were more episodes of extreme weather, resulting in a dearth of food and in famine. What with floods and poor weather, the environment was gravely at risk. Storms, hail and rain flattened crops, while drought and interminable heatwaves shrivelled up plants and scorched the vines. The topsoil of former marshes dried up and cracked.

The area worst affected by the Po floods and bad weather appears to have been the Polesine of Bondeno, to the west of Ferrara. In 1478 the entire area was devastated by tremendous storms. In 1481 heavy rain swamped the Polesine and was followed by a devastating thunderstorm which lasted a quarter of an hour and ravaged the entire area, as well as Veronese and Paduan territory. Hailstones the size of a fist fell, ruining the vines and tearing the leaves from the trees so that they lay deep on the ground and on the roads, while hailstones filled the channels beside the fields. In the Ferrarese, meanwhile, the Po had swollen and had breached its bank at Ficarolo, where the local inhabitants were immediately mobilized 'to watch over the Po'. In April 1489 corn was dear 'because the Po had risen and burst its banks in many places and had flooded the fields', while at the end of June a great storm blew up, with gales and downpours, bringing down trees and chimneystacks and sinking many watermills on platforms in the river.

The winter of 1490–1 was so severe that it appears that the Po was frozen for a whole month. The vines began to die and when in August it was clear that the grape harvest would be poor, wild plums were used instead to make a bitter wine. The chronicler who tells us this goes on to describe how the year 1497 saw a heatwave in the late summer during which dysentery broke out in Ferrara and many children died. In 1499 the Po was exceptionally high, throwing all the inhabitants of the adjacent villages into a state of alarm.

Floods left pools of stagnant water, which affected the grass and made the hay poor in quality and unsaleable. There was little point in trying to improve fields by clearing meadowland of weeds if it was to be flooded and spoiled every year. At other times drought dried everything up, causing great cracks to open up in the earth and killing off the grass. The situation varied: in the Ferrarese and in many other places it was perhaps worse still. Although the Po delta suffered greatly from floods, flooding was not a phenomenon restricted to this eastern section of the Po plain. An economy increasingly dominated by cereal production and viniculture demanded the gradual elimination of all wild areas, woodland and marshes which had traditionally absorbed excess water. In addition it appears that the climate deteriorated in the fifteenth century. There was increased rainfall which swelled the streams flowing down from the mountains and into the rivers. These streams in turn were no longer maintained, putting extra pressure on rivers. The entire Po plain was to continue in varying degrees to suffer severe flooding for centuries, giving rise to the great drainage and reclamation efforts at the end of the nineteenth century.

Chronicles regularly recorded floods: in November 1280 there was 'a great volume of water' and floods inundated Mantua and Cremona, and in 1293 the Po swelled so much that no embankment could contain it and a third of the town of Mantua was under water. The following year the entire area around Cremona, Brescia and Mantua was flooded. In 1327 the Po again overflowed its banks. In 1331:

> causing untold damage to Ferrarese and Mantuan territory and bringing about the deaths of more than 10,000 people, who all perished in the floods, the river impetuously left its bed and ravaged the entire territory for miles around. Two Sienese engineers, Agostino and Agnolo, were accordingly sent for as talented and able men. By confining this terrible river with embankments and most useful defences they found a way to return it to its rightful course. All this brought them great honour and profit because as well as the renown they gained they were granted most generous rewards by the lords of Mantua and by the Este family.

In an emergency, therefore, when local skills could not suffice to repair the dykes, outside experts were evidently called in and generously rewarded. Yet even their intervention could only offer a provisional solution. The skills of such engineers were prized, but over time high water-levels and flooding became a perennial problem and the task of countering them ever more intractable, for all the reasons we have seen.

'In 1386 it happened that the rains had swollen the waters of the Po and of the Adige beyond measure.' Bernabò Visconti exploited the fact that the embankments had been steadily raised over many decades to protect agricultural land near the river: 'he had the embankments of the great and swollen river broken down and in this way flooded all Mantuan territory.' 'At the same time the Scaligeri lord of Verona had the Adige diverted, directing it towards Paduan territory.' In the constant struggle between neighbouring cities, where a pattern of local and regional powers, all keen to establish their authority over the surrounding territory, was emerging, the rivers were widely regarded as a legitimate weapon.

However, it was the extensive network of watercourses in the Po plain, the vulnerability of the embankments, and the serious consequences of flooding in a region which was ever more intensely cultivated, which conspired to make it tempting to use the waters as weapons, whereas in the largely silvo-pastoral world of the early Middle Ages floods had not presented a problem to the economy. Nor had they impeded the movement of armies then, since war was generally on a much larger scale, within the vast reaches of the Carolingian empire up to the ninth century and between the nascent national states after that. In any case, marshes, secondary channels of rivers and land waterlogged for months on end occupied so large an area that deliberately increasing the volume of water would have made little perceptible difference.

In the fifteenth century, however, floods were much more frequent and had a disastrous impact. As in 1385 when most of the town of Mantua and nearly all its territory were flooded, so in 1440 the lowest-lying parts of Mantuan territory were again under water. On 2 November 1454 the river Secchia burst its banks, with devastating consequences. The floodwaters formed a great lake and it was possible to travel from Guastalla all the way into the centre of Mantua by boat; 'everywhere was water.' On 7 October 1467 the area was again flooded when the inhabitants of Guastalla broke down the embankment of the Po near Quingentole to release the waters and save themselves. In the spring of 1481 the level of the Po began to rise and the river remained dangerously high all through May and June. In 1493 and 1496 the Po burst its banks and continued to so, even more dramatically, in the sixteenth century.

The endless cycle of high river levels and flooding led to desperation. It was hard to accept that disasters could be so frequent and that nothing could be done to counter them. They threw the economy into crisis. Those in power failed to intervene, since they were those least affected, and acted only when it was apparent that they too might suffer. Inexorable and terrifying natural disasters, starvation and destitution all generated fear and hysteria, which was whipped up by sermons. The anxiety caused by the strain of the economic situation and by frequent ominously high river levels and flooding fostered an obsessive, paranoid atmosphere in which scapegoats were sought and witch-hunts flourished. In 1493, after repeated floods of the Po, an old woman found guilty of witchcraft was imprisoned and then burnt at the stake in the piazza of San Pietro in Mantua. The period saw the beginnings of a sustained attack by the Church on misunderstood elements of peasant life, with innocent rural customs being seen as the hand of the devil.

As the economy changed and agricultural production increased, the fragile balance of nature was disrupted and land was more at risk from natural disasters. A balance between agricultural development and control of the waters lay in the future: the landscape was being transformed but without any corresponding attempt to regulate the forces of nature. Reclamation, for instance, had gone at a faster pace than had attempts to control the watercourses and to ensure systematic drainage through dykes and canals. In many areas of the mountains and lowlands, especially the latter, much of the tree cover had been removed. Earlier, trees and undergrowth had absorbed rain, but without them rainwater ran straight off the hillsides. The natural ecological controls which prevented calamity were gradually being eliminated but without any corresponding attempt to control the waters and the environment. A classic instance of this instability, the precarious relationship between cultivated land and the waters, is the series of floods of arable land which reached a peak in the sixteenth century.

Efforts at the very beginning of the general clearance of wild areas to ensure an adequate balance between rough and cleared land and to avoid over-zealous clearance would have prevented affairs reaching this pass. Unfortunately, as early as the twelfth century, so much of the ancient forest of the lowest-lying parts of the Po plain had been cleared that legislation to limit the felling of particular species became necessary. Communities went to law over the ownership of the remaining woods and the rights to them, or sought to lease them from the large churches and monasteries. This was an inevitable result of the continued and profound dependence of the economy on timber. Any sense on the part of any individual or institution, ecclesiastical or secular, of a general need to retain an equilibrium between cultivated land and wild areas seems, however, to have been absent. Otherwise city legislation would not have had to concern itself, sometimes in urgent tones, with the survival and use of the remaining woods belonging to the cities.

One of the clauses of the Reggio Emilia statutes of 1242, revealingly headed 'Prohibition on the export of timber from the diocese of Reggio', laid down that a guard was to be placed on those woods which formed an irregular semi-circle to the north of the town, while an addition of

1266 re-emphasized the responsibilities of the *podestà* (city governor) in this area. Again, the Imola statutes of 1334 made the *podestà* responsible for defending the city's rights to the 'Via Lata' forest and to the other woods belonging to the town, and for reasserting rights which had been allowed to lapse. The *podestà* was to ensure that the boundaries of the woods were clearly defined by fences and that dykes were dug in order to deter trespass and the unauthorized removal of timber or anything else on carts. One of the woods belonging to Imola, the 'Argine' wood, was to be protected with especial care, to the extent that there were orders for it to be entirely surrounded by a moat to prevent the entry of carts and the removal of timber in them. Just one entrance to the wood was to be left and this was to be secured by chains which could be unlocked only by the guards on duty.

This contraction of woodland put the silvo-pastoral economy in difficulty. Many people still depended on the forest for food, but increasing restrictions and prohibitions on hunting reflect the steady contraction of forests and marshes where hunting was possible. That the fourteenth-century Imola statutes established a close season for quail, partridge and pheasant (between 1 May and 1 August) suggests that there was indiscriminate slaughter during the breeding season, putting the survival of the birds at risk. Similar statutes proliferate and strongly suggest an urgent need to limit hunting in order to protect game. No such legislation survives from the early Middle Ages. In part it would have been unnecessary since wildlife was abundant and hunters few and scattered, but the later frequency of legislation indicates, too, the extent of the acceleration of the destruction of natural habitats.

As in so much else, there was a stark contrast between the early medieval centuries, up to the end of the eleventh century, and the later medieval centuries from the twelfth century onwards. In the later period the environment was increasingly manipulated and there were systematic and massive efforts virtually everywhere to eradicate the wild areas, with little respect in any way for nature. Ecological disasters comparable to those of today were perhaps only avoided because the technology available was unsophisticated and could have only a limited impact.

From the twelfth century onwards an increasingly pragmatic and utilitarian view of nature emerged and became entrenched. The natural world was regarded as peripheral, to be exploited, and areas associated with a less productive economy were regarded as alien. This can be explained in part by the rise in population and the consequent need to cultivate more land to ensure increased food supplies. The transformation from the markedly silvo-pastoral economy of the sixth and seventh centuries to the primarily agrarian economy of the late Middle Ages was achieved in the main not by technical developments to enable better yields but by the easiest method, that of merely expanding the acreage available for cultivation through clearances and the use of a vast amount of human labour. The reasons for this choice have still to be explored. Given the primitive nature of tools, however, and the unsophisticated farming methods, a huge amount of labour was required and the increasingly utilitarian outlook meant that the leasehold agreements of peasant farmers tended to become harsher and more exacting.

This does not mean that the economy declined or that living conditions for the lower groups in society worsened. The cultivation of so much land meant that a much higher population could be supported than in previous periods, and so most people's standard of living did not worsen. However, the excessive rise in population made for an increase in the area of cultivated land and vice versa; a balance between the two was never reached. In Italy, as early as the end of the twelfth century the need to guarantee food supplies for their own citizens obliged cities to invest capital and labour in drainage schemes, sometimes of very unpromising land. The cities laid down regulations for agriculture, drainage and the construction and maintenance of canals and ditches. The inherent fragility of the economy and of society is, however, indicated by the continual crises of famine and terrible floods. The cities would then be obliged to intervene, at times with statutes which demonstrate that despite the intense colonization which was transforming the landscape there had often been little thought of regulating the watercourses as land for cultivation had been robbed from forest and fen. There had been neither the desire nor perhaps much awareness of the need to modify the watercourses in proportion to the transformation wrought in the countryside. Open marsh had been left adjacent to or surrounding land which had been cleared for agriculture with no provision for drainage or the protection of the new farmland. In 1311 the town council of Reggio Emilia had to pass a law obliging the rulers of Correggio to dig a drainage channel fourteen *braccia* wide to allow for water run-off in an area which had lost most of its woodland.

Not only the requirements of agriculture but also the increase in trade and travel between cities meant that roads needed to be kept clear and well drained. Legislation began to concern itself with them: the Reggio Emilia statutes of 1248 made it a crime to damage the drainage ditches along the public highway. The preoccupation with the problem of drainage for both agriculture and the roads was at its greatest in Modena since the town and its *contado* were particularly low lying. In 1336 all the laws concerning the construction and maintenance of canals and ditches in the town and *contado* were collected together into one comprehensive statute (principally from the fifth book of the city's 1327 statutes, which is concerned with this topic alone). City statutes in general are full of injunctions that streets in the town are to be paved or gravel is to be spread on roads in the country, mainly with a view to the speedy drainage of rain and floodwater and the avoidance of impassable morasses. It is clear from the 1288 Bologna statutes that a further perennial concern was that high water-levels would make canals unnavigable or the roads impassable.

This concern with road drainage and the problem of high water-levels in canals in general is frequently voiced from the fourteenth century onwards. It reflects the increasing need for intervention to allow dispersal of the surplus water; with the reclamation of areas into which rivers and marshes might overflow this became imperative. Yet it was a hopeless enterprise since the cycle of clearance and drainage went on regardless, though we do not know at what rate. The changes in the pattern of farming, with an increase in share-cropping, or *mezzadria*, accelerated the process because the consolidation of small units into self-contained holdings increased the need for drainage. As time went on, the combination of factors which meant that arable farming came ever more to dominate had the result that marginal lands and the activities dependent on them such as rough grazing and hunting lost importance. The restrictions on hunting were intended not only to conserve the remaining stocks but also to protect arable land; this is clear from a clause of the 1334 Imola statutes. 'We decree that no one, whether on foot or on horseback, may enter any vineyard, orchard, smallholding or arable field belonging to any citizen of the city of Imola or its territory with the intention of hunting animals or fowl while the grapes and other crops are still in the fields.'

If we remember that in addition to the land that was being cleared to make way for fields and vineyards, vegetation was also being cleared along the roadsides in order to make travel easier, we can gain an idea of the extent to which huge areas of the Po plain were losing their natural cover. The fourteenth-century statutes of Piacenza shed light on the practice of eradicating trees beside or in the vicinity of roads. Parma, Reggio Emilia, Modena and Bologna passed laws which vary in detail but which have the same end in mind. Such laws were based on the conviction that there was a need to disencumber agriculture of the natural habitats which had long been a burden and whose overwhelming presence had hindered attempts to establish new settlements.

All this coincided with an increase in cultivated land. Trees and vegetation were considered an impediment to agricultural development, but they soaked up rain and without them the risk of flooding increased. The inexorable rate of the clearances, of the unremitting campaign launched against trees and all undergrowth with the intention of freeing cities, roads, fields and canals from triumphant nature, upset the natural balance and passed the critical threshold. It is hardly surprising that the early modern period saw the destruction by the forces of nature of work which had taken decades to complete, particularly in areas where change had been most rampant and shortsighted. In the Ferrarese, floods brought devastation:

> Our crops are ruined, both the young shoots and the ripe corn. Often we sow twice, yet lose both. Our houses are destroyed . . . Our embankments are washed away, and without them we cannot last a year, so we constantly have to rebuild them. Our vines and our fruit trees are ruined before our eyes. Nowhere is so poorly supplied with trees and vines as our land, and yet with every breach of the banks we have the expense of replanting and have to begin anew.

20

The City and the Dead

Whereas in the early Middle Ages ruins were to be seen everywhere, over the centuries almost everywhere churches and abbeys rose, constructed from their stones. Gradually ruins disappeared from cities and country until by the beginning of the eleventh century they were a rare sight. Once common, they were now few and far between. Memories of massacres and martyrdoms meant that these lonely spots were associated with the dead, although as settlements developed around monasteries and churches the dead came to be linked with them as well. Until about the eleventh century no sharp distinction between the living and the dead was made. When people went to church they worshipped alongside previous generations who lay buried near the tomb of the local saint. Moreover, the souls of the dead, it was believed, retained some form of link with the body resting in the grave, and at the Last Judgment with the Resurrection of the Dead the body would rise anew.

Earlier it had been thought that forests and wild areas in general were populated by the spirits of the dead, who would often appear to people. This was not, as today, because forests were felt to be intrinsically eerie but simply because it was known that the graves of Christian martyrs lay there among the ruins or that Christians had been massacred there. In this period many forests were far from deserted: up until the eleventh century at least they supported a thriving silvo-pastoral economy, and the later stereotype of alien and empty forest, untracked and inhabited by spirits, is misleading. Those who lived from hunting, fishing and herding animals knew these forests intimately. The forest teemed with a large population of shepherds and woodcutters, while even less frequented forests sheltered the occasional hermit or band of outlaws while the Hungarians and other invaders sweeping from the northern, eastern or southern fringes towards the old Europe also passed through them.

Attitudes began to change only with the growth of agriculture and the ever more drastic expansion of cultivated land, fields, meadows, farmsteads, villages and towns after the twelfth century. The pace of change was far from uniform but the general trend was unmistakable and irrevocable. Forests were eroded particularly in central northern Italy, where the impetus for clearance came from the powerful towns well able to intervene in their surrounding territory. The result was that forests came to be regarded as different, as strange and frightening, and everything connected with them, and with wild areas in general, began to be feared and to assume monstrous proportions. This was the case with wolves, around which a daunting mythology grew up. Once common almost everywhere, they became more and more scarce and were hunted and feared to the point that they acquired a fantastical and unreal image. Stories of giant wolves, or ones which imagination made grotesque, with docked or unnaturally white tails, were common. The fierce wolf that terrorized the citizens of Gubbio in St Francis's lifetime belongs to this tradition, one in which the popular imagination ran riot.

In this way forests began to be intimidating places, entered only with reluctance and skirted warily by pilgrims on their long journeys and by shepherds. This image of the forest gradually came to embrace all forests, even those which were entered and traversed, though these too were becoming less and less familiar territory. It was believed that the spirits of the dead were at large in them and manifested themselves as ghosts, even if other places came to be associated with them, too, such as, much later, graveyards. Change came only with the Napoleonic reforms which laid down that cemeteries had to be sited well away from centres of population. Though these decrees were not applied uniformly and took a considerable time to be put into practice, they marked the beginning of the period in which the dead have been associated with graveyards rather than with forests.

One of the earliest accounts of the dead appearing to the living in a remote spot occurs in Orderic Vitalis's *Historia ecclesiastica*. Orderic describes how in the year 1091 a priest walking at night along a lonely path some distance from the village of Saint-Aubin-de-Bonneval heard the sound of an approaching procession. It was making as much noise as an army on the march. In it men and women, some on foot and some on horseback, were being tortured by demons. At their head walked a man of huge stature, carrying a mace. All were people who had died, and the priest recognized many of them: unfaithful women, murderers, even priests and monks who until then were believed to be enjoying eternal bliss.

The apparition described by Orderic is an example of 'Hellequin's hunt', a genre with a long history. One hundred and fifty years earlier the German monk Reginus of Prüm had condemned it in one of his didactic works. This time the procession was of people who had died young or by violence and who, tormented by the thought of their premature deaths, in their anguish at having seen their life cut short were raging against the living. In Orderic's later version, by contrast, the dead return in order to reveal to the living the punishments of the next world and to dissuade them from leading a life which will result in such awful retribution. The story exists in many versions and is clearly a Christian version of a pagan belief. Moreover, the differences between these two accounts are revealing: in Reginus's version the apparition takes place in a village and is intended to terrify the living, but by Orderic's time a remote spot was regarded as a more appropriate setting for the desperate plight of the hapless victims, tormented by unendurable punishment.

Writers often used landscapes to symbolize states of mind. In the popular imagination forests came to be daunting and alien, an image which was firmly established by the time of Dante. In the *Inferno* Dante placed those who had committed the sin of suicide in a sombre wood, also the site of the punishment of the spendthrifts, pursued and torn to pieces by a frenzied pack of black hounds in a chase which repeats itself endlessly. The forest setting is an integral part of this punishment. In the *Divine Comedy* Dante several times uses forests to symbolize the dark side of life. They are represented as frightening places, associated with anguish and death. Dante chooses the image of the 'selva selvaggia', the wild and tangled wood, of the opening canto of the *Divine Comedy* to reflect his mental turmoil as he wanders, disorientated, until Virgil comes to him near the edge of the dense forest and leads him out and away. Only one forest is described in positive terms, that in the Earthly Paradise (and therefore close to God). With its trees, airy glades which are pleasing to the eye and lawns and avenues, it is open and spacious, both literally and metaphorically. Unlike the tangled, inaccessible forests described earlier, this is open and welcoming. For it Dante draws on the conventional and time-honoured image of Paradise, found as early as the *Dialogues* of Pope Gregory the Great.

In time the primitive and uncomfortable aspect of wilderness, in part a consequence of the decreasing familiarity with the forests, came to be used increasingly to symbolize states of mind. Descriptions of forests in literature are of dark, forbidding places. In Tasso's *Gerusalemme liberata* night and sinister forest are the prelude to Clorinda's tragic death (disguised as a knight, she is killed in a duel by Tancredi), while after her death the scene in Canto XIII where Ismen summons the forces of evil is set in a dreadful forest, gloomy and forbidding even by day and a refuge for witches and demons. The bravest of the Christian knights do not dare enter the forest or remain there long. Tancredi, the most valiant of all, ventures in and comes to a broad clearing overshadowed by a tall cypress. There he sees hieroglyphs carved into the bark of the tree, warning him that the forest is the realm of the dead, not the living, and that the living should keep away.

> O hardy knight! who through these woods hath pass'd,
> Where death his palace and his court doth hold,
> O trouble not these souls in quiet plac'd!
> (Edward Fairfax translation, 1600)

In Tasso we see the culmination of the trend associating the forest with dark forces. The effect of the passage depends on the widespread belief, which Tasso shared, that such forests were inhabited by the spirits of those who had died by unnatural means; the extent to which forests had become associated with witches, ghosts and devils by this period is clear. The Catholic Reformation would reinforce this emphasis on the real and appalling existence of the forces of evil.

A more restrained, if still violent, manifestation of the trend can be seen in Boccaccio, writing two centuries earlier. In the *Decameron*, the eighth story of the fifth day is set in a forest. It concerns Nastagio degli Onesti, a young man from Ravenna who is unrequitedly in love and who witnesses a macabre hunt. While he is wandering in broad daylight in the pinewoods near the town, the silence of the forest is suddenly broken by cries. He sees a young woman fleeing from a young knight on horseback, who is urging on two fierce mastiffs. Nastagio looks on aghast as the mastiffs seize the maiden and the knight dismounts, rips her back open with his rapier and tears out her heart, dripping with blood. The knight tells Nastagio that because the woman had not returned his love when they had been alive he had killed himself in desperation, thereby condemning himself to eternal damnation. Both he and the woman he had loved were doomed to repeat this ritual once a week for ever more. Despite his fright Nastagio is able to turn this disconcerting experience to good use. He ensures that the woman he himself loves witnesses the scene the following week, upon which she realizes the error of her ways and finally agrees to marry him.

The episode has pronounced similarities to the ancient 'Hellequin's hunt' of pagan origin, although it differs in that here the man who had died a premature death avenges himself on another person who has died young, not the living. The story is also influenced by the basic theme of the *dolce stil nuovo*, the 'sweet new style' of lyrical love poetry, the duty to reciprocate love. All the same, the growing association of the forest with apparitions of the dead to the living is a dominant feature.

The Franciscan tradition offered an alternative image of the forest, as benign and serene. Many of the most intense mystic experiences of St Francis and his followers occurred in forests, while in the *Fioretti* of St Francis ancient forests are constantly portrayed as places ideal for contemplative prayer: their remoteness and silence made them conducive to an intimate relationship with God through prayer, while they offered an antithesis to the bustle and noise of centres of habitation, both in the country and, especially, in towns. For St Francis there was a deep affinity between men and women and the natural world. Although for the Franciscans the dead still appear to the living, they are benign, not frightening, and seek to help them. Death is seen as a friend, not an enemy, an image which offered a counterbalance to the prevailing unease about the wilderness and wild animals and to contemporary fears surrounding death.

This contrasted with the situation in the early Middle Ages, when many areas had reverted to nature. Within the towns themselves vegetation and undergrowth were rampant, choking buildings. This was especially marked north of the Alps where the ruins of many towns had all but vanished beneath dense vegetation. Then, too, religious people eager for solitude and also for a site for their monasteries had sought out such places. The solitude and tranquillity to be found had been a factor, but more so was the desire to find a site for a monastery. Moreover the forests had in the early Middle Ages sheltered a large population of foresters, shepherds and hunters, but with the shift to a predominantly arable economy and the growth of the towns this population had diminished dramatically. In France and Germany, however, the forests long continued to support such populations.

In the early Middle Ages it was supposed that the dead remained close to where they had been buried. Though they might make themselves visible or bring about miracles, they would never stray far away. Gradually, however, the idea that the soul became divorced from the body at the moment of death became widespread, and by the late Middle Ages the spirits of the dead were associated with a much greater variety of places and were thought to be all around. It is at this time that the phenomenon of haunted houses developed in earnest; it was evidently sufficiently common for it to appear in legal textbooks in Italy. In his commentary on the *Institutes* of Justinian of the first half of the fifteenth century, the lawyer Giovanni Cristoforo Porzio argued that in the case of a house being haunted the tenant was not obliged to pay rent. The problem was to arise frequently in both legal theory and practice over the next two centuries and there have even been cases in recent years in Italy. Legal theory generally upheld the rights of the tenant, but in practice courts seldom found in their favour: the gap was largely due to the difficulties of providing proof.

The issue appears to have declined in importance up to the nineteenth century, when there was a sharp drop in the number of cases, although Italian legal textbooks continued to treat the subject. In 1868 and 1927 courts in Italy found in favour of tenants and as recently as 1959 an Italian legal textbook on tenancies (Visco, *Trattato delle case in locazione/Leaseholds*) devoted two pages to the topic, citing cases from 1915 (12 October) and 1928 (14 January) in Naples and one from 1927 (13 March) in Pomigliano d'Arco, a suburb of Naples. According to Visco, report of ghosts is not sufficient in itself to invalidate a tenancy agreement; there must be actual material proof of their existence. If it can be established incontrovertibly that disturbances exist, that they are inexplicable in normal terms, and that they existed previous to the tenant moving in, then the tenant has a right to terminate the contract. In addition, if the landlord was previously aware of the situation the tenant is entitled to compensation. If, however, the phenomena appear to be produced through a spiritualistic medium, perhaps through a third party, the tenant cannot make a claim.

The beginnings of a perception of the dead, particularly those who died young or violently, as malevolent spirits dates from the twelfth and thirteenth centuries. It parallels the spread of the belief in the ability of the dead to manifest themselves where they chose, and especially in remote spots. It is principally a consequence of the desire to separate the dead from the rest of human society, in the context of a 'rational' transformation of society as people steadily became divorced from the forces of nature and from the entire early medieval environment, and above all from the wild areas which were gradually cultivated and colonized. Death, which was part of nature, was increasingly regarded as alien and the gulf between the living and the dead widened. The period also saw the beginnings of a distinction between those who were useful (active and productive) and those who were not, or who were no longer so. It is at this time that the cities of central northern Italy passed draconian measures against such people, who found themselves increasingly marginalized. Beggars were restricted to specific areas of the town and cripples, conjurors and sorcerers were expelled, while the gallows for murderers and other criminals were to be sited well away from frequented parts of the town.

Funerals also came to be controlled at this time and legislation sought to tone them down. Evidently they were thought to have become too ostentatious and extravagant and to play too dominant a part in daily life. For example, regulations limited the number of women who could take part. It appears that women wept and keened too loudly and beat their breasts or collapsed and had to be supported, all of which was 'a shameful sight'. Both in Italy and elsewhere death was increasingly feared, and where regulations did not impede it, funerals therefore became more elaborate. In particular, mourning and grief was highly visible and theatrical. Stunned and helpless in the face of death, people had responded by emphasizing the place of weeping and lamentation. For a long time the dead continued to be buried inside churches or near them but the era of amicable coexistence between the dead and the living was coming to an end.

In this context the city statutes of Bologna, dating from the second half of the thirteenth century, are telling. They sought to ensure that at the very least the procession to the grave should be more discreet and less dominant in the life of the city. The origins of the trend which has resulted in our modern desire to suppress the fact of death – a few cars following the hearse, a brisk cremation or burial – lie here. In Italian cities such regulations, motivated in part by a desire to curb what was seen as unnecessary expense or extravagance, offer indirect evidence for the extent of the practices they denounce: conspicuous funerals and the involvement of a wide circle of people, outsiders as well as relations and friends. Death provided a focus for the life of the community. All gathered together to participate in mourning at the dead person's house, all accompanied the funeral procession and attended the burial. Since the dead continued to be buried in or next to the church, they were felt to be very much present and those attending mass were surrounded by past generations. The restless spirits of those who had died by violence were associated with remote and wild places, and as the abandoned ruins and derelict churches containing martyrs' tombs developed into thriving towns, the dead were felt to be present there as well. The Bologna city statutes of 1288 were severe:

> No one resident in the town may bring anyone in from the country . . . to attend a burial, to mourn or to stay in their house. The fine is 100 *libbre* . . . Relations up to the fifth degree will be exempted on condition that they comply with the above ordinances as to weeping and the beating of breasts. Similarly, no one is to employ more than eight priests for a funeral in a church belonging to the family, or any priests or clerics over and above those attached to the church if the funeral is held elsewhere.

The Bologna laws also laid down that a maximum of two crosses and four candles of one *libbra* weight each might be carried. After the funeral, only relatives up to the fourth degree were allowed to remain at the home of the dead person. The statutes were especially severe as regards women. Only the mother, mother-in-law, wife, daughters, granddaughters, sisters and sisters-in-law could stay; all the rest had to leave. Women were singled out because, the statutes claimed, they made an exhibition of themselves, even fainting and having to be held up in public by men, which was 'not seemly'.

Such legislation sought to discourage mass participation in funerals and to reduce their central role and their profound importance as ritual. It represents the first expression in a formal context of the shift in the attitude to death. Death had a diminishing place in the everyday life of the city and mourning was a private affair for friends and family. Only in our day has the process reached its logical conclusion, a result of the gradual disengagement of wider social groups from participation in mourning for a relative, a friend or a fellow citizen. The sense of death as a collective event involving all citizens has vanished, and nowadays it is felt to be a matter only for a few people closely connected with the dead person by blood ties or by affection. Ultimately individual, not collective, participation came to be the norm, although elements of the latter long survived.

In Italian cities in the late medieval period a consequence of this gradual distancing of death from the community was a perception of the dead as different and, increasingly, as unnatural and even grotesque. The 'dance of death', a parade of skeletons with putrefying flesh, eye-sockets gaping wide in skulls from which all the flesh has fallen away, and gaunt bony fingers, all surrounded by the stench of death, is above all a consequence of this marginalization of the dead. This is the new and terrifying image of death which is found at the opening of Boccaccio's *Decameron*. As the plague rages in Florence, the young Pampinea, appalled at the prospect of such a death, proposes to her comrades that they flee the city.

> And if we return to our houses, what happens? I know not whether your own experience is similar to mine, but my house was once full of servants and now there is no one left apart from my maid and myself. I am filled with foreboding and feel as if every hair of my head is standing on end. Wherever I go in the house, wherever I pause to rest, I seem to be haunted by the shades of the departed, whose faces no longer appear as I remember them *but with strange and horribly twisted expressions that frighten me out of my senses*. (trans. G. H. McWilliam; emphasis added)

Banished from the city, the dead had only the countryside to roam. Their natural home was increasingly felt to be the areas least touched by human intervention, untamed forest and moor. In time it would be believed that the witches' sabbath took place there, in desolate forest clearings where witches gathered to communicate with the dead, and that the dead would make contact with relatives and friends only in specific places and through particular intermediaries. Increasingly the living went in fear of the dead. Within the still huge areas of wild and empty land some especially isolated and lonely places might be associated closely with them. The mountain of Tonale near Trent, for example, was infamous for hundreds of years as the site of sinister encounters of supernatural forces, male and female witches, devils and the spirits of the dead. Even though the bodies of the dead might remain buried among the living, their souls wandered at will, free to appear to men and women where they chose, though they preferred solitary, seldom visited places like forests and moorland. Later, when they became associated with graveyards, these in turn became places to avoid at all costs at night. The dreadful forest described in Canto XIII of Tasso's *Gerusalemme liberata*, a horrifying evolution of the bleak wood of the suicides in Canto XIII of the *Inferno*, yet more ghastly still, reflects the changing image of the forest.

Increasingly every part of the countryside had to serve a purpose. Society was moving towards what for convenience we may call a rationalistic use of resources, while at the same time the demands of economic production required that all should contribute, or at least be prepared to do so. In Italy the cities were growing in size while their populations swelled and 'pre-capitalist' activity increased. The cities increasingly distanced themselves from the countryside and steadily eradicated uncultivated areas and unwanted trees inside their walls. The same period saw the beginnings of the exclusion of women from the management of their own affairs, from rights of inheritance and landholding in the feudal system and from civic and political life. Simultaneously the increasing ill-ease in face of the natural world meant that women, who because of childbearing seemed more closely connected to nature, were viewed with hostility. Fear and criticism of them became common. In any case, women, less physically strong and hampered by repeated pregnancies and the demands of childrearing, were unable to keep up with men in work, particularly in the area of urban crafts but also in agricultural work, where the need for increased production and therefore for increased participation was strongly felt.

The changes in the landscape were a tangible expression of the new economic situation. As fields expanded at the expense of wilderness, so wild areas became peripheral and thus ever less frequented. A patchwork of cultivation and settlements developed over wide areas and the remaining forest was seen as an alien and strange element. However, forest and marsh were not everywhere on the retreat; large expanses of forest and marsh survived in remote areas in the mountains and on the fenland, far from towns and villages and difficult of access. As well as being economically backward, such areas were culturally conservative. Here it was impossible for the forest to be 'different'; there was no constantly evolving landscape and intensive, homogeneous agriculture to contrast it with.

On a cultural level the message of the Church that the dead were inimical and the next world alien had little impact here. But even in the most economically and culturally conservative regions, such as Friuli at the end of the sixteenth century and the beginning of the seventeenth, efforts by the Church to combat ancient harvest rites had some impact on popular culture. The Church's policy was to portray such practices as witchcraft, and the world of the dead came to be seen as macabre and frightening. On the other hand, even in the areas most influenced by urban culture, the existence of a popular culture linked to ancient pagan beliefs and the presence of the dead in or next to churches are evidence of the survival in the sixteenth and seventeenth centuries of old beliefs about the nature of the next world.

On the whole, however, the influences for change which have been discussed above prevailed, and wild areas and the dead increasingly came to be regarded as alien and unnatural. The underlying trend was clear, even if it varied abruptly between different places and times. Efforts were still made to rid the dead of their fearful associations and to make the next world appear less hostile. Different social groups had dramatically different perceptions of death: cleric and layman, townsman and peasant each had a widely differing mental world, while a shepherd, who had a primitive way of life and who inhabited an ancient mental and physical landscape, might have an entirely different set of beliefs again.

21

Animals in City and Country

One of the features which distinguished the early medieval centuries from later ones was, as we have emphasized, the presence throughout Europe of huge areas of wilderness. Vast forests and desolate heathland, marshes and pools were to be found everywhere, especially north of the Alps. In many areas wilderness exceeded cultivated land, and what cultivated land there was might well consist of meagre patches of cleared land on the edge of the forest. Deer, boar and wolves outnumbered domestic animals. For centuries wolf-hunts had to be organized: as late as the fourteenth century the statutes of Mantua envisaged the possibility of wolves coming right into the town, while in the mid-thirteenth century Salimbene of Parma told how packs of wolves besieged the towns at night during a severe winter when people and animals alike went hungry. He described how they would howl outside the city defences and sometimes even manage to get in and kill many people. Centuries earlier, Charlemagne had appointed *luparii*, men who were employed specifically to hunt wolves.

Other wild animals were considerably more numerous than wolves and posed a constant threat to cultivated land and domestic animals. From contemporary documents we learn of the erection of fences and thick high hedges to protect vegetable plots and animal enclosures, and of heavy fines for anyone damaging them. The relationship between people and animals in the early Middle Ages was still marked by the need to safeguard oneself and to protect property and farm animals from wild beasts. However, it was not always possible to defend land against animals. North of the Alps, and especially in central Europe, huge swarms of grasshoppers might descend on anything that grew. Andreas of Bergamo, writing shortly afterwards, lamented an invasion of them in 873, when a dense mass swarmed over much of northern Italy from

Vicenza to Brescia and Cremona and as far as Lodi and Milan, devouring 'many smaller grains, that is, the different kinds of millet'. Andreas echoed Proverbs: 'The locusts have no king, yet go they forth all of them by bands.' In the same year they descended on Germany too: 'There were so many of them that in one hour alone they destroyed one hundred *iugers* of grain near the town of Mainz. When they rose into the sky they formed a cloud a mile long, so great that they almost entirely shut out the light of the sun.'

In the early Middle Ages, however, many animals posed no kind of threat and could in fact be a valuable source of food. The peasants of the Po delta were obliged to give their lords a certain number of birds each year and the endless marshes there must have then sheltered many hundreds of thousands of migratory birds. Similarly, those who lived along the Po could find fish in abundance. Even large sturgeon were plentiful: in the eleventh century the inhabitants of Sermide, on the Po east of Mantua, had to give their lord an annual tribute of a certain number. But the most sought-after animals were boar and deer. Hunting was a congenial activity since it fostered qualities and abilities essential in battle. Animals abounded in the endless forests of northern and central Europe, but they were also common in the mountains and plains of Italy and were often to be found at only a small distance from towns and villages, or even within them. The Edict of Rothari of the mid-seventh century shows that deer were being reared in villages and cranes and storks kept in captivity; it imposed heavy penalties on anyone who harmed stags in enclosed areas during the rutting season, when they would deafen the villagers with their belling.

Evidence for such domesticated wild animals survives throughout the Middle Ages and beyond. The life of St Matilda, wife of Henry I of Germany, written in the second half of the tenth century, describes a tame deer which wandered as freely as the domestic animals in the enclosed fields of the convent where the queen lived; it would come right into the convent buildings and into the nuns' living quarters. Such familiarity with wild animals was common in the lands north of the Alps, a natural consequence of the greater area of wilderness there compared with southern Europe. The silvo-pastoral economy was stronger there and the presence of these great forests meant that hunting was much more common than in Italy. There was felt to be little distinction between wild and domestic animals and wild animals might well be fed where necessary.

According to the life of John of Gorze, who lived in north-east France near Metz in the tenth century, John, concerned to ensure a regular food supply for the monks and other residents of the monastery and for guests, would order that not only the domestic animals and fowl belonging to the monastery, but also the wild animals and birds were to be fed. Wild animals would be tended almost as carefully as domestic ones. In any case we know that herds of domestic pigs lived alongside wild boar in the forest and mated with them. (The size of forests was generally calculated according to the number of pigs they could support.) Thus pigs ran alongside wild boar, shepherds and herdsmen also hunted, and stockraising was pursued alongside hunting. The consequence was that when early medieval chronicles mention epidemics among animals, it is often not clear whether only domestic animals were affected or animals in general, while there are many instances of sick wild animals which were looked after or cured by a saint.

Of all animals, most attention was paid to horses. In a society ever more dominated by the feudal code, ownership of a trained battle horse, costing much more than a mere packhorse, was proof of status. Penalties for injuring horses are found as early as the Edict of Rothari and the so-called barbarian law-codes. The relationship between horses and their owners, whether the horse was used in battle or to travel, was close and led to horses taking on something of the prestige of their riders, especially if they were of high social status or even saintly. The monk Folcuin from the abbey of Saint-Bertin near Calais, round which the town of Saint-Omer later developed, wrote of how a particular horse which had been ridden regularly by a saintly man itself acquired sanctity. The horse had obeyed its master just as if it were human and was so devoted to him that when he died it died shortly after. Its carcass was left in open country to be eaten but no animal ventured to touch it, a mark of their respect. Eventually 'people decided to bury it as if it was human, considering that no fowl of the air or animal on the earth had presumed to touch the body.'

As well as showing the respect felt for the horse, the story reveals how dead animals were treated. The contrast at the centre of the story between burial, reserved for humans, and exposure to the ravages of wild beasts, the fate of animals, suggests that it was not normal for animal carcasses to be buried, and given the many wild animals then living close to towns, carcasses would have been picked clean very quickly. Much later, during the age of the Italian city-republics between the thirteenth and the fourteenth centuries, town statutes frequently forbade the depositing of animal carcasses within or near the town or near the city walls. The need for such laws suggests that the habit of dumping dead animals, skins or unwanted parts of slaughtered animals inside the town was all too prevalent. At the same time as removing dead animals, the city sought through legislation to ban living animals, especially strong-smelling ones such as goats and pigs, from the city. As the cities grew in area and population, much open space inside the walls was lost and there was no longer room for living animals, let alone dead ones. In this too, and not only in Italy, the late medieval city was beginning to differentiate itself sharply from the countryside and from towns of the early Middle Ages.

In the early medieval centuries death took a heavy toll of people and animals alike. Chronicles refer constantly to death, especially to epidemics of fatal diseases against which there seemed to be no remedy. In 791, at the end of one of Charlemagne's campaigns, disease broke out among his horses and out of many thousands 'scarcely one-tenth survived'; in 810 cattle throughout the Carolingian empire succumbed to a bovine epidemic which was widely believed to be the result of witchcraft, a belief which demonstrates both the ignorance of the nature of disease and also the strength of religious fears. St Agobard, Archbishop of Lyons and author of one of the chronicles which mention the epidemic, deplored the atmosphere of superstitious terror as the epidemic raged and during its grim aftermath:

> A few years ago, during the cattle pestilence, a superstitious belief spread. It was claimed that Grimoald, Prince of Benevento, had sent people to sprinkle certain powders everywhere, on fields and meadows and in the mountains and rivers, and that these powders were the cause of the cattle dying. Grimoald's motive was said to have been hatred of the most Christian Emperor Charlemagne. As a result people seized many whom they held responsible and proceeded to bind or nail them to boards which were then cast into the river. In this way they died. I have heard this told and saw it with my own eyes. What was most remarkable was that those seized gave evidence against themselves, confessing that they had had these deadly powders in their possession and had spread them on the ground ... Everyone believed this, save a very few who thought it an absurdity. People did not stop to consider what manner of powder might kill cattle alone and not other creatures, and failed even to ask themselves how it could have been spread over so great an area ...

Many pagan beliefs in magic persisted into the ninth century. Agobard was astonished and bitter that Christians should believe in such things. Yet behind these beliefs, which derived from a mentality still deeply influenced by magical practices, lay a feeling of utter helplessness in the face of epidemics, and the fear that for some unknown reason no remedy was possible. Epidemics, especially those affecting cattle, were common: ten years later, in 820, people and cattle again died of plague throughout the Carolingian empire. According to Einhard's *Annales regni Francorum*,

> in that year the excessive rains and high humidity caused great problems. Indeed pestilence broke out among both people and animals over huge

areas, to such an extent that hardly any part of the empire of the Franks was unaffected.

For the year 823 Einhard records that 'then there was a great pestilence which raged all through the lands of the Franks . . .' Some epidemics struck down only animals, others people, many both, but invariably they seemed terrifying and inescapable. At other times other forces struck down people and animals: in a vulnerable environment like that of the early Middle Ages, extremes of climate – drought, heat and, above all, cold – were perilous. The year 824 saw 'a very long and harsh winter, so bitterly cold that not only animals but also many men and women perished'. In a silvo-pastoral, largely non-agricultural economy where most food came from the forest or from unfarmed land in general, people and animals alike were vulnerable to the vicissitudes of the seasons. Cold, drought or late frosts inhibited plant growth. Contemporary chronicles record disastrous late frosts which killed the buds and new growth, and deprived people and wild and domestic animals of food.

Since domestic animals depended entirely or almost so on uncultivated areas for food and were given no extra food in winter, they were much smaller than later ones. Analysis of cattle, pig and sheep bones found in archaeological excavations makes this clear. Even the carved images of animals on church facades of the later Middle Ages show how small they were. Pigs appear to have reached a maximum of seventy kilogrammes in weight and to have averaged much less. The fact that only a very few animals were kept inside for any time militated against their increasing in weight and size: the oxen used for ploughing cannot have been as useful as the bigger and more powerful ones of later centuries.

None the less, bearing in mind the relatively insignificant role of agriculture in the early Middle Ages compared to later, the limited tools and animals available were probably adequate; over great areas, grazing, hunting and fishing and collecting wild fruits and nuts were as, or more, important. After the twelfth century in Italy, mainly through the initiative of the towns, animals were increasingly kept inside and cattle became larger and stronger and able to work the land more efficiently. At the end of the thirteenth century Bonvesin della Riva boasted of the many thousands of sturdy oxen which were used to plough the land around Milan.

An examination of the image of animals is essential to understanding the place of animals in the early Middle Ages and the relationship with them. A consequence of the intimate relationship with nature was that animals were seen as the most authentic and forceful expression of nature, and at the same time as emblematic of the arcane forces which lay behind the natural order. Dogs, for instance, were held to exemplify the

virtues of courage and faithfulness, associations which go back as far as
the Lombards and which were still alive in the time of the powerful
Scaligeri of Verona. Their members adopted the names of dogs –
Cangrande, Cansignorio, Mastino (*cane* = dog, *mastino* = mastiff) – and
their battle helmets had a visor in the form of a dog's head, evidently a
survival of a usage in combat of ancient origin: Paul the Deacon had
written of the cynocephali, legendary warriors with dogs' heads and
human bodies, who were born to slaughter the enemy but who in the
absence of an antagonist were fated to tear each other to pieces.

The story has a kernel of truth as it is an echo of the ancient custom
of ritual dances before battle performed by warriors who covered their
heads with the heads of animals renowned for courage and ferocity such
as dogs, wolves or bears. This is the explanation of the fantastical
exploits of the cynocephali and of Germanic personal names such as
Wolfetan ('wolf helmet'). In Italy the Lombard custom of calling male
children *Lupo* (wolf) was widespread for centuries, persisting long after
the Carolingian invasion and the defeat of the Lombards. When nicknames began to be common from the twelfth century onwards (and often
became surnames), they were frequently taken from animal names. Usage
is much more precise than before: the range of animals referred to is
much greater than in earlier centuries, while there is a rich diversity of
diminutives, pejorative versions and other variations. Animal names
were used to suggest ugliness or attractiveness and good or bad traits of
character, while the aristocracy were given sobriquets deriving from
those animals held to symbolize military virtues such as ferocity or
courage. The central place of animals in the medieval world picture is
clear.

In both town and country, animals and people lived in close contact.
As early as the thirteenth century, as we have seen, town councils
energetically sought to ensure that the city was disencumbered of the
presence of animals, but despite these efforts they remained in large
numbers. City governments were concerned above all to remove animals
from the streets and open spaces and they threatened offenders with
heavy fines. With the growth of trade and of fairs and markets, it was
important that city centres should be cleared of animals and that passage
not be impeded by obstructions. Such measures are but one aspect of the
growing self-consciousness of the town as a distinct entity markedly
different from the country; the city became, in a sense, antagonistic to
animals.

Evil forces were also viewed in terms of animals. Demons were imagined in the guise of animals, as were heretics or overweening nobles.
In moral tracts the strong who oppress the weak are described as wolves
or as aggressive and lumbering rhinoceroses, whereas heretics who

undermine the teaching and institutions of the Church are called foxes or wolves.

The symbolism attached to animals can vary and can even be superficially inconsistent, one animal being used to exemplify different, even opposite qualities. This happened because the associations of an individual species might depend on the background of a writer, whether he was clerical or aristocratic. The wolf, for example, which for the aristocracy represented strength and courage, in clerical eyes stood for the negative aspects of those characteristics, violence and force. Despite the radical differences in outlook, animals had a central role in the medieval world picture, to an extent which can seem obsessive to the modern mind. Though there was an intimate relationship with all animals, varying according to the species and milieu, horses were particularly important. Not all peasants owned a pair of oxen but every nobleman had a horse. The knight's most important means of combat and his constant companion was his horse, and the partnership of man and horse in battle is a dominant feature of contemporary chronicles. Both might well meet the same bloody end. Liutprand wrote of how, in a hard-fought battle in the mid-tenth century, Anscar, Marquis of Spoleto, eventually found that he and his horse were cut off and surrounded. Though greatly outnumbered, he resisted to the last and could be overcome only when his horse slipped into a deep hollow, and horse and rider died there together in a hail of arrows and spears.

A century and a half later, in his history of Matilda of Canossa, the monk Donizo painted a blood-curdling picture of the savage battle between Boniface of Canossa and his brother Conrad in about 1020, describing how the horses' hooves of both sides splashed and trampled in the blood of the dead and wounded. Because of their crucial role in battle, the best breeds and finest examples were much sought after, like the hundred bay horses which – according to Donizo – Albert, Viscount of Mantua and Boniface's vassal, gave to the Emperor. Horses are again in the foreground in Donizo's description of Boniface's journey to meet his second wife, Beatrice of Lorraine. Determined to impress those he met, Boniface had silver placed under his horses' shoes and ensured that the nails were loose so that at a certain point on the journey the horses shed silver on the road and the people in that land, rushing to retrieve them, were suitably impressed by this evidence of Boniface's wealth.

Nobles spent a good part of their lives on horseback, frequently meeting their death in battle or while hunting. In the autumn of 898, Lambert, Marquis of Spoleto, rode into a branch while galloping after a boar and was killed, though some said that this was merely the official account and that in reality he had been murdered. Whichever version is true, he died on horseback out hunting. Also on horseback, according to tradition, was Boniface of Canossa when he was assassinated a century and a half later. On horseback, too, died the hosts of the Italian nobility who fell in the battle which raged between Berengar I and Rudolf of Burgundy at Fiorenzuola in 923; a dispirited Liutprand commented that many families lost so many of their members that they took generations to recover. The horse was also, as we have seen, the frequent companion of saints from aristocratic families. As described above, a horse was the loyal companion of a saintly man when St Gerald of Aurillac rode through a bitterly cold night to punish himself for his lustful intentions, which he had succeeded in resisting only through divine intervention.

If the horse was associated with many virtues, the ass, in the eyes of the aristocracy and the Church, had quite opposite associations. In the mid-ninth century the sons of the Emperor Louis the Pious fought each other in one of the bloodiest battles of the whole period. George, Archbishop of Ravenna, had been on the losing side and paid for his involvement with a grotesque humiliation: he was hoisted on to an ass whose ears and tail had been cut off and was dragged past jeering soldiers. Elsewhere, Adalbert, the powerful Marquis of Tuscany, was urged by his ambitious wife to rebel against the emperor. After his defeat he was discovered hiding among the animals in a byre. He was taken before the Emperor, who taunted him, saying, 'I think Berta your wife was quite right when she prophesied that your shrewdness would make you either king or an ass. And since she wouldn't – or couldn't – make you king, she has made an ass of you so as to ensure that her prophecy would come true.'

The worst insult that could be directed at a noble was to suggest he could not ride. During the battle between Berengar I of Friuli and Guy, Marquis of Spoleto, in the late ninth century, a Bavarian soldier in Berengar's army jeered that the Italians could not ride; speared in the chest by an Italian horseman and unhorsed, he paid for the insult with his life.

If horses were prized in war, mules were preferred for travel, particularly over inhospitable terrain. In particular, bishops, abbots and clerics in general favoured them for their journeys between cathedrals and monasteries, often to other countries. Mules and donkeys appear in the sources above all in the context of transporting goods. Donkeys, too, were ridden by peasants, especially in southern Italy where cultivated land lay far from villages and towns but could be reached by this more modest means of transport. They were well suited for this harsh, frequently arid, hostile terrain and moreover were cheaper to buy and feed. We also know of some tougher breeds of horse which could stand up to arduous journeys through remote country. The horse ridden by a deacon from Novara for his arduous journey over the Alps to the monastery of

St Gall in present-day Switzerland in the second half of the tenth century must have been one of these breeds. The deacon left a description of the hazards of the crossing:

> We passed steep mountains and sheer valleys until we finally reached the monastery of St Gall. I was in such straits from the bitter cold we had encountered in the mountains that my hands were numb with cold and all through the journey I could not manage to mount or dismount by myself. Instead the others had to heave me on and off. When we finally reached our destination the thought of the peace and tranquillity I would find in the monastery consoled me.

Unfortunately, after a journey which had taken him to the threshold of endurance, things did not go as he had hoped.

As well as horses of good quality for journeys and, above all, for battle, the aristocracy kept other animals. These were wild, or in any case fierce, and often brought from far afield. They were intended as a tangible symbol of the lord's power and of the awe he should inspire. Lions, the supreme symbol of power and strength, were especially popular (and later would be much used on coats of arms). The great feudal lords often kept lions in captivity. In Mantua, for example, the palace of Boniface of Canossa was graced by lions chained up outside to impress visitors before they had even met the powerful Boniface, who we know was indeed valiant in battle. A seventeenth-century print depicts the legendary fight between Henry the Lion, Duke of Bavaria, and a lion. In addition, hunting dogs themselves included some particularly fierce breeds. A passage in the life of St Gerald of Aurillac describes how he was taken hunting when a boy and was taught in particular to handle Molossian hounds. This was an ancient and particularly strong and fierce breed of dog which the Romans had used in battle, as well as for show fights in the amphitheatre. In the Middle Ages they must have been used chiefly for larger quarry such as deer and boars and in wolf-hunts.

In the history of the relationship between humans and animals the use of animals in agriculture is particularly important. Among these animals the most important were oxen, used for ploughing since time immemorial. While horses began to be used only in the early modern period, and only in some areas, oxen retained their central role until the mechanization of agriculture in recent years. They are still used throughout the developing world and help us, despite the differences, to envisage how early medieval agriculture would have appeared. The parallel is useful for it reminds us that then as now oxen would have been relatively uncommon. Few peasant families owned one, and land had to be laboriously prepared and dug for sowing. Indicative of this is the economic status of small landowners, who became dependent on others and were obliged to offer their labour-services to the lord from whom they rented their land as well as the beasts to work it. Elsewhere poorer peasants, whether they owned their land or not, had to borrow an ox from a neighbour fortunate enough to own one.

At times it was the peasants themselves who worked the plough, one pushing and one pulling, using a light plough in the friable soil of southern Europe, a method still seen today in the developing world. Thus ploughing in the early Middle Ages was often carried out with primitive tools, even without one or two oxen or other animals. The lack of oxen even on the great estates suggests that the situation was general, even though it varied between different social groups. The reason is clear: epidemics, as we have seen, could be devastating, wiping out cattle over wide areas, and afterwards it must have been difficult, often impossible, to build up stocks again. Cattle prices, always high, would soar when diminished numbers made them sought after, and in such circumstances only those with large estates and therefore money can have been in a position to acquire them.

As well as epidemics, a further cause of the loss of oxen by peasants was raids during war. The result was that freemen who owned land might decide to enter the service of others, perhaps with onerous labour-services. This is what appears to have happened to a certain Stavelene from the Piacenza area. In 784, when the effects of the war between the Franks and the Lombards were evidently still felt in Italy, Stavelene contracted himself to rent and cultivate a holding; in addition to the usual rent in kind of a proportion of the yield, he was to work on the owner's land for as many as three days a fortnight. Stavelene may have still been a free man but he was evidently in dire straits: the contract lays down that the landlord would loan him a pair of oxen and a yoke and plough to work the land, as well as a sheep, a she-goat and a young pig.

Already at the end of the Dark Ages, in the eleventh century, the face of Europe was changing, a trend which would become ever more marked in the following centuries as virgin land steadily came under cultivation. The changes also resulted in drastic change where animals were concerned. With the contraction of rough land, populations of wild animals fell dramatically and far fewer domestic animals were left to roam semi-wild. At the same time the growth in fields and in cultivated plots made for an increase in the number of animals kept indoors. Many of them, especially oxen, were used to work the fields or to transport agricultural produce. As the silvo-pastoral economy steadily yielded to settled agriculture, especially around the Italian towns, so information about domestic animals begins to proliferate in the sources. Details about their purchase and care and about their loan to peasants by landlords are increasingly found. In the later Middle Ages a cow's colour, peculiarities

of its horns, its breed and other distinguishing marks might all be
recorded, as well as its age, state of health and consequent value.

In the early Middle Ages, on the other hand, prices of animals remained unchanged for centuries. In part this was because there was less
awareness of potential variations in their price and in that of land, but
the general economic stasis, linked to the frequent religious overtones
and symbolic content of custom, was also significant. Between the eighth
and tenth centuries, in much of Italy large pigs are almost invariably
recorded as costing twelve *denari*, and small ones six, with few exceptions. In practice, however, there must have been variations; it was
simply that little attention was paid to them. This rigid system was
already beginning to collapse by the eleventh century, to be gradually
replaced by a hardheaded pragmatism about the prices of material goods.
Italian local chronicles of the thirteenth and fourteenth centuries are
crammed with figures about agriculture and crafts; the city had committed itself to accounting and profit.

As the wilderness decreased and cultivated land increased, the animal
population fell. Animals also lost a crucial role, that of a unit of measurement of land. Until the beginning of the eleventh century, while forest
and fen were still extensive and supported great herds of pigs, the size of
forests was frequently estimated according to the number of pigs they
could support. For example, in the second half of the ninth century a
large forest belonging to the monastery of St Columbanus at Bobbio near
Piacenza was measured in terms of the 2,000 pigs which could be grazed
and fattened there, and towards the end of the tenth century the abbey of
Nonantola on the Po plain, also near Piacenza, owned a large stretch of
forest which was assessed at 1,000 pigs. Obviously in the case of land
of poor quality a larger area would be required to support the same
number of pigs, but all the same the method was commonly used to
measure uncultivated land in many areas of Italy and elsewhere in the
early Middle Ages. In the eleventh century it began to yield to the modern
system of measurement by surface area and the shift was complete by the
twelfth century. This change is evidence that land was by this time used
primarily for arable fields and orchards rather than for rough grazing
since it was valued primarily by area. Even the vanishing forests and
uncultivated areas began to be estimated by the new method rather than
by the number of swine they could support.

The most striking feature of the transformation of the animal world is
the decrease in the number of wild animals. They needed ample space,
and their natural habitat of forest and marsh, once extensive and found
on flood-plains, was diminishing. By the eleventh century populations of
several species had already fallen drastically, while some had become
extinct. The great deer of the Po plain, for example, became rare as the

forest and fen disappeared. Once hunted by all, they became the prerogative of the aristocracy. In time the aristocracy began to allow forests which had been cleared to grow anew purely for hunting, and to stock them with animals from far afield to make up for the gap left by the advance of agriculture.

As for wolves, the expansion of agriculture restricted them to ever smaller pockets of wild land and they found themselves circumscribed by the growth of settlements. Finding that their normally ample prey of wild beasts and domestic animals left to graze in the wild had been reduced, they turned their attention to humans; in the low-lying areas, most amenable to clearance, they found themselves increasingly trapped, as if in a pincer movement. Short of food at the best of times, when there was war or famine and animals vanished from the countryside, wolves would prey on people and even gather outside the towns, sometimes managing to get in during the night and to attack anyone who was not sleeping under cover. This happened in the winter of 1247–8 at the height of the war between Frederick II and the city-republics of the Po valley which had devastated much of northern Italy. In the low-lying area around Modena there were wolf-hunts even in the early modern period; they would culminate with the capture of the cubs, a fact which suggests that the wolves were well established there, since they had had time to breed.

Once wolves began to attack humans they were ruthlessly hunted out throughout Europe. The hatred they inspired is indicated by the rituals which often surrounded their killing: frequently they were strung up alive, a practice attested by surviving place names such as *Loupendu* in France and *Lupompesi* in Italy. In any case, the spread of a mythology which throve on tales of giant or freakish wolves suggests the feelings of fear and loathing they inspired. In earlier centuries, in contrast, the higher wolf population, which meant that they were a familiar sight, as well as the abundance of other wild animals for food, had prevented the development of such a fearful, often hysterical, attitude.

By the late Middle Ages, not only wolves but other animals too were beginning to be regarded with apprehension and hostility and to acquire similar fearful connotations. People frequented wild areas less and such regions were increasingly perceived as different, alien and hostile. Cultivated land came to be the norm, and people felt ill at ease in forest, moor and marsh. Devils were believed to have their ghastly abode there and the spirits of the dead were thought to appear; everything associated with such areas gave rise to anxiety and fear, though there were exceptions in regions where the landscape was still largely wild and had changed little, such as in mountainous areas. Nevertheless, even in areas which had seen dramatic change, the response to wild areas was still not as wary as it would be in later years and not all wild areas were regarded with such apprehension. Forests which were still frequented, which had well-defined tracks to reassure the traveller, and which still sheltered pigs and sheep were felt to be quite different from impenetrable and neglected forest where people ventured only to hunt, to seek solitude or to escape the law.

To conclude, in most of Europe the relationship between people and animals changed entirely between the early and the late Middle Ages; it altered radically around the year 1100 as the countryside finally began to shrug off the wild aspect it had taken on in late antiquity and the first medieval centuries, a taming of the countryside which affected animals too. Just as people began to lead a more settled existence, so their animals were left to wander less and were increasingly kept close to the villages. The byre replaced the forest, the enclosure the open countryside. Wild animals and those semi-wild ones left to roam wild were increasingly outnumbered by domestic animals, a shift parallel to that undergone by peasants, who steadily left behind their early medieval existence as hunters, herders and farmers at one and the same time.

PART III

The Solitude of the Flesh

Solitudo carnis, the solitude of the flesh. The phrase suggests a melancholy awareness of the shamefulness of part of oneself, an oppressive sense of imprisonment, as it were, within the body. Authoritative voices had long stressed the inferiority of the body, its imperfections and cumbersomeness, its hostility to the soul. The very idea of beauty itself was dominated by an unrelenting stress on abstract geometric forms, a coldly intellectual tradition which scorned any deviation from perfection. Rigorous and elitist canons of beauty which emphasized order, proportion and symmetry prevailed for centuries, although their influence naturally depended in part on the particular place and time and on the social group or culture concerned.

Yet this disdain was only one cause of the solitude of the flesh, the sense of wretchedness. No less oppressive, and the cause of much suffering, was the burden of the condemnation of everything physical which weighed down the human spirit. The body was identified as the enemy of the soul, as its inferior partner and the principal impediment to spiritual excellence; it was regarded as responsible for weaknesses, failings and shameful lapses. This was as intellectual and bleak a view, although its proponents frequently had recourse to religious arguments to justify it. For instance, Christ's message was interpreted in a spiritual sense, as an argument for monasticism, and came to be a rallying cry against the imperfections of the world: 'all flesh is as grass, and all the glory of man as the flower of grass. The grass withereth, and the flower thereof falleth away' (1 Peter 1:24). At the beginning of the tenth century a monk in France quoted the passage in the context of an exhortation to turn one's back on the life of the flesh, with its specious pleasures and shoddy temptations, and to choose instead a monastic life.

In the early Middle Ages western Europe clad itself with a dark mantle of religious houses. Found in the most remote and desolate areas, they were a stark and constant reminder of the renunciation and rejection of the world. A rude and violent society, in which even relations between men and women were marked by brutality, and the ruling class was dedicated to war, had scant space for hopes and dreams; it seemed impossible to make the world more human and tolerable. This harshness cannot alone account for the existence of monasticism but monasticism undoubtedly gained from it, increasing in authority and influence and in its appeal. Violent and peace-loving nobles alike would take the irrevocable step of entering a monastery, turning their backs on their former life, a trend which disrupted both the exercise of power and its continuity. Even those who did not renounce their position and remained in the world felt the influence of the retreat to the cloister, a silent reproof of all abuses of power.

The view that a truly Christian life could be led only in a monastery was not the only one to be expounded by the Church, though it was the position held by its most outstanding members; some of them did strive to understand the role of the laity, stressing their merits and their responsibilities and emphasizing the need for them not to renounce their position, particularly if they were good Christians as well as powerful. Nonetheless, it was generally accepted that no lay person could ever attain spiritual perfection.

Towards the end of the early medieval centuries, a new way of looking emerged. Considerably more attention was paid both to people themselves and to the world in which they lived as an awareness grew of the ability not only to improve houses, clothes, food and the land, but also to refine manners. There was a greater tolerance of weakness and an increased trust in individual abilities. This changed view was current chiefly among those who lived in the secular world, not among those who still lived in large, though declining, numbers in monasteries and who clung to an older view of the world. It was in this period that the great Pope Gregory VII, who before becoming pope had been a monk, sharply rebuked the Abbot of Cluny, the foremost abbot in Europe, for accepting into his monastery a pious noble.

> My brother, do you not realize how difficult these times are for the Holy Church? Where are those who for the love of God fight against evildoers and do not fear death in the name of justice and truth? Alas, so many of those who fear God eschew Christ's battles and neglect the security of their brethren, loving themselves alone and seeking tranquillity . . . In welcoming a duke into the peace of your house at Cluny you have deprived one hundred thousand Christians of succour!

The severity of Gregory's reprimand not only reflects his immediate concern but also grows out of a new position, one maintained by many clerics, that the message of Christ should be spread through the world in order to change it. In contrast to the past, the Church was now seeking to make its mark on the secular world outside the monastery not in order to ally itself with the powerful, but – or this at least was generally the aim – in order to modify their behaviour.

Among both laymen and clerics there were many who were determined to improve not only themselves but also the society and the economy, and who struggled to tame the very countryside, transforming the great expanses of forests and woods into fields, meadows and vineyards and establishing villages and towns. Rudolf Glaber commented on the transformation he saw around him: 'As the third year after the millennium approached, almost everywhere, but above all in Italy and in France, new churches were built . . . It was as though the world were shaking off old age and clothing itself in a white mantle of churches.'

People were changing even more than their surroundings, as a monk in the abbey of Brauweiler near Cologne, writing in the second half of the eleventh century, noted: 'Christ said, "In truth, in very truth I tell you, he who has faith in me will do what I am doing." And no one, man or woman, of any condition of life, even married people (if the virgins and widows will forgive me!), can be excluded from the words of Christ.'

Christ, then, wanted everyone, men and women, married and celibate, laity and secular and regular clergy, to imitate him. The 'superbia' of celibate monks was challenged and a new interpretation of the Gospels energetically propounded. Between the eleventh and thirteenth centuries, this new position would confront the traditional monastic ideal and result in its decline while leading to new attitudes to the human condition, to the body and to the material world. Though acceptance of them varied between time and place and between different groups within society, the distant origins of the modern outlook lie here.

Many different strands of belief were interwoven – old, revived and new, peasant, aristocratic and intellectual. None the less, there are basically two possible views of materialism, of the entire physical world of humans, animals and plants: acceptance or rejection. Either it is regarded as self-evidently good or it is condemned as indisputably inferior to the needs of the spirit and of reason. The two positions were not confined to the religious context, since both gave rise to secular patterns of thought, becoming increasingly complex but remaining essentially true to their origins up to our day. Nowadays, more than ever, we have seen confrontation between those who believe absolutely in the possibility of improving humanity and the world, and those who are aware of the limits of intelligence and who seek social change without destruction and suffering. Increasingly we distrust uncompromising ideologies and grandiose systems of thought which claim to offer comprehensive solutions but which are authoritarian and dishonest in their attitude to individuals and their physical and spiritual needs. Similarly, we are ever more reluctant to look to others for guidance on how to live. Yet war, grim and dark times, oppressive dogmatism and intolerance of diversity still, as in the past, thrive.

22

The World Contemned

In the early tenth century a monk in France exhorted his readers to follow the example of a young woman who, on being widowed, had unhesitatingly entered a nunnery. 'Hasten . . . and trample underfoot the pleasures of the flesh. It is as grass and its glory is as fleeting as the flower of grass.'

In western Europe the long-standing monastic contempt for the body and for the earthly world was at its greatest in the tenth century, the 'century of iron'. Many churchmen regarded it as inevitable that they should reject a society which was more violent than ever and more disrupted by political upheaval as it was thrown into confusion by the Hungarian, Viking and Arab attacks. Nobles and lords, preoccupied with defending themselves and their people, found themselves obliged to use force routinely. They might well feel revulsion from this and give up their position for the cloister even though they were aware of the difficulties and restrictions of the monastic rule.

One who did so was William, Duke of Normandy, one of the most powerful figures of the tenth century. His forebears had been Vikings and accordingly he was heir to a tradition which emphasized prowess in battle. William told his story to Martin, abbot of a monastery in Jumièges, near Rouen, within his duchy of Normandy, a region then characterized by great forests and rolling downs. Appalled by the bloodshed for which he had been responsible as duke, William had spent long days and sleepless nights weeping before he eventually knocked at the door of the monastery, one which he had for a long time protected and enriched. Abbot Martin saw the duke approach and abruptly demand to know: 'Why is Christianity divided into three different orders of the faithful? Will all Christians have the same reward in Heaven even though they have all carried out different tasks, assigned to them by the Church?'

Faced with William's evident agitation, Abbot Martin promptly replied:

> All will be rewarded according to their works. However, as I see that you doubt this I will explain more clearly. You should understand, then, that Christianity is divided into three orders – the laity, the secular clergy, and the regular clergy – which are the foundation of all Christendom. These orders reflect the Trinity and, as our faith tells us, together they reflect the unity of God.

Duke William persisted. He could not believe that as a layman he could attain in the world a degree of perfection equal to that of monks, or that he would gain the same reward in heaven. He told Abbot Martin of his desire to enter a monastery:

> In the flower of my youth I followed the wide and broad way of the world. Yet though I desired with all my heart to take the rocky and narrow way of the monastery, my father and his principal vassals obliged me to take on the responsibilities of the dukedom. But now I am my own master, and I intend to withdraw from the world and put on the monk's habit. I wish to ascend to the heights of the contemplation of God and to enter upon the training ground of sanctity.

Abbot Martin begged him not to renounce his dukedom since it was his very piety and faith which made him so valuable to all.

> How can you have thought of becoming a monk, you who are the protector of this our country? Who will stand up for the clergy and the people, who will fight the pagans, who will rule over the people and administer law as a father? To whom can I entrust your flock? To whom else can I hand over the duchies of Normandy and Brittany? Divine providence cannot approve of this desire of yours and you will not succeed in becoming a monk – at any rate not with my approval.

William retorted that 'My son Richard will be duke in my place and my vow to God will soon be fulfilled.' Then, refusing the food the hospitable monks offered, he went angrily away. Though he suffered terribly because of what had occurred he stood by his decision, summoned his vassals and told them that he would soon become a monk and pass on his worldly possessions to his son. Astonished, they nevertheless had to accept his decision.

However, violence and disorder broke out anew in Normandy as one lord seized another's castle and the king did nothing to help. Nor did William, until he felt obliged by his ducal responsibilities to intervene. It was a period when regional powers were developing, though the process

was painful and powers found themselves undermined by internal con-
flicts and by the lack of protection from the crown, a consequence of the
weakness of the monarchy. William defeated his vassal, believing that
this would be his last worldly action before entering the monastery. But
one of his enemies, one of the many local lords who were uneasy about
the establishment of a strong duchy in Normandy and Brittany, betrayed
and killed him, brusquely ending his dream of a monastic life. 'And so the
great Duke William, glorious witness of Christ, received the martyr's
crown.'

As William's lifeless body was carried away, a key was discovered
among his clothes and found to open a chest in which he had kept ready
his unworn monk's habit. He had often gone to the chest to gaze at the
habit. For William the monastery had represented the summit of perfection, a spiritual training ground, but it had been a forlorn hope; the
world, governed by violence, had refused him entry.

The story of Duke William's life was written down less than a century
after his death by Dudo of Saint-Quentin, a town not far from the
monastery of Jumièges which William had planned to enter. Dudo, a
canon, does not give an idealized picture of the duke, let alone emphasize
his aspirations to become a monk. The period in which he was writing
saw the first skirmishes in what was to be a bitter dispute between the
secular and regular clergy about their roles: monks were accused of lofty
disdain for secular affairs, which they left to the secular clergy and the
laity. Dudo, not in any case a monk himself, if anything played down the
strong desire to enter a monastery which dominated William's entire life
until his tragic death. Moreover, he chose to put the arguments against
becoming a monk into the mouth of an abbot, Martin of Jumièges, who
in reality may not have taken as negative a view of the Duke of Normandy's wish to become a monk.

It was fifty years later, in the late eleventh century, that the Abbot of
Cluny found himself severely reprimanded by Pope Gregory VII for
having accepted Hugh, Duke of Burgundy, into the abbey. The irre-
sponsibility for which Gregory censured the abbot was that of having
removed from one of the most important positions of the time a man
who was profoundly attached to the Church and to its teaching. In this
period the Pope and the Emperor were in dispute over the right to
appoint bishops so that the papacy was in urgent need of reliable supporters. Indeed, only a few years earlier, it had been Gregory who had
dissuaded Matilda of Canossa and her mother Beatrice, who had inherited what was perhaps the strongest state in Italy, from entering a
nunnery.

In the early Middle Ages, until around the year 1000 when the Church
itself began to discourage the practice, it was common for those in power

to relinquish the world and enter a religious house. The belief that a truly Christian life was possible only within the cloister began to be eroded as the need became felt for a greater involvement of clergy in the secular world so as to spread the message of Christ more effectively to more people. In addition, with the enhanced position and prestige of the papacy and of the bishops, the role and importance of the Church itself in secular affairs was growing. The Church was also closely associated with the emerging dominant groups in society; we need only think of the ever closer relationship between the bishops and the cities.

In the background, as a cause for change after AD 1000, was the widely shared desire to transform society, the economy, political institutions, and even, with the removal of inconvenient forest, scrub and marsh from large areas, the countryside. Where clerics had once condemned the body, now many began to accept the physical nature of human beings and the flesh, and the needs, pains and pleasures of the body. Ultimately, clerics and laity were in fact to give the human race a privileged position at the expense of the natural world, as people sought to transform the environment to their own advantage, ignoring the complex and delicate mechanisms which controlled it. The outcome of that was a converse phenomenon of a growing lack of understanding of and of a rejection of the natural element in the human race, the physical and emotional side. As a result women came to be marginalized, since they were regarded as uncomfortably close to nature.

But this is to jump ahead. In the tenth century the contrast between the secular world and the monastic ideal, between the violent turbulence of the ruling classes and the tranquillity of the cloister, the laws of the flesh and those of the spirit, had become sharp. Moreover, the metamorphosis of the ruling laymen into professional knights was by now irreversible, while the higher echelons of the Church developed the celebrated theory which relegated the laity to the task of warfare, effectively denying them the possibility of a truly Christian life. The outcome was the spiritual crises and sufferings of many powerful figures and their decisions to seek shelter from the buffetings of the world in the cloister.

Those whose secular responsibilities made it impossible for them to enter a monastery might well find themselves leading two entirely separate, and mutually opposed, lives. Resigned to exercising the responsibilities of their high office during the day, at night they were finally able to lay aside their weapons and the trappings of power and put on a coarse monk's habit. They would pray deep into the night and subject their bodies to harsh penitence. However powerful they were, they found themselves marginalized from history, obliged to lead a double and near-intolerable life and to find themselves worn out, derided and ignored, perhaps even murdered. These 'monks by night', ascetic and frequently disorientated disciples of a fearsome, over-exigent God, began to live fully only as dusk fell.

> At night he would be as awake as if it were day. He did not know what sleep was. Hardly had the first hour of the evening rung than, spurning his splendid royal bed, he would secretly arise. He would wake a servant-boy, take his much-thumbed pocket prayer-book and, with only the boy for company, slip out of the palace. The guards never noticed him as he would avoid them by going out in the dead of night. Ceaselessly chanting the psalms and visiting the churches along the way, he would go barefoot up into the mountains, along ice-encrusted and rocky paths and tracks and down steep mountainsides, his tender feet lacerated and his path marked by blood. At dawn he would return to the palace, lost in thought, and there put on his resplendent royal robes. Underneath, however, his purest flesh was rent by a hairshirt.

This description comes from a life of the martyred King Wenceslas of Bohemia, written in the mid-tenth century by the German Gumpoldus, Bishop of Mantua and a member of the court of Emperor Otto I. Wenceslas was familiar with the mountains at night, when the dark peaks were outlined against the moonlit sky and the cliffs lost in shadow. Chapels and oratories would loom up before him in his lonely wanderings along the tracks and icy rock-strewn paths in the silent and deserted expanses as night's shadows hid the world, just as they hid the everyday life he endured.

Such nocturnal scenes, of an astonishing degree of asceticism, are surreal and disconcerting. They reflect the ideal of those who abhorred daylight because it was associated with violence, extravagance and pleasure, of those who lived at night and those who recorded their actions. The attraction of night-time prayer, which could be heard rising from monasteries as the world slept, grew at this time, fostered by the revulsion felt by many at the excessively violent society. Prayer and penitence helped to counterbalance the sins of Christians and monks' prayers rose, veiling, as it were, sin from God's eyes.

The 'iron century' appeared to present a stark choice to nobles: since violence was commonplace and inescapable, it was necessary either to flee it, finding refuge in a monastery, or to seek to atone for their own actions at night, as, it is recorded, did St Wenceslas.

23

The Elusiveness of Perfection

The violence of the age prompted the great abbot Odo of Cluny, discussing the descendants of Cain, the first murderer, to write in his celebrated moral treatise:

> First of all there are those who do not hide their wickedness: such are the powerful who oppress the weak. Typically they surrender to the pleasures of the senses or use the authority given them by God in violence against others or in destroying themselves by extravagance and lasciviousness . . . The generations of man are two, and originate in the sons of Adam, that is, in Cain and Abel. These generations, until their last descendants, which are now and will be, are at times distinct, at others indistinct . . . The good have their own city, Jerusalem . . . The wicked also have their own city, Babylon . . .
>
> The race of the virtuous, or elect, is two-fold. The first consists of the 'perfect' . . . who despise the comforts of this life, regarding them as ephemeral and as deficient in what truly counts . . . There is also a second group of the virtuous. These are, however, 'less perfect' for they cannot fully discern things of the spirit and are dominated by the five physical senses of the body.

The flesh was therefore an insuperable obstacle to the attainment of Christian perfection, even for the virtuous and even where the urgings of the body were by and large repudiated. Odo described these 'less perfect' as compassionate towards the poor and weak and as rejecting violence; they were, he said, 'as concerned with their spirit as with their flesh'. All this was, however, insufficient for perfection, and Odo followed convention in urging a rejection of the world. His writings reflect the Benedictine position as well as the aspirations of many to a monastic life. For those who remained in the world, therefore, only a compromise was possible;

they could hope merely to become 'less perfect', not 'perfect'. Baulked by the demands of the flesh, which laymen as well as clerics denounced, they could go only some of the way on the path of spiritual development. However virtuous a layman was, even if he rejected violence and was not given over to unbridled pleasure-seeking, as a layman he could not aspire to perfection.

This rejection of the secular world, a rejection which Odo of Cluny sought to counter in another of his works, the *Life* of St Gerald of Aurillac, needs to be seen in the context of a more general mode of thinking current in the Church. There was a constant tension between this position and the opposite one, which did not regard the secular world as inferior to the monastic life in any way, and which was more open to it and prepared to sympathize with the needs and virtues of lay society. The influence of each view has fluctuated but in the long run the view that spiritual perfection is attainable only within the cloister triumphed and has exerted an influence up to the present day, though it is certainly not the only possible option nor, in the view of many, the better one.

None the less, during the 'iron' tenth century the violent and oppressive nature of the social structure meant that withdrawal from the world was widely seen as a congenial course of action, and the only prudent one. Indeed, the foundation of countless monasteries, teeming with monks in communities of perhaps several hundred, ceaselessly at prayer, was a highly visible sign of reproach. It came naturally to most churchmen, regular and secular, inheriting as they did the rigidly ascetic interpretation of the Gospels, to urge the merits of the monastic life; they were unable to conceive of any other choice for those who wished to live in the secular world without being at a distinct spiritual disadvantage.

The late tenth century was a difficult period for the French monarchy, emerging painfully from obscurity after it had lost the prominence it had enjoyed under the Carolingian kings. One of the few on whom the king, Hugh Capet, relied, was a knight called Burchard. A life of Burchard survives, written in the mid-eleventh century by a monk from the Benedictine abbey of Fosses, between Charleroi and Namur in present-day Belgium, which describes how Burchard was taken to the royal court as a boy and entrusted to Hugh to be trained in the use of weapons. (It was common practice for the sons of the aristocracy to be sent to be trained by a more powerful lord.) Later Hugh arranged a marriage between Burchard and the widow of a count; Burchard was happy to comply, partly because 'the natural instincts of youth as well as of human nature itself impelled him to do so.' Hugh made him a count and he became one of the king's intimates. His life was that of a powerful layman, within the framework envisaged by monks:

He was a stalwart defender of the new churches which were being built in the kingdom of the Franks. He was a constant benefactor of the poor, a comforter of the wretched, and a champion of pious monks and clerics and of the widows and virgins who had consecrated their lives to God as nuns.

Moreover Burchard 'governed his subjects according to the laws of God'. He had the abbey of Saint-Maure at Fosses restored and, with the support of Mayeul, third abbot of Cluny, reformed it, introducing the Cluniac rule. Burchard was responsible for reforming other monasteries as well, including that of Saint-Pierre in Melun, in southern Brie, southeast of Paris. But then, so his biographer tells us, a serious illness intervened. The count's illness coincided with dissatisfaction with the life he was leading, as he realized how incompatible it was with his own path to spiritual perfection as well as with those of others.

> Even though he strove to please God through his many virtues, as far as was compatible with his position as one dedicated to the profession of arms and absorbed by worldly concerns, the greatness of his soul, which was devoted to the King of Kings, could not remain hidden from the rest of the world. It was not right that the candle should be hidden under a bushel; instead it should shine out brightly from the candlestick and cast its light over all Christians.

To the consternation of his vassals, as well as of the poor and weak whose protection had been entrusted to him, Burchard became a monk. Yet again the monastic ideal had triumphed.

In that long-ago tenth century, similar 'defections' of powerful aristocrats for the peace of the cloister were common throughout France, in the north and southwards to Lorraine and as far as Burgundy and Aquitaine. At the beginning of the century among the knights of the Count of Namur in Lorraine was one Gerard, from the neighbouring region of Brogne. He was soon sickened by what he saw of the world; with his father's permission he began to build a monastery on his land, although he did not yet feel ready to become a monk himself. The time came when his lord sent him to Paris to join the retinue of Count Robert. There he visited the famous monastery of Saint-Denis, the burial-place of the kings of France, originally built by King Dagobert in the seventh century and dedicated to the patron of the city. The abbey, a celebrated example of the strict observance of the Benedictine rule, made a deep impression on Gerard and on his return to Brogne he reformed the monastery he had built there and entered it himself as a monk. His reputation as a pious monk rapidly spread and powerful lords such as the Duke of Lorraine and the Count of Flanders invited him to come and reform their monasteries so that they were restored to strict observance of the Benedictine rule.

St Gerard of Brogne and his compatriot from Lorraine, John of Gorze, were great monastic reformers. Others too, as we have seen, decided to relinquish their position among the aristocracy or, at any rate, the ranks of the military, for a monastic life. During the late ninth century and throughout the tenth an unprecedented crisis convulsed the aristocracy of western Europe. Spiritual crises were common, inspiring many to seek desperately for another way of life as clerics or monks, even as hermits. One individual might well end up passing through all these stages: Odo, who was to be one of the most famous abbots of Cluny, spent his youth as a knight with Duke William of Aquitaine before becoming a canon of the church of St Martin of Tours and, eventually, a monk. We learn of Odo and Adhegrinus that

> there was no place within the confines of France where, once they had learned of the existence of a monastery, they did not either go themselves or send others to visit and inspect it. But they could discover no monks who observed the rule and among whom they could finally find the peace they sought and put an end to their efforts. And so on each occasion they were obliged to return to their poor monastic house.

This comes from the life of Odo by John of Rome. John had met Odo in Rome and had been inspired by his example to become a monk himself. His gloomy remarks on the lax observance of the monastic rule in the houses visited in vain by Odo and Adhegrinus derive from his concern to urge the merits of the Cluniac reform movement.

However, both the Empire and the national monarchies were going through a period of crisis. Separatist interests had triumphed, only to collapse as a result of the hostility of local lords. The monasteries, frequently controlled by such lesser lords, entered a period of serious decline in which the position of abbot might well be filled by a layman, while abbots (lay or clerical) and monks alike increasingly led a life which was no different from that of the aristocracy. Like the feudal lords, their days were taken up with hunting and with military exercises. The state of affairs in most religious houses was such that any lord who wished to enter a monastery with the intention of adhering scrupulously to the monastic rule had few options. Only with the monastic reforms of the tenth century, and above all with the Cluniac movement, did the religious houses again observe the Benedictine rule strictly. The initiative commonly came from laymen who had become monks or who had remained in the secular world but protected the interests of those who had opted for the monastic rule. Dozens and then hundreds of religious houses everywhere became affiliated to Cluny, whose authority and prestige can be gauged from the fact that even at the end of the tenth century the Abbot of Cluny was called 'Rex Cluniacensis', King of Cluny.

The region most affected by the breakdown of central authority, and where royal officials were most at risk from threats and violence from local lords, was central southern France. It was here, in the Cantal, that Gerald of Aurillac, a royal vassal, lived between the second half of the ninth century and the early tenth. After his death he was widely said to have been a saint, and stories circulated of his extraordinary self-denial in protecting the weak and of his generous mercy for thieves, bandits and for all manner of marginalized people whom the peremptory and brutal justice of the time had condemned to death or to grim mutilation. A bishop and an abbot from nearby towns proposed having the story of Gerald's life written as an example to other figures in authority and chose Odo as author. This was probably in the period before Odo became Abbot of Cluny.

Initially Odo had serious qualms about the enterprise, since he was reluctant to believe that a layman worthy of being a saint could exist. He argued that there were two obstacles which to him seemed insurmountable: the flesh, and blood. No layman could ever hope to avoid being ruled, at least in part, by his physical needs and desires, and if he was powerful he could not avoid shedding blood.

A further difficulty for Odo was that he had not known Gerald personally. However, he decided to accept the commission and began by conducting detailed interviews with everyone who had known Gerald well, questioning them all separately. As one of his aims was to present a portrait of a powerful layman which could serve as a model for Gerald's peers at a time when one was sorely needed, he above all avoided trying to find monastic traits in Gerald's everyday life. Indeed he repeatedly warned monks against condemning Gerald for practices forbidden to clerics but permitted in a layman: eating meat, bearing a sword, or wearing clothes appropriate to his status which served to symbolize his authority. Gerald's significance as a model lay in his moderation where such things were concerned, the result of his faith. And yet for Odo this was not enough to make Gerald 'perfect', a saint. As we shall see, considerably more would be required of him before he could aspire to 'perfection'.

Odo's life of Gerald is a striking example of an attempt to explore how far a life according to Christian principles was possible outside the confines of the monastery; given Odo's position as a monk and the period in which he was writing, the tenth century, we should expect nothing different. Odo describes Gerald's handsome appearance, his physical strength and his skill with weapons and in riding and hunting. There is only one monk-like element in this description: Gerald's unusually white neck which all close to him felt the desire to kiss, an unlikely feature in a man who spent all his time in the open air. There are occasional such monastic touches in the life and it is hard to avoid the conclusion that Odo, listening to those who had known Gerald, exaggerated these stories, quite possibly unintentionally.

Gerald always refused to marry; his celibacy was doubtless a great relief to Odo. Marriage and bloodshed were the two insuperable obstacles which prevented a layman, however virtuous and devout, from attaining full sanctity, equal to that available to a 'perfect' monk. Odo particularly stressed Gerald's staunch refusal ever to succumb to physical desire, whether in the form of his early rejection of 'the shipwreck of purity' as a youth or his later repression of the passion he felt for a young woman. Moreover, Gerald had refused a proposed marriage to the sister of the Duke of Aquitaine and had always been dismayed by the involuntary emission of semen during sleep, which he was helpless to control. Even after death, when his body was stripped in readiness for the shroud and burial, his hands were seen to move as he sought to cover his genitalia and continued to do so however many times his arms were stretched out by his sides, proof that he had overcome the flesh and was as saintly as those who had taken the monastic vow of chastity.

Odo's life of Gerald is an attempt to bridge the gap between the monastery and the secular world. He gives a detailed description of the ideal layman but what finally confirms Gerald's saintliness is still his virginity, the virtue 'which makes monks akin to angels'. Had Gerald been responsible for bloodshed, though, his chastity would not have been sufficient for sanctity, but he had never, according to Odo, injured anyone or permitted anyone to be mutilated or executed in his presence in accordance with the harsh laws of the time.

For contemporaries, Gerald's rejection of violence would have been the more striking given the echoes in popular memory of the grisly death of St Denis, patron saint of France. According to legend, at the time of the first Christian martyrs St Denis had been beheaded on the hill of Montmartre, but he had picked up his severed head, walked down the hill and walked some distance in the empty countryside, carrying his head, before falling to the ground and expiring. A church was built in his honour on the spot where he died, and in the seventh century King Dagobert had a monastery built there which became the most famous in all France, while St Denis came to be the patron saint of Paris. The story of St Denis's macabre perambulation through the deserted countryside may well have had its roots in Celtic ritual, where decapitation was common; it was clearly a memorable event from the early Christian history of France and left bloody echoes.

In his well-known moral treatise Odo noted that aristocrats had received their sword from none other than Christ himself, and he reminded them that it was their duty to return it unsullied by blood. Gerald himself, he wrote, not only had never bloodied his sword but had even prevented his men from bloodying theirs, ordering them to fight using the blunt wooden handles of their lances, not the sharp blades. Many mocked 'this strange way of fighting', Odo continued, but with God's help Gerald had invariably won his battles.

24

Man's Disgrace

For monks, night began early, as their rule laid down that they go early to bed, but it was interrupted by the office and by individual prayer and watch. The night was long and fraught with danger: during sleep the body could escape the vigilance of the mind and respond to the unleashing of instincts produced by all the desires and lusts which had passed even momentarily through the mind during the day. It was necessary to spend the entire day in preparation for the night, when the devil lay in wait for monks the instant they fell asleep. Sleep and dreams represented the severest trial in the battle against the flesh, since during sleep all the physical desires which had been repressed by the conscious mind during the day could rampage unchecked.

In the fifth century the monk Cassian was obsessed by the trials he and his brothers had to face once their eyes closed and they drifted into sleep and unconsciousness. The prospect of succumbing to the flesh at night after a day spent in ceaseless struggle against it appalled him. He discussed the problem of nocturnal emissions (the more clinical modern term) in several passages in his writings and devoted the whole of the twenty-second chapter of his *Collationes*, a celebrated treatise and an important source for the development of monasticism in Europe, to the subject.

Cassian first distinguished between 'voluntary' and 'involuntary' nocturnal emissions. Voluntary emissions were triggered by desires which had not been suppressed before sleep; involuntary emissions occurred independently of any action by the victim, though they were still to be considered a grave failing. Moreover, Cassian argued that even involuntary emissions were not always entirely so. They might be the consequence of thoughts and actions of the previous day which had not been adequately suppressed at the time and could therefore emerge at night to rampage through a mind, now unconscious, which had not been in control during the day. Excessive eating, lustful thoughts and other weaknesses were behind the feverish dreams and nocturnal emissions to which ill-prepared laymen and, he regretfully noted, monks were vulnerable. Cassian considered that the only nocturnal emissions to be entirely involuntary were those which occurred during dreamless sleep and without any awareness on the part of the sleeper, had purely physiological causes, and had not been provoked in any way during the day. Only then were they not due to sin and weakness, though they were still a cause for bitter regret and a failure over which the devil gloated. The most saintly, assured of the constant presence of divine grace which was stronger than nature, were immune to such tricks from the devil, since they had succeeded in completely mastering their bodies and in vanquishing desire.

It was at night, then, that the aspirations and fears of monks took shape, in their search for perfection and for the final triumph of the spirit; it was at night that the devil and divine grace competed with each other over the body. Only divine grace could liberate the body from the ultimate obligation to surrender to its natural urges. Cassian was stern: 'We must ensure that certain thoughts passing through our minds, as well as the passions of the flesh, are repressed; it is permissible for the body to fulfil its natural function but no pleasure may be felt.' True perfection, the ultimate goal, entailed a refusal to yield to any natural instincts which were not essential to keeping the body alive. Any urges which derived from sexual desire were therefore to be quashed. In contrast, the desire for food was acceptable since food was necessary for existence.

Though Cassian's exhortations, which grew out of the tradition of complete subjugation of the body of eastern monasticism, had a considerable influence on the development of western monasticism, they were never entirely accepted. Odo of Cluny used the same title as Cassian's work, 'Collationes', for what was to be his best-known treatise but was less extreme. In his life of St Gerald of Aurillac, who, as we have seen, adhered as resolutely to celibacy as any monk, Odo never sought to claim that Gerald mortified his flesh to such a degree that he was free from nocturnal emissions. Instead he considered them as an inevitable misfortune which could befall even one as virtuous as Gerald, who had not only reached manhood without succumbing to lust but who had also, with God's help, succeeded in resisting the tempting soft complexion of a girl and had refused ever to marry, vowing that he would remain a virgin. Yet despite all these triumphs Gerald was still vulnerable to nocturnal emissions, which troubled him deeply and were a cause of intense self-reproach:

How much he abhorred the vileness of the flesh can be comprehended from his anguish at these night dreams. For every time that this weakness of man took him by surprise during sleep, a servant who slept close by would bring him clean underclothes which were kept ready, along with a napkin and a basin of water. Gerald was unwilling for the servant to see his nakedness as he entered and the man would leave immediately, shutting the door behind him. The saint, who rejoiced in the purity of the soul, could not accept that his body should be soiled and so would wash out this, the sole stain to mark it, with water and with his own tears to boot, behaviour which seemed absurd, but only in the eyes of those whose minds were clouded by sin. When such people defile themselves, either intentionally or unintentionally, they fail even to wash.

In Odo's description the horror of everything generated by sexual desire is apparent: Gerald is 'soiled' and must wash immediately. The psychological tension between the monastic ideal and the coarse physicality which characterized contemporary society helps to account for the general insistence on the strict repression of sexual urges and also of any intense physical pleasure. The flesh was too alive; it was tyrannical and crushed the spirit. Since its instincts and unpredictable urges hindered spiritual development, it had to be repressed and mastered, even purified. According to Odo, as Gerald saw his spirit grow, so his body wasted away. Odo, we should not forget, regarded the body as a cumbersome sheath for the soul, which was imprisoned within the body just as the foetus was within the womb. Over the years Gerald watched as his body weakened and became ever more insubstantial and feeble as his spirit triumphed over it.

The body, then, was increasingly marginalized, the *solitudo carnis*. No concessions or allowances were to be made to it and perfection could be attained only through the complete rejection and abrogation of one's own flesh. Though Odo, a monk, also attempted to be receptive to the demands of the secular life, especially to that of powerful laymen, his assumptions derive from a tradition which could brook no compromise in the pursuit of perfection and saintliness, and for which monasticism offered the sole route to perfection. The Cluniac reform movement, which was in its infancy in Odo's time, would become yet more rigid and uncompromising. Not all clerics shared this view, but in the long run, and despite setbacks and the emergence of different, even diametrically opposed, positions, the monastic ethic came to be regarded as the ideal one for a good Christian.

In the eleventh and twelfth centuries, however, a different, more worldly notion of sanctity developed which opened the door to the possibility of reconciling the spirit with the flesh and the Church and the teaching of Christ with the secular world. It centred on the need to establish the kingdom of God in this world, among the men and women who were listening in ever greater numbers to the teachings of the Gospel. Tension between secular and regular clergy found a focus in the debate whether it was better to live as a good Christian in the world or to flee it, a debate which often flared up, with a wealth of insults and accusations from each side. Yet by the close of the thirteenth century the monastic ideal had triumphed again. The rejection of the world was sharper than before, more wary of all things material and of the flesh.

In the mid-sixteenth century, at the time of the Council of Trent, the ascetic tradition reasserted itself. Even the leading figures of the Catholic Church, regarded as modern and innovatory – which in their own way they were – were involved. In the second half of the century St Philip Neri, or 'Pippo the Kind' as he was called affectionately by the Roman people, using the diminutive form of his name, was far from kind to his own body and to those of others. He would refuse to eat at the same table as women and was reluctant to hear their confessions or to try to reform them if they had fallen into sin. On one occasion, having made a great effort to overcome his apprehension, he visited a prostitute in order to urge her to change her ways, but he fled, terrified of falling into temptation, as soon as he saw her. In the most important life of the saint we read that:

> The Almighty was so pleased with this deed that thenceforth He granted him the grace of no longer feeling physical desire and even spared him nocturnal illusions. Baronius asserts that the saint told him himself that he would have died of grief if such a misfortune had befallen him. Indeed, St Philip said that in this area he had become as insensible as a log. Thanks to God, he would say, touching a woman would have been to him as touching a stone.

St Philip could not even tolerate the occurrence of 'nocturnal illusions' in others. 'He could tell from the smell alone when they had suffered night dreams . . . and could recognize this failing merely from looking in their faces.' His disgust at such impurity was so great that it was said of him that, 'He had the ability to discern impurity (if it can be termed thus) even in animals.' The wheel had turned full circle; we are reminded of Cassian's zeal and his assiduous advice to monks how to avoid such nocturnal defilement. But St Philip went yet further: where Cassian, in extending his advice to the laity, had been content merely to recommend that they do their best to avoid sin, St Philip was adamant that they must do so. He was aghast at the thought of what the night held in store for the unconscious sleeper, precipitating him into sin and defiling him both literally and morally.

The *solitudo*, or emptiness, of the flesh was greater than ever, the body utterly marginalized. It was the duty of a good Christian to despise the flesh as irredeemably depraved. Mortification of the flesh was the sole possible course – and the word 'mortification' derives, of course, from the word for 'to kill'.

25

From Mortification to Insensibility

The rejection of the impulses of the flesh was to become much more insistent, while the mere presence of temptation came to be regarded as undesirable, a grave lapse in saintliness. St Luigi Gonzaga was never tempted by sin and, according to his confessor, who wrote a celebrated biography of the saint, enjoyed a near angelic nature.

> As far as chastity is concerned, we can confirm that his nature was close to that of the angels . . . Indeed his body never suffered any agitation and his soul was so pure that it did not retain even the faintest impression of any impure form . . . He revealed this to me while we were speaking of a great servant of God who was then still living and was often tormented by this kind of temptation but had nonetheless remained a virgin. Luigi confessed to me that God had dealt very differently with him, inasmuch as he did not even know what such temptation might be.

The philanthropy and deep humanity of St Luigi and of others like him is not in doubt. St Philip Neri's charitable work among the poor and those who had suffered injustice, and his concern for needy families and his scrupulous efforts to inform himself about them so that all necessary help could be given, demonstrate this. He would weep over all these people and grieve for them, just as he would be racked by sorrow when he meditated on Christ's passion. Yet he refused to make the least concession to his body or to allow others to treat their own bodies kindly if doing so would entail any pleasure. Above all, to surrender to sexual desire was anathema. This prevented St Philip from seeking to reform the prostitutes of whom Rome was full. Similarly, he was unable to dine in the presence of women, while in his youth he had always been unwilling to hear women's confessions for fear of being tempted.

In the first place, like St Antony, he would never leave his skin uncovered, and he preferred others, too, to ensure that no part of their bodies, such as their arms and legs, was left uncovered, save in extreme necessity. He was particularly concerned that people were not to look upon their own nakedness ... and he kept strict control over his own eyes ... For the same reason, when he began to hear confessions he was reluctant to confess women; indeed he always heard more confessions from men than from women ... When speaking to women he was somewhat abrupt and stern, never affable, and he would keep his face turned away from them, though in old age he was less austere. Once a penitent of his took him to dine at the house of a gentleman. At the end of the meal the saint turned to the penitent and said to him, 'You have had me do something I have never done before. I have eaten in the presence of women.'

Such an attitude was common among members of religious orders at this time, the second half of the sixteenth century. The spiritual adviser of St Teresa of Avila was Peter of Alcantara, a Spanish Franciscan, who died in 1562 and was later canonized. Not only did he advise St Teresa during his life but he continued to do so after his death, appearing to her in visions. According to St Teresa, relating what he had once told her, 'It was many years since he had looked a woman in the face' and even 'By then he was not troubled whether he could see or not.'

Four hundred years earlier, St Francis of Assisi, the founder of the order to which Peter belonged, had behaved very differently:

He and one of his followers chose a certain area. When they reached it they entered an inn to rest. And there was a woman there, most beautiful of body but dissolute in spirit. This wicked woman sought to lure him into sin. And St Francis said to her, 'Very well then, let us go to bed.' And she led him into the bedroom. And St Francis said, 'Come with me and I will show you a most beautiful bed.' And he led her to a great fire which was burning in that room and in the fervour of his spirit he stripped naked and lay down on the fire which was blazing on the hearth, and invited her to undress and to come and lie with him on that splendid bed. And when St Francis had been lying quite some while with a cheerful countenance, not burning in the least or even toasting, the woman, astonished by this miracle and full of contrition, not only repented of her sin and of her wicked intentions, but was completely converted to the Christian faith and became so devout that through her many souls were saved in those parts.

The episode, which occurred during St Francis's mission to the Muslims, as well as glorifying the victory of St Francis over the flesh, also shows how he had no fear of it, to the extent that he was willing to confront female temptation naked. As is well known, this was not the only occasion on which St Francis was partly or completely naked. Yet several centuries later a Franciscan such as St Peter of Alcantara had so little trust in himself that he did not dare to look a woman in the face. This 'blindness' corresponded to the mortification of all the other senses, 'windows of the soul through which the impulses to sin enter', according to a traditional and obviously monastic definition. St Teresa described how Peter hardly slept, refused to protect himself against the heat and the cold, scourged his flesh, ate only once every three days, and spoke but rarely.

> When I first knew him he was already very old and was so gaunt that he seemed a tree root . . . After his death it pleased the Lord that he should be even more precious to me than he had been in life, for he continued to counsel me on various matters. I saw him quite often in a shining glory. The first time that he appeared to me, one of the things he said was 'Blessed be penitence, which has earned me such a reward'.

It was Peter's desire for penitence which lay behind his custody of the eyes, as he shut his eyes to people and to objects in an absolute rejection of life and of the entire physical world.

> He told me that as a young man it had happened that he stayed in a house belonging to his order for three years, during which time he recognized the friars only from their voices because he never looked up save once to go on a journey. Even then he did not look where he was going but was content to follow in the steps of his brothers.

According to St Teresa, Peter hardly slept but would stay awake in prayer almost all night, sleeping at most for an hour and a half. Since he saw nothing during the day, he had extended night's shadows into day; all was unrelieved darkness.

The monastic emphasis on night and the hours of darkness as a privileged time, the opposite of the everyday and a time when the failings of the day could be redeemed, had become complete. Night had succeeded in taking over day, like the dark brown haze which obscures the landscape in paintings from the second half of the sixteenth century, the period when these saints lived. In Guido Reni's paintings the outlines of the countryside, houses, mountains or those labouring in the fields can be glimpsed only indistinctly, masked by a heavy dark veil. Villages, castles, people and animals are obscured and almost hidden by a mask of dark pigment. This is the unregarded landscape, a timeless night scene. The physical world was all but snuffed out.

Fear and mistrust of the physical world and a distancing from it are increasingly apparent in literature and art as early as the late fifteenth century and the first half of the sixteenth, a trend which grew inexorably.

This fear coincided with the separation of many educated people from the rhythms of the physical world, from the seasons and the countryside, a gradual divorce from nature which touched many more people than we can imagine.

This accounts for why nature might appear as a cruel taskmaster rather than as a benign guardian. It was increasingly viewed coldly and intellectually, as the object of study and analysis. Leonardo da Vinci's paintings and drawings of landscape and of natural phenomena leave the impression of one tormented by the possibility of disastrous events. His detailed drawings of the human body, which meticulously record grotesque deformities, frequently reveal extreme horror. In the same way, behind Leon Battista Alberti's writings on the family and society lurks the shadowy but dark and troubling presence which he calls *fortuna*, the malevolent and chill deity who is responsible for the downfall of cities, countries and families and for the loss of wealth, who overturns the social and political order and unleashes the forces of nature. It was in this period that Niccolò Machiavelli wrote down his pessimistic conclusions on human nature, associating it with irredeemable moral iniquity.

This was an ancient way of thinking, which developed principally in the central years of the Middle Ages. Though a more positive attitude towards the human condition and to physical and mental attributes emerged between the eleventh and thirteenth centuries to challenge it, it survived intact, even spreading. Yet it was increasingly associated with an unlikely companion, fear. Fear of the natural world, generated by the unconscious remorse of those who had overplayed their hand in the transformation and adaptation of the natural world for their own needs. Vast areas of western Europe had seen their trees ravaged and as a result the soil, deprived of its protective mantle, suffered. Though it could now produce more grain and wine, foods and fruit, the dramatic decrease in tree cover meant the earth was 'naked', vulnerable to the elements which wore it down more and more. From the thirteenth century human affairs were frequently interrupted by flooding in the Po plain which had lost its forests and where even the foothills were virtually denuded of cover. Not all this change can be attributed to human intervention since climatic change also played a part, bringing extremes of rain, drought and frosts, but the main reason for the flooding of the rivers was the excessive removal of tree cover by local people, which must also have had an adverse effect on the climate. Never before had so much vegetation been removed in western Europe, never before had so much damage been wreaked. Countless forests were reduced to dismal wastelands where the cleared land was used for pasture rather than for cultivation, or where cultivated land was exhausted. Vast tracts of desolate scrub came to be a feature of the landscape everywhere, sometimes to the exclusion of all else.

26

In Defence of the Body

The monastic ideal spread above all in northern Europe, and in particular in that great area between the Loire and the Rhine which also saw the emergence and domination of the feudal aristocracy. The strength of monasticism here was in part a response to the way of life of the nobles. As early as the first decades of the eleventh century, however, this very domination of the monasteries had encouraged the development in this region of a new, non-monastic model of life. In particular, the figure of the saintly aristocrat emerged. Dudo of Saint-Quentin, canon of the church in that town, to whom we owe our knowledge of Duke William of Normandy's yearning to be a monk, also left a description of William's son and successor, Richard.

Richard was an example of a powerful member of the laity who succeeded in attaining perfection even though he had never become a monk and had remained duke. His Christian exercise of authority was sufficient for him to be saintly, so much so that Dudo called him 'magnificent in his condition and in his secular life' and reminded his readers that, though rich and powerful, Richard had been poor in spirit and, as the New Testament declared, 'Blessed are the poor in spirit for theirs is the kingdom of heaven.' Even though Richard never became a monk or even sought to follow the monastic rule in any way, as did some, he could still be saintly. Dudo tells us that: 'He never abandoned his leadership of the duchy of Normandy, not because he was attracted by the glory of the position, glory which is fleeting, but in order that he could defend God's holy Church from the pagans and their raids.'

Richard retained the dukedom and 'as a layman maintained God's law in purity of heart . . . He should be counted among those who are called children of God because of their faith and their imitation of Christ.

Indeed he carried out the responsibilities of his high office with great faith, aware that God wishes many to share in his grace.'

Such grace and absolute Christian perfection was available not only to the regular and secular clergy but also to the laity. The attainment of saintliness was not therefore an impossibility for those who lived in the world, since life as a member of the laity did not necessarily imply any neglect of Christian morality. Even the body itself did not have to be rejected; instead it could be redeemed and made holy, just as men and women were purified through the marriage ceremony. Such was the case with Matilda, daughter of Otto II, and Ezzo, the wife and husband who founded the abbey of Brauweiler, east of Cologne. In the second half of the eleventh century, a monk from the abbey countered those who argued that Matilda and Ezzo, being married, could not have been perfect Christians and saints; he asserted that 'It is not that which is spiritual which comes first, but that which is animal,' and pointed out that 'Elsewhere, too, we read in the Scriptures of the man and woman who symbolize the marriage with Christ and with the Church.' To cut short any doubts as to whether the couple had been true Christians and saints, he concluded: 'Christ said, "He who has faith in me will do what I am doing." And no one, whether man or woman, of whatever condition, even if married (if the virgins and widows will forgive me!), can be excluded from the words of Christ.'

Christ, then, allowed all to imitate him, men and women, married and single, the laity as well as the regular and secular clergy. The passage is highly critical of the *superbia* of monks, whom the writer, a monk himself, calls *virgines*. The implication is that the conviction that sanctity was attainable only through a total renunciation of the world and of the flesh was by this time, the second half of the eleventh century, weakening even in the monastery. It was in this period that Pope Gregory VII, a monk by origin, urged Beatrice of Canossa and her daughter Matilda not to enter a religious house and bitterly reproached the Abbot of Cluny for having accepted Hugh, Duke of Burgundy, one of the few virtuous men in a position of authority, into his monastery as a monk.

Throughout Christendom the issue of how the monastic world should react to the secular world was debated. In this context the German cleric St Norbert of Xanten (Xanten lies on the right bank of the Rhine), who at the beginning of the twelfth century challenged the very basis of the monastic ideal, is typical. Norbert founded the Premonstratensian order of regular canons (the name comes from Prémontré in France) with the intention of training men who would devote themselves not to prayer and contemplation but to preaching and pastoral work outside the monastery. Norbert was concerned, however, that living as a community with a rule would turn them into monks – and that is indeed how it tended to turn out later in France. Two lives of Norbert survive. In the first, written in Germany, the description of the saint and his life is suffused with fervent evangelism and abounds with references to the epistles of St Paul and to the early Church of Christ and the Apostles. The second, very different, life was written in France and stresses the monastic side of Norbert; but although it emphasizes the difficulties and trials suffered by Norbert, these clearly were in fact the result not of penitence carried out with perfection in mind but of persecution which Norbert suffered in the name of truth. It is certainly not the lonely mortification of the monk: for Norbert, penance, study and meditation were relatively unimportant.

In the German life there is a lively account of an episode which occurred during a visit by Norbert to the school of the masters Anselm and Rudolf in Laon in northern France. During this visit Norbert was apparently accused of seeking to turn the order away from evangelism towards contemplation, whereas the order should be inspired by evangelism alone, as in the early Church.

> At that time the school of the brothers and teachers Anselm and Rudolf was prospering in Laon. The man of God [Norbert] decided to listen to their exposition and commentary on the psalm, 'Blessed are the undefiled in the way.' At that time Drogo, a most religious man, was prior of the church of the Blessed Nicasius of Rheims. He had been at school with Norbert and had known him well. Drogo heard of this action of Norbert's and wrote indignantly to him: 'What is this I hear of you? You, who were instructed in the school of the Holy Ghost, who constantly teaches us, have abandoned it and have crossed the threshold of a lay school . . . ? [The order] you have built did not begin in this way so that Rachel [the contemplative life] should follow Leah [the active life] . . . I must tell you, my dear brother, and you should regard me as a prophet, that if you wish to love them both you will end up with neither.'

In France the Premonstratensian order slipped into a more traditionally monastic pattern, evident from the second, French life of Norbert which revealingly omits the above episode.

It is no coincidence that the diversion of the movement towards strict monasticism should have occurred in northern France. Here, in the forest of Coudy some twenty kilometres west of Laon, Norbert established the first community in about 1120, around which later developed the village called Prémontré from which the order took its name. France, cradle of both the aristocracy and the monastic movement, and northern France in particular, saw constant conflict between two antithetical visions of the world, two different paths to Christian perfection: a Christian life in the world, or life as a monk or nun. The second invariably prevailed as the

ultimate ideal and goal. Despite temporary setbacks, it was this view
which affected religious thought. Norbert sought to reform the clerics
responsible for the care of souls, and to elevate their spiritual life,
distancing them from political involvement and from the ownership of
wealth. The essence of his evangelical message was to change the world,
not to reject it. This new attitude emerged in a period when not only
popes and bishops, clerics and the laity, but monks too were attempting
to bring the Church back into the world – Pope Gregory VII, after all,
had been a monk. The result was an anti-monastic polemical tradition
and a constant appeal to the charity and love of the early Church and to
a 'truly apostolic' life.

This can only be understood in the context of current social and
cultural change. From this point of view the millennium is more than a
convenient benchmark; the years around it saw profound changes in
western culture which affected every aspect of life. Despite regional
variations, most of Europe saw irreversible change. The extent of
awareness of this varied according to the social group people belonged to
and their level of education. All the same, some were astonished by the
innovations and looked on bemused, seeing the signs of the transformation in the landscape, now covered by new towns and villages, by
monasteries and great cathedrals. In their travels between different regions and countries, clerics and monks observed these changes as they
occurred, and recorded them. They interpreted the transformation in a
religious key, noting that the millennium, the thousandth anniversary of
the birth of Christ and a momentous date, was approaching. The Cluniac
monk and chronicler Rudolf Glaber described western Europe as covered
by a white mantle of churches as the saints 'rose again', and remarked
that the proximity of the millennium inspired people to hunt out saints'
relics, which were everywhere uncovered and venerated.

> Eight years after the millennium, when the whole world was resplendent
> with restored and gleaming white churches, countless signs permitted many
> saints' relics to be rediscovered in the places where they had long lain
> hidden. At a sign from the Lord they appeared before the eyes of the
> faithful, as if they had been awaiting a glorious resurrection, and gave
> everyone great cheer.

The history by Rudolf Glaber from which this passage is taken is
unusual. Rudolf had a lively, rebellious turn of mind; he had not become
a monk through any sense of vocation and he was little inclined to
obedience. His history, full of passion and vehemence and marked by
impulsive opinions and prejudice, is deeply original and very different
from the other histories written by monks at that time.

Yet despite his idiosyncrasies his attitude must have been shared by many. In the mid-tenth century, for example, the atmosphere of change and the rapid transformation of social structures alarmed another, the Bishop of Verona. A northern European by origin (a Fleming), and moreover a monk, he found himself in one of the cities of Italy most in turmoil as a result of the rise of the class we call the 'bourgeoisie', and he was troubled to the point of obsession by such social mobility. Events in Verona were typical of changes in the second half of the tenth century in the central part of northern Italy, where the most important development was the dramatic growth of the towns, the steady increase in wealth of the bourgeoisie and its acquisition of power by means of alliances with those elements of the aristocracy intimately associated with the city. Very soon the citizens of Pavia would shut the city gates before the Emperor, forbidding him entry into his capital, and destroy the imperial palace, having already treated Arnulf of Germany with equal disdain a century earlier.

In an attempt to curb the influence of the great rural monasteries, the bishops of this area built religious houses inside the city walls. Outside Italy the eleventh and twelfth centuries saw the consolidation almost everywhere of territorial principalities or duchies both large and small, and an extension of lands and cities subject to the monarchies. In northern Italy, in contrast, towns were shaking off the overlordship of the powerful rural aristocracy and of the bishops, and the power of the bourgeoisie came to equal, or even surpass, that of the urban aristocracy itself. At the same time, as they became independent city-states, the towns once again began to exercise authority over the surrounding area, in many cases with complete success.

Over much of Italy, then, the city was asserting itself. Elsewhere, in contrast, the aristocracy and the monarchy were increasingly prevailing and towns saw their hard-won independence end abruptly at the city boundary. Independence was gained at a cost, often wrested from the local bishop after hard bargaining or conflict, and towns still always had to recognize an overlord, whether lay or ecclesiastical. In northern France associations of townspeople sprang up. Here the inhabitants of towns were called 'bourgeois', because they lived in a mere *burgus*, and not 'citizens', as in Italy and in southern France, where people lived in a *civitas*, or city. Such associations were established in Le Mans in 1070, in Cambrai in 1077, and in Beauvais and Saint-Quentin. They were resisted by the overlords of the towns, but in 1115 the inhabitants of Laon rebelled and killed their bishop. There were uprisings in Germany too. However, the townspeople gained only limited privileges – the right for citizens to join together in associations, exemption from excessive taxes and from any military service for their overlords, and freedom from any kind of personal dependency – and never succeeded in gaining political independence. Above all, they had no control over the surrounding territory, where the aristocracy remained undisputed masters. Apart from the Flemish towns, which had withdrawn their allegiance to the aristocracy and enjoyed the right to self-government and to defend themselves militarily, only in central northern Italy and in southern France did cities achieve a distinct degree of power; elsewhere towns usually gained only economic privileges.

In central and northern Europe far-reaching change was nonetheless occurring, the result of pressure from the towns. Agricultural colonization promoted by the aristocracy and religious houses went on apace. After AD 1000, forest and moor yielded to field and vineyard, though compared to central northern Italy clearance was limited; even today France, Germany and England still have extensive uncultivated areas in both hill country and lower-lying areas. In the later Middle Ages the aristocracy in these countries was much more powerful than in Italy and jealously guarded such areas of forest and open land for their hunting. Above all, the feudal nature of society here militated against a new relationship with the natural world as a result of the drastic transformation of the environment.

However, even if repopulation was limited and slow in comparison with Italy, northern Europe saw decisive change. Market villages, later to become towns, grew up around nobles' castles, religious houses and bishops' seats. This made for considerably more intervention in the natural world and for a greater subjugation of the environment than in the past. At the same time there was increased regard for the physical body, and a higher degree of realism. In the artistic sphere, these changes reached their highest expression in the great cathedrals. In the cities the old artistic models were adapted to express the changed world: a host of men, women, animals and plants can be seen carved on the doorways of the great northern Romanesque and Gothic churches, whereas in Italy, apart from scenes from nature and the agricultural year (especially the latter), representations of the different crafts practised in the cities, of the world of the bourgeoisie, are common on religious buildings. In Italy the powerful corporations of artisans, merchants and bankers all built themselves splendid halls, while the city councils erected grandiose public buildings. The churches of the Italian city-republics differ from those north of the Alps, which tend to stand apart from other buildings and to dominate the town and the surrounding countryside.

In the ferment of change in Italy, new ways balanced the old, or fast superseded them. It was in the Italian city-republics, in the first decades of the thirteenth century, that the new religious orders, especially the Franciscans, first challenged and then triumphed over Benedictine monasticism, and then went on to spread through Europe. But even before the emergence of the new orders, in the twelfth century, there had been a deep-seated shift in religiosity. The urban culture of central Italy, from Tuscany and Umbria to the Po plain, produced lay saints from merchant families. They urged poverty and charity for the dispossessed (whose numbers were increasing in towns) and preached against political conflict and factional splits in the towns; theirs was a more humane and kindly vision of the Christian faith. In painting, Christ in majesty, triumphant and regal, was supplanted by a suffering Christ, and both in literature and in painting and sculpture Christ came to be represented as a weak and emaciated figure. The earliest representations of holy men and women of the period, lay as well as clerical, are similar: St Raymond of Piacenza, St Homobonus of Cremona, St Francis of Assisi. Spirituality was marked by the cult of the Passion, by lamentation and weeping over the dead Christ and over the poor and wretched, who were particularly identified with Christ. The saints of the city-republics in the twelfth and thirteenth centuries are concerned above all with their fellow men and women and their physical and psychological vulnerability.

This new religious outlook did not emerge without warning but had its origins in the ferment in the eleventh century when antagonism towards the monastic movement first emerged in northern Europe. The new spirituality shared many common features with the urban mentality – a sense of humanity and of concrete realism, a desire for peace, an attention to the things of this world – but at the same time it set itself staunchly against the utilitarian individualistic philosophy which stressed profit and which resulted in widespread poverty and marginalization. The new stress on rationalism rejected the natural world and its laws. The dominant religious outlook was mistrustful of the body and of its passions and, since women were regarded as more physical and more dangerously close to nature than men, was deeply misogynistic. Those who resisted these changes, like St Francis of Assisi, were in a sense going against the tide of history.

27

The Body Vindicated

When Our Lord Jesus Christ spoke with us as a man He said, among other things, that the tongue is prompted by the heart. Therefore, all those of you who have a noble and gentle heart make your thoughts and your words pleasing to God, and honour, fear and praise the Lord Who loved us even before He created us and before we ourselves loved one another. And if we should happen to speak, then let us do so with the greatest propriety and courtesy, so that we may not give displeasure to God and may give delight to our bodies and be of succour to them.

This passage is from the opening of *Il Novellino*, the earliest Italian collection of *novelle*, or short stories, dating probably from the end of the thirteenth century. It is permeated with a serene acceptance of the human body, which is to be spoken of with propriety and delicacy. This view reflects the culmination of a long period during which a positive image of the body had asserted itself, although the development was fitful and uneven, and much that was coarse and gross remained. It was in lay culture above all that a new attitude towards the human body had developed, often adopting survivals of popular beliefs. Monks dismissed such notions, as they had always done, regarding the body and the physical world as flawed, ephemeral and mortal.

Despite the pious words of the prologue, not all the stories of the *Novellino* are informed by propriety and courtesy. Physical beauty, sexuality and all the pleasures of the senses, rescued from centuries of repression, abound. Those who disapproved found themselves over-whelmed; evidently moderation was as difficult to achieve in practice as it was in theory.

This was a period in which all western Europe saw the advent on a huge scale of the use of nicknames. Eventually these nicknames became surnames and many still survive today, though generally in a more respectable form, having shed the crude references to physical appearance which originally inspired them. In Italy such nicknames were common in the first years of the communes and are found in extraordinary variety and number in the twelfth and thirteenth centuries. In a period when few can have been particularly physically attractive, they were inspired by individual failings and foibles. Any physical oddity, any disconcerting physical shortcoming or disagreeable trait, was mercilessly highlighted. Repellent physical or mental characteristics appear to have aroused more interest than agreeable ones. It appears that despite the increasingly favourable attitude to the flesh the view of both body and mind was unrelentingly harsh. Notarial documents are full of nicknames, and their ubiquity suggests that along with greater civility and regard for the body went a continuing obsession with individual peculiarity and physical difference. Nicknames are found indiscriminately through all social groups, and physical features are a frequent target. This disparagement of the body was an established feature of both clerical and popular culture. Names appended to personal names in legal documents in the twelfth and thirteenth centuries include 'Goatgob', 'Mouseface', 'Big Nose', 'Cowgob', 'Tiny', 'Baldy', 'Dog', 'Hen', 'Loopy', 'Goat', 'Ne'er-do-well', 'Scarecrow' and 'Scabby'. As changing social conditions generated a need for family names, such nicknames came to be used as surnames and lost their associations with particular individuals.

The minute attention paid to ugliness nevertheless implies a concern with attractiveness; an awareness of beauty and a preference for it made people more aware of its absence. Although pejorative nicknames are in the majority, there are also some which refer to pleasing features or to personal qualities such as kindness and honesty. The trend towards stressing good qualities was slow and was seen in primarily the higher and middle groups of society. In miniatures and paintings from the thirteenth century to the fifteenth these people are represented not only as well dressed but as physically attractive, much more so than people from lower social groups, who were presumed to be ugly because of their humble origins (poverty and hardship may well have made this true). The idea of beauty was a construct, emerging among the aristocracy and the more prosperous citizens over generations as affluence made for a higher standard of living and a steady refinement of manners. The bourgeoisie rejected violence and from the twelfth and thirteenth centuries became wealthier, as the cities, which in contrast to the aristocracy had seldom been involved in violence, also became richer. Diet and clothes improved, houses were better heated and more comfortable, work was less onerous and there was increasing time for learning and private pursuits. All this is clear from miniatures, paintings and frescos, and though it

was a phenomenon particularly of Italy, with its affluent and powerful merchant class, it was also true of northern Europe and of the
aristocracy there.

Women's dress became richer and more ostentatious, so much so that
in the thirteenth and fourteenth centuries Italian city councils passed
sumptuary laws in an attempt to limit display. The late thirteenth-
century Bolognese laws laid down that 'No noblewoman or any other
woman in the city of Bologna, in the market towns and throughout
Bolognese territory may venture to . . . wear furs or any article of
clothing with a train of more than three-quarters of a *braccio*.' Forbidden
articles included gold and silver necklaces, gold brocade and kerchiefs
with gold thread in them, and strings of pearls, as well as pearls in any
form except in rings. Such legislation had little effect, as contemporary
images demonstrate. Conspicuous consumption in clothes and at feasts
and all public occasions continued.

Behind the desire to curb it lay not only a wish to limit spending and
to stop extravagance, which harmed the city economy and the economy
in general, but concern at the increasingly aristocratic manner of life of
the merchant class – its growing aloofness from work and trade threatened the prosperity of the city, as the city had originally waxed rich and
powerful as a result of the enterprise of merchants and artisans. The
triumph of the bourgeoisie in many north Italian towns towards the end
of the thirteenth century, when it succeeded in displacing the aristocracy,
had resulted in its adoption of a way of life which was akin to that of the
nobles. In many parts of Italy the aristocracy went into dramatic decline
at this time, whereas north of the Alps it maintained its wealth and
dominant position as well as its conspicuous display. The standard
of living of the Italian merchant class was equal to that of the northern
European aristocracy: in the fourteenth century the clothes worn by
Italian merchant families were as sumptuous as those of the French
nobility, while with the crisis in republican government families of merchant origin gained control in many Italian cities and entire regions. They
even made marriage alliances with non-Italian ruling houses, which,
some thought, debased the ancient monarchies. In *The Guermantes Way*
Proust describes the astonishment of the parvenu Bloch when the Mar-
quise de Villeparisis, a *grande dame* of the ancient house of Guermantes,
asserts that the French monarchy had been thus demeaned (by the
marriages of Henry II to Catherine de' Medici and of Henry IV to Marie
de' Medici):

'What is rather amusin',' said our hostess, 'is that in these chapters [con-
vents] where our great-aunts were so often made abbesses, the daughters of
the King of France would not have been admitted. They were very exclu-

sive chapters.' 'The King's daughters not admitted!' cried Bloch in amaze-
ment, 'why ever not?' 'Why, because the House of France had not enough
quarterin's after that misalliance.' Bloch's bewilderment increased. 'A misalliance? The House of France? When was that?' 'Why, when they married
into the Medicis?' replied Mme de Villeparisis in the most natural tone in
the world.' (trans. C. K. Scott Moncrieff and Terence Kilmartin)

The special place accorded the French aristocracy is suggested by the
title Proust gave to this volume, *The Guermantes Way*. The great majority of the Italian aristocracy was of relatively recent and bourgeois
origin, or at any rate had been 'contaminated' by bourgeois forebears.
Even today most Italian aristocratic families can trace their history only
to the late Middle Ages. Here the important element to stress is that in
the thirteenth and fourteenth centuries the ceremony and show of the
merchant class was at its height, though some were nostalgic for a past
supposedly more glorious and less marked by extravagance. This made
for competition with the aristocracy, but also for a 'rebellio carnis', a
reassertion of, and pride in, the body after centuries of tireless condemnation by most churchmen. The condemnation of churchmen was to
continue: the background to the sumptuary laws was a wave of
preaching by the Dominicans as early as the last quarter of the thirteenth
century. Their attack on rich clothes and extravagant feasting was intended not so much to point out that many lived in penury as to urge
penitence and self-abasement: the ancient theme of suffering and a denial
of the body. The timeless exhortation to 'Repent and do penitence'
emerged with renewed force, like a dark curtain falling to shroud the
gaudy world of the merchants.

28

Forbidden Pleasures

Between May and September of 1233 the Dominican preacher Giovanni da Vicenza preached in the towns of the Po plain and the Veneto. His impact on the crowds who came to listen to him in these few months was great and he succeeded in persuading the city governments to introduce an emphasis on penitence into their legislation. The German Dominican Theodore of Apolda, writing at the turn of the thirteenth and fourteenth centuries, described the events of that summer:

> There was so much grace in preaching at that time and so many good works by the friars of the Dominican order, not only in Italy but elsewhere too . . . that all Christendom was astonished and burned with the love and praise of the Saviour. Indeed the reputation of Brother Giovanni da Vicenza, a most religious man and an outstanding preacher from the Dominican order, first spread as a consequence of miracles he performed in Bologna. With God's help he brought ten dead people back to life, and the all-mighty and merciful Lord condescended to perform a further two hundred wonderful miracles through him. When Brother Giovanni began to preach about the divine revelations he had received about our father St Dominic . . . and after Brother Stephen, prior of the province, began to press for the translation of St Dominic's body, from that moment even greater grace of benediction shone forth from the brothers who preached as well as from those who listened to them. In the cities of northern Italy a great number of contumacious heretics were burned at the stake and more than one hundred thousand people who had been undecided between the Holy Roman Church and heresy were converted to the Catholic faith by the Dominican friars. These people now persecute heretics and abhor those whom they formerly protected. The cities of northern Italy, including many towns in the Veneto, entrust their laws and the regulation of their everyday conduct to the Dominicans so that they can rewrite their legislation and bring their advice and judgement to bear on affairs.

The passage reveals the intense involvement of the populace in Giovanni da Vicenza's sermons and the reassertion of religious orthodoxy in large areas of Italy and in other countries. Much Dominican preaching was directed against heresy, but their popularity was also boosted by Dominican involvement in the vast movement for peace which has been called the 'Great Hallelujah'. This movement, which affected the whole of northern Italy, began in the late spring of the year Theodore writes of, 1233, and its impact was felt until September. Many factors lay behind it: weariness of the wars between cities and of factional conflict within the towns themselves, as well as of the campaign of Frederick II against the towns of the Po plain; unease at change as the merchant class acquired power and the feudal nobility declined; alarm caused by the growing dynamism and upheavals in urban society; the serious repercussions of increasing intervention by towns in their rural territory and of the growth of agriculture; and, finally, the high incidence of flooding and therefore of famine. Crowds descended into the towns to demand peace, led by lay preachers, like the Benedetto whom Salimbene of Parma, a Franciscan, described in the late thirteenth century.

The Mendicants, Minors and Preachers (that is, the Franciscan and Dominican orders) took over the leadership of the religious 'Great Hallelujah', but though they shared the general desire for peace they rejected the sense of elation which had hitherto dominated the movement. They argued that the way to peace lay instead through penitence and the rejection of material goods. The Dominicans played a much larger part in the movement than the Franciscans, who despite their rejection of extravagance in clothes and food and in material goods were quite content with a serene and optimistic view of this world. Thomas Cantimpratensis, a Dominican from the Low Countries, and a contemporary of Giovanni da Vicenza, recounted a characteristic episode from the Dominican milieu:

This story was told to me by a brother of the order of St Dominic called Nicolas, who came originally from Dacia and was studying law at Bologna. He had not yet taken holy orders when he saw with his own eyes what I am going to tell you. Brother Giovanni da Vicenza was preaching to the people, who had come from every part of the city to hear him, when he saw something which grieved him deeply, namely that almost all those seated around him were wearing wreathes of roses on their heads. Giovanni stopped talking, paused a moment, and then cried out that they ought all to be ashamed to wear wreathes of roses and flowers since they followed Christ who had had a crown of thorns placed on his head. He went on to say, 'I excommunicate these wreathes of roses. Not the people themselves, but the wreathes, for they lead the people to sin.' When they heard his words, everyone, from the most powerful to the most humble, took off their wreathes and stopped wearing them, for none dared to disobey the saint's command. After some days, however, a wedding was held in the city. Among those present was a boy who was carrying a rose wreath. A swaggering and fashionably dressed young man snatched it out of his hands and put it on his head. Immediately it caught fire, and before he could take it off his hair was all burned. The people were dismayed and thus learned to respect the words of the saint.

This episode occurred when Giovanni was first preaching in Bologna in May, the season when roses and other flowers appear and when, following ancient custom, garlands were worn to celebrate the return of summer and the burgeoning of nature. Giovanni regarded the wearing of such wreathes as sinful; his denunciation of the practice, described in Thomas Cantimpratensis's rather smug account, is the first recorded instance of clerical excommunication.

In the wealthy Italian cities such festivities reflected the emergence in the thirteenth century of a more serene and cheerful view of the world, but they were deplored by those who stressed a religion of pain and suffering, of the cult of the Passion and the instruments of the Passion (the crown of thorns, the nails, sponge and lance). Undoubtedly a degree of sobriety was needful – life is not all roses – but the wearing of the wreathes was an entirely innocent amusement which the stern Giovanni was unable to overlook. His zeal was long remembered by the citizens of Bologna. Local chronicles record his desire that women should wear veils when they went out and that people should greet each another in the name of Jesus Christ. Giovanni changed the city statutes, inserting a penitential stress; the citizens obeyed him – or feigned to. As late as the sixteenth century Leandro Alberti, a Dominican from Bologna and a celebrated geographer, wrote of Giovanni:

> He forbade women to wear rich clothes and instructed people to greet each other in the street in the name of Our Lord Jesus Christ . . . He organized a barefoot procession, in which the clergy as well as the laity participated, through the whole city on the thirtieth of April . . . The citizens were transfixed by his powerful sermons on the need for peace and harmony and for honesty. One day, while he was praying, a cross shone on his forehead and could be seen by all. It moved on to his head and an angel could be seen speaking to him. This occurrence spurred many to penitence.

Alberti's account adds nothing new to the description by Thomas Cantimpratensis, Giovanni's contemporary, who told how 'an angel of the Lord descended from the sky, and a cross the colour of bronze shone bright on his forehead.' Central to these two accounts, which stand at the two ends of a long period, from the first years of the Dominican order to the sixteenth century, as well as to other Dominican sources, is an insistence on the role of penitence. On the other hand Salimbene of Parma, a Franciscan, wrote that the Dominican Giovanni was arrogant, and had even advised a friar who was shaving him in the friary to keep the bristles as they would become relics. The rivalry between the two orders, Dominican and Franciscan, was intense, not surprising as although they shared some common features they were driven by essentially opposite impulses. However, the divisions and splits within the Franciscan order suffice to demonstrate the strength and vigour of St Francis's beliefs and of the commitment, often with tragic results, with which his followers tackled contemporary problems.

The Dominicans were renowned for their study of the natural world. Albertus Magnus, a German, is celebrated for his treatise on plants, *De vegetabilibus*, as well as for his philosophical writings. Thomas Cantimpratensis is less well known, beginning his career as a regular canon and later becoming a Dominican. A pupil of Albertus Magnus at Cologne, like him he taught at Louvain until his death around 1270. Thomas was a great student of the natural world and the author of an encyclopaedia used by Albertus Magnus himself and, later, by Vincent of Beauvais. He also wrote an idiosyncratic work in which the ideal Christian life is described, taking its inspiration from the strictly ordered world of bees; Thomas's scientific interest led him to a vision of an ordered community which he extended to human society. Dominican scientific and ethical thought was characterized by rigour and a strict sense of rank, as in Albertus Magnus's *De vegetabilibus*, which sees the plant world as a rigid hierarchy in which some plants are inferior to others: 'In any wood where the oak and beech trees have been removed, we can see that only aspens and tamarisks, which are ignoble compared to oak and beech, will grow.'

Thus some trees were noble, some not, exactly as in society and in the whole of Creation. The Dominican outlook was very different from that of the Franciscans, who stressed an empirical approach and a minute and serene observation of nature but who had a benign view of the human body. The Dominicans, in contrast, clung to the austere, penitential interpretation of Christianity.

Monasticism was changing. Where once monks had prayed and kept vigil at night, now they adapted to a changing society and new demands; they took an interest in science and the natural world and in the workings of the body. None the less, the material world was strictly subordinated within an ordered hierarchy in which the soul was still supreme and detached from all things physical. Neoplatonism re-emerged. This viewed all creation as a descending order, a hierarchy of essentially separate entities: angelic spirits, souls, bodies, plants and, last, minerals.

Since Neoplatonism also held that the soul was not truly part of the body but was imprisoned by it, one consequence was an increasing rejection and marginalization of the body, which was regarded as still more inferior than in earlier centuries. Science, more rigorous than it had been in the earlier Middle Ages, could prove its baseness. The ideas, or forms, of all living beings were held to be in God, but also to be distinct from each other, while God, it was believed, had not created humans and the rest of the animate world out of love but had merely generated them dispassionately.

In contrast, for the fourteenth-century Franciscan, William of Ockham, who was born in Surrey and spent his life between Pisa, Avignon and Munich, the world was easily compatible with rationality. Universal abstractions and predetermination were of less importance for him than the individual. It is telling that William, along with Michele da Cesena, the general of the Franciscan order, and Bonagrazia da Bergamo, should have been accused of heresy and excommunicated – though under the protection of the Emperor in Munich he was able to write several books. Nicola Abbagnano, the great twentieth-century philosopher, has commented of William: 'Although he lived in the age of scholasticism he was able to break the bounds of its dogmatism. Through his critical thought, based on experience, he effectively foreshadows British empiricism, and his critical outlook makes him the first great figure of the modern age.'

Elsewhere in the same book, in a chapter entitled 'The Absolute and the Smell of Fish', which argues against all schematism and predetermination and against all abstractions which make physical or psychological demands on the individual, Abbagnano recounts a delightful personal anecdote:

Sixty years ago, when I used to wander around Naples breathing in the salty air amid the shouts of the fish-sellers, I certainly never ran into that Absolute Spirit which moves onward through History by means of its dialectic consisting of thesis, antithesis and synthesis. All I encountered was many-sided reality, with its pleasures and pains ... Perhaps it was the Absolute which was the subject of the real world and of history, or perhaps rather the multiplicity of individuals, each with their very real needs.

29

Brother Ass the Body

One night, while all the brothers were asleep, one of them cried out, 'I am dying of hunger.' St Francis rose and had the table prepared and joined him in eating so that he would not be embarrassed to eat alone . . . And the other brothers ate with them too. When they had finished St Francis said, 'My brothers, each of you must consider his own constitution. If another can manage with less food than you then you must not try to imitate him. If your body requires more food then you must give it more; you must respect it and give it what it needs so that in this way a stronger body can serve the spirit. It is true that it is our duty to abstain from over-indulgence in food, which harms our bodies and our souls, but we should guard against excessive abstinence since it is mercy which the Lord requires of us, not sacrifice.' And he went on, 'My dearest brothers, we have eaten in company with my brother for his sake so that he should not be ashamed to be the only one to eat and it is our duty of love and charity which has moved me to do so.'

This story comes from the *Legend of the Three Companions*, written some time in the thirteenth or fourteenth centuries and difficult to date precisely. In it one of the characteristics of St Francis, his concern for the physical side of men and women and his respect for everything created by God as good in itself, is clear, an aspect of the saint which made a deep and lasting impression on his many followers. The origins of this attitude lie in the new view of human nature which was to be found in many sectors of society in the twelfth and thirteenth centuries. Despite forceful opposition from many, including some Franciscans, mainly from the late thirteenth century but also before, it was destined to last. As the Franciscan order developed there was conflict between those who interpreted the teaching of their founder St Francis as entailing a general acceptance of society and its problems, and those who felt the renewed attraction of penitence and monastic withdrawal and who would brook no compromise with the world and with human frailty. By the end of the thirteenth century many Franciscans, in place of love for their fellow men and women and an acceptance of human weakness, were emphasizing the need for harsh penance and complete poverty; they viewed this life as essentially worthless.

Iacopone da Todi, a Franciscan, subjected his body to the most rigorous torments. Obsessed with death and decay, the inevitable fate of everything on earth, he took pleasure in suffering, disease and death and fantasized on the thought of decomposing flesh. He could see earthly objects only in terms of their grim fate.

> Where are my eyes, now purified? They have fallen from their sockets and worms have eaten them. Never fear, now, the sin of pride. My eyes are no more, those eyes with which I sinned every time I walked along the street, every time I looked on others, every time I greeted them. O woe is me! Now do I suffer grievously! My body is eaten up and my soul is burning. Where is my nose, which once served me to smell? What blow made it fall? You could not save yourself from worms and now you can vaunt yourself no more. This nose of mine which served me to smell has fallen off and gives forth a foul stench. Did I not warn you of this, in the days when I used to revel in this false world, full of filth . . . My flesh has fallen away and only my bones are left . . . Look at me now, O you who still live, and shun folly while you are in the world. Remember, O heedless ones, that all too soon you too will be wracked by pain.

Death is seen as a loathsome and shameful vanquishing of the flesh and is evoked in order to cast a long shadow over everyday life and to intimidate and warn. There is an uncrossable gulf between Iacopone da Todi and the teaching of St Francis, founder of the order to which Iacopone belonged. For St Francis 'Sister Death' was a serene passing away, akin to sleep, and decidedly not an abrupt end. 'Praise to thee, my Lord, for our sister Bodily Death, from whom none can escape.' Francis regarded the body as created by God and therefore to be respected. Its strengths should be admired and its frailties tolerated, as is apparent from another story from the *Legend of the Three Companions*: 'On another occasion the Blessed Francis learned that a sick brother had a fancy for grapes but was too shy to ask for them. He was moved by compassion and decided to take the brother to a vineyard. There he sat down beside him and started to eat grapes himself lest the brother feel awkward to eat alone.'

The *Legend of the Three Companions* and other lives of St Francis include many such episodes which testify to the absence in Francis of any rigorous condemnation of physical needs, an aspect of the saint which clearly made a strong and lasting impression on his followers and which long continued to characterize the Franciscan order. St Francis's kindliness and his sense of the intrinsic value of the physical side of humanity extended to a calm acceptance of the entire natural world as good both in itself and as the mirror of God. St Francis was happy to look nature in the face, unlike some of his followers whose view, even during his lifetime, was impeded by a dark veil and whose attitude was to triumph in the second half of the sixteenth century.

The *Mirror of Perfection* gives an instance of St Francis's openness:

> We who were with him have seen him take inward and outward delight in almost every creature, and when he handled or looked at them his spirit seemed to be in heaven rather than on earth. And not long before his death, in gratitude for the many consolations that he had received through creatures, he composed *The Praises of the Lord in His Creation* in order to stir the hearts of those who heard them to the praise of God, and to move men to praise the Lord Himself in His creatures. (trans. Leo Sherley-Price)

St Francis's interpretation of the physical world is naturally in religious terms; given the age he lived in, he could hardly have thought otherwise. But it is important to stress that for Francis nature did not exist simply for the benefit of humans and to prove the existence of God. For him the physical world had an independent existence and its own beauty. Moreover its beauty made it an important bridge between God and humans since it was the first step to the knowledge of God. This view of the natural world, of men and women, animals and plants, largely corresponded to contemporary lay thinking about life and poverty, but also contrasted starkly with a significant strand within the collective consciousness, where for some decades ancient notions of evil had re-emerged.

The heresy of the Cathars, or the *perfecti*, however much it varied between different parts of Europe and over time, in essence lay in an insistence on a belief in Good and Evil as two opposing, and dominant, principles. This was in the tradition of gnosticism and Manichaeism, dualistic philosophies which were at their strongest around the time of the emergence of Christianity. Though there is no trace of such dualistic thought in the Synoptic Gospels, it had a growing presence in ascetic and penitential readings of the Gospels. During the decline of the ancient world, this interpretation of the world cast long shadows over Europe. Christianity offered a glimmer of hope but this too was overshadowed by the dualistic view, which influenced Christians, including some eminent figures.

Monasticism was affected by such views more than any other institution, and it thus had a lasting and dramatic effect on the culture of western Europe. Stoics, Neoplatonists and Manichaeans all believed in the existence of evil and identified it with matter and hence with the body. In his life of Plotinus (died AD 270), Porphyry wrote that, 'It was as if he felt ashamed to have a body', while St Augustine, discussing marriage and sexual relations within marriage which were not intended solely for procreation, was adamant: 'Why not forbid marriage, if you wish to take away that [children] which makes it such? For indeed, if the intention of procreation is absent, husbands are but foul paramours and wives but prostitutes, the marriage bed a brothel and mothers-in-law bawds.'

In his youth Augustine had been a follower of Manichaeism, but after his conversion he fought vigorously against it, denying the real existence of evil and asserting that matter did in fact contain good, merely less than did spirit. This did not prevent him, however, from maintaining that original sin was transmitted through sexual relations: 'Christ was conceived and born without physical pleasure. Therefore he was always undefiled by the stain of original sin.' In his *Confessions* Augustine bemoaned the images of pleasure which assailed him at night:

> It cannot be the case, almighty God, that your hand is not strong enough to cure all the sicknesses of my soul and, by a more abundant outflow of your grace, to extinguish the lascivious impulses of my sleep. You will more and more increase your gifts in me, Lord, so that my soul, rid of the glue of lust, may follow me to you, so that it is not in rebellion against itself, and so that even in dreams it not only does not commit those disgraceful and corrupt acts in which sensual images provoke carnal emissions, but also does not even consent to them. (trans. Henry Chadwick)

Augustine was obsessed by the strength of the flesh and of the impulse to yield to physical urges, even more than the monks of the tenth century would be: 'Men go to marvel at the high peaks of mountains, the great waves of the sea, the vast currents of rivers, the circuit of the Ocean, the course of the stars, and yet they neglect themselves.' For Augustine, nature distances us from God, even the magnificent and awe-inspiring landscapes he preferred which could in some way reflect the greatness and impenetrability of the soul. His was a view very different from that which St Francis would hold.

Although throughout the Middle Ages churchmen were less obsessed by the presence of evil than they had been during the rise of Christianity in late antiquity, the idea of evil nevertheless sporadically emerged, as for example in the twelfth and thirteenth centuries with the Cathars. The Cathars believed that the soul is imprisoned within the body and the flesh, and is not therefore regenerated by procreation. For them, all matter was evil and they therefore stressed poverty and penitence. This attracted many Christians who were deeply troubled by the spread of wealth and luxury goods, in short, by the new, positive view of earthly existence.

As a result of the intense persecution they suffered in the south of France and the campaign of the Dominican friars from 1233, the year of the 'Great Hallelujah', the numbers of the Cathars decreased dramatically. Yet the principal reason for their steady decline and eventual disappearance was their aloofness and their withdrawal from a world which they regarded as hostile and irrelevant and governed by the laws of evil. In contrast, the new orders, the Franciscans and Dominicans, in Italy and elsewhere confronted the problems of a rapidly changing society, albeit in different ways.

None the less, the rallying cry continued to be penance and the struggle against sin and the flesh and, ultimately, a condemnation of all things physical. St Francis's significance lies in the fact that he had the courage to go against the mainstream at a time when those who thought differently were increasingly marginalized and quashed, and when the prevailing current of thought was so strong that even the Franciscan movement itself was eventually sucked in. It is no coincidence that the Dominican order should also have emerged at the same time. It was quite different from the Franciscans, as we have seen, and its early history was not marked by the crises, tragedies and struggles which are found in the Franciscans, intimately bound up as they were with society and its problems and contradictions.

30

Women, the Fragile Sex

'She lifted the veil which covered her and revealed her graceful body and long arms and her slender white hands with their long fingers.' This comes from a short poem by Marie de France, who wrote in the late twelfth century. Describing the woman who is the subject of the poem, Marie suggests an elusive beauty which is a blend of the physical and the spiritual. The flesh is sublimated, although the woman's graceful body houses a disconcertingly headstrong passion. 'As they spoke of many things she looked with ardour into his face and on his body and gazed on his whole form, thinking that he was quite perfect . . . Love sent her a message, commanding her to love him, and made her turn pale and sigh.' Her knight was to go through countless dangers for her sake, as she would for his, as he braved perils in distant lands and at sea as well as in his feudal domain in northern France. 'His castle lay close to the sea, only a morning's ride distant, and was surrounded for thirty leagues by forest.'

In France and elsewhere the kind of beauty generally favoured in women at this time and later was a slender, northern European type, so much so that in the late sixteenth century Montaigne would complain of the plumpness of Italian women, their ample breasts and large thighs. Within this feudal society, in the twelfth century a sophisticated notion of what constituted handsomeness in men developed, as well as more demanding ideas of beauty in women, although the traditional virtues of courage and self-sacrifice continued to be regarded as essential: in Marie de France's poem, as in so many others, the man and woman go forward to meet a harsh fate with stoicism. The woman is represented as resolute and strong, except when she surrenders to passion, an emotion to which in any case the man also yields. There are certainly many poems of courtly love in which the woman is portrayed as a temptation which the man manages to resist, but these refer to a sophisticated game with set rules that make love identical to physical passion, so feared by the Church and by the bourgeoisie, and frequently regarded as the only possible expression of the relationship between the sexes.

The emphasis on the military prowess of a knightly class meant that courage was regarded as equally necessary in women, and indeed they might well find themselves obliged to fight in their husbands' absence. Later, when tournaments came to supplant war as the theatre of virtuosity, women watched enthusiastically, urging on their knights against their opponents. Breathlessly watching single combat, they threw articles to the knights as favours until they were bareheaded and gloveless. In the late Middle Ages such tournaments were a feature of countries which had retained a strong aristocracy and where the idea of chivalry was still very much alive on both the cultural and the institutional levels. It is difficult today to appreciate the central role that such tournaments and competitions between knights had for the nobility. They had nothing in common with modern sporting events, which are largely irrelevant to the everyday lives of the spectators as well as, by and large, to those of the participants themselves. In contrast, tournaments and single combat between knights, either as ritual or on the field of battle, were a deeply ingrained part of contemporary culture and involved almost everyone in some way, including women, regardless of whether they were of the knightly class or not.

Some particularly celebrated encounters lived long in the collective memory and a memorial might be erected where knights had met in single combat, a practice which continued into the fifteenth century. The well-known 'Pilgrims' Cross' near Saint-Omer is an example. Fifty years after its erection, Bayard, 'chevalier sans peur et sans reproche', made a pilgrimage to this celebrated cross on the eve of a tournament. The chivalric and military tradition also gave rise to the custom of hanging pieces of armour and trophies from single combat or battle on the walls of famous churches, a practice which in France persisted long after the Middle Ages: the column erected in Place Vendôme in Paris by Napoleon was cast from cannons captured at the battle of Austerlitz. Italy and other countries never shared this enthusiasm, which was peculiar to France. As the great historian and French patriot Marc Bloch pointed out with pride, the true homeland of chivalry had been northern France and it was always most at home there.

The military ethos and the idea of women converged in France to produce the ideal of the female warrior. No myth has ever sprung up as fast, or retained its potency for so long, as that which developed around Joan of Arc. The sober monument to her on the site where she was burned alive in Rouen in deepest Normandy is still much visited, and the huge modern church close by is built in the tradition of the great French cathedrals. French fifteenth-century culture gave birth to the myth of Joan of Arc, the clearest and the most striking result of the fusion of the two ideals, of woman and of war. The myth could have emerged only in France. Elsewhere the factors which fostered such a myth were absent: feudalism; an enormously popular monarchy which to the common people and the dispossessed appeared to offer some hope; a long-established but still thriving nobility intimately associated with the land, whose seigneurial castles and churches were to be found in every corner of rural France. From here the most celebrated knights of the time emerged to fight in almost every corner of Europe; from the tenth century they were involved almost everywhere in wars or crusades.

In Italy, towards the close of the Middle Ages, St Catherine of Siena came to be the advocate of entirely opposite values to St Joan of Arc in France. In her letters and discourses she constantly urged peace, which the new merchant ethic also regarded as imperative. The many female and male saints of this period, foremost among them St Raymond of Piacenza, St Homobonus of Cremona and St Francis of Assisi, all insisted on the need for peace and denounced faction.

Although it was two women, the valiant soldier St Joan of Arc and the great peace-maker St Catherine of Siena, who came to stand for the two ideals of war and peace and whose influence spread far beyond their immediate circles, the image of women as weak and as the cause of sin continued unabated throughout the Middle Ages and beyond, though the particular nuances varied according to time and place and between different social groups and occupations.

In Italy, during the period of the city-republics, a new concept of what constituted saintliness in both men and women developed which stressed the need to take an active role in the world by evangelizing and seeking to modify or prevent behaviour which did not accord with the teachings of the New Testament. Towards the end of the twelfth century, however, the situation changed as the majority of clerics, and particularly members of the regular orders, largely withdrew from this commitment. This coincided with an increasing exclusiveness of the ruling groups, now dominated by the aristocracy, and with the gradual exclusion from government of members of the middle-ranking groups. It is true that those in power continued to pay attention to their interests, particularly as individual families came to control the cities and a chequerboard of competing states emerged, but their concern was merely that of rulers towards their subjects, with all that that implies.

The increasing aloofness of those with political and moral respon-siblity and the withdrawal of many clerics from any involvement in the secular world, even with its more congenial elements, left the way open

for less savoury tendencies within society. The merchant class of the cities
of Italy were proponents of the new ethic which stressed the acquisition
of wealth and the exploitation of others and even of the environment
itself. Those who were unable to play according to the rules of the game
of production, or who had no economic function, found themselves
marginalized within society and swelled the numbers of poor and sick, of
beggars and outlaws. Disease itself came to carry a social stigma and
could be regarded as a mark of moral failing. Those sections of society
who were perceived as closer to nature and its laws, such as children and
peasants and, above all, women, were despised. This was consonant with
a growing alienation from the natural world and everything connected
with it either in reality or in the imagination. In the fourteenth century
the Florentine, Paolo da Certaldo, in his celebrated manual of advice,
urged prudence on his readers: 'Be careful never to leave your house at
night if it can be avoided . . . Never visit the house of a woman of
doubtful virtue at night.'

Values were shifting: obligatory among the merchant class were prudence, caution and a fear of danger and of the night, not courage.

> Women are of weak character and when their husbands are away they are
> in great danger. If you have women in your household, watch over them
> and return home often. Ensure that they go in awe of you . . . Ensure that
> they are kept busy. Idleness is full of perils for both men and women, but
> especially for women . . . Do not fall in love with any woman apart from
> your wife; simply remember that all women are made in precisely the same
> way and that there is therefore no reason for you to prefer one to another.

Evidently the bourgeois insistence on economizing could well extend
to women too. Women were commonly regarded in terms of their
productiveness alone: they ran the household and produced children.
Although this was not the only view, it was the one which came to
prevail. It is understandable that women should have rebelled against this
degrading treatment and should have found their own means of escape;
the explosion in the number of female saints after the late thirteenth
century, the so-called 'feminization of sanctity', is a response to the
situation in which women increasingly found themselves. Many women
found their best option was to leave their families to live in a convent, or
at any rate to become tertiaries, living in close contact with members of
the religious orders. The phenomenon was especially marked in Italy
from the time of the crisis of republican government in the thirteenth and
fourteenth centuries, but it was also apparent elsewhere, among the
Béguines of northern France, for example. The Italian female saints of
this period left their families as soon as they could, preferring divine love

to conjugal love. Their descriptions of the love of God are suggestive of a sublimated physical passion:

> On the following Holy Saturday this soul devoted to Christ revealed to the present writer, a friar, the joy which God had granted her. Among much else she told me that on that day she passed into ecstasy and was aware of being in the tomb beside Christ. First she kissed His chest as He lay with His eyes closed just as He had been after death. Then she kissed His mouth, feeling an indescribable sweetness which came from it. After a brief pause, she rested her cheek on His cheek, and He touched her other cheek and pressed her to Him.

This is from an account of one of the mystical experiences of the Blessed Angela da Foligno. Born in the mid-thirteenth century, Angela became involved with the Franciscans while married and with children, and after the deaths in rapid succession of her mother, her husband and her children towards the end of the century. She became a Franciscan tertiary. She spent the remaining twenty years of her life between her home and the Franciscan house. She died in 1309 in her sixties after a life taken up by frequent mystical experiences as well as by tireless involvement with the poor and sick.

Their commitment to the world through their involvement with the marginalized and their dedication to peace distinguished the saintly women of Italy from those of northern Europe, preoccupied sometimes to the exclusion of all else with mysticism and penitence. Yet the most remarkable feature is the number of women in Italy at this time who dedicated their lives to God, a higher number than in any other country. Many of them, though they were never canonized, became the subject of popular devotion; crude images of them were painted on the walls of houses and they were invoked in prayer. The cult of these saints was an outlet for much frustrated ambition among women. One explanation advanced for many of their mystical visions has been neurosis, but though many women did indeed go to the limit in prayer and vigil and in charitable activity, choosing to suffer extreme privations and pain or even to push themselves beyond endurance until they died, all were of strong mind. Night was the favoured time for their visions and mystic experiences, their prayers and lamentations, though these might also occur during the day. For Angela da Foligno there was little difference between day and night: 'The vision stayed continuously before me for three days. It did not prevent me from eating or from any other activity, though I ate but little and spent the time lying down without speaking.'

In Angela's ecstasy night was as day since she saw everything around her illuminated by the dazzling light which emanated from Christ. And yet for mystics the world was in a sense becoming an irrelevant and darker, less substantial place. Angela prayed for death so that she could leave the earthly world behind for ever and devote herself entirely to the adoration of God:

> She sought the intervention of the Blessed Virgin and prayed to the Apostles to kneel down with her so that together they could supplicate the Almighty to spare her the torments of that death which is this life on this earth and grant her to go to Him, to Him Whom she could already feel within her.

From the mid-fourteenth century onwards profound social and economic change and the upheavals in religion and institutions, as well as the consternation caused in much of Europe by the Black Death, made for an increased sense of the transitoriness of this material world and of the instability of institutions, social groups and families. Mystics, too, saw the world in shadowy terms, as can be seen in a letter from St Catherine of Siena to the Countess Benedetta Salimbeni: 'But do you know what sight, the love of this world, is? It is a clouded vision, full of shadows . . . For darkness enwraps the fleeting objects of this world when we behold them unmindful of the love of God but for the mere pleasure of the senses . . .'

It was still, just, allowable to look on the things of this world since they could be seen as the product of God's munificence. From here, however, it was but a short step to an insistence that the faithful should turn their eyes away from the world entirely. Peter of Alcantara's voluntary blindness lay only a hundred and fifty years in the future and already by the end of the fourteenth century many mystics had eyes only for God; for them the things of the world were redundant, dark and benighted. The body was spurned and marginalized; so, even more so, were the senses. The *solitudo carnis* reigned supreme.

In the fourteenth century the theme of death began to appear in literature and art. The figure of death, ever ready to snatch away the living, lurks in scenes of festivities, whether set indoors, in the increasingly comfortable houses, or outside during *fêtes champêtres*. The beautiful maidens in Luca Signorelli's colossal frescos of the Last Judgment in the Duomo in Orvieto have a strange expression of despair and utter sadness. In the fresco skeletons jostle naked men and women as angels blow trumpets above their tormented bodies. Only the saved venture a timid smile. By the time of Signorelli the Middle Ages were drawing to their close. In the past lay its hopes and aspirations, the tentative beginnings of science, almost constant misfortune, the grim torments of the flesh. The flesh of Jews, witches, lepers, peasants and wage-labourers was doomed to repression, segregation and death as a result of political calculation and social upheaval, religious fanaticism, popular hysteria born of instability and the collapse of values.

On 30 April 1389, in Florence, Brother Michele da Calci was tried and condemned to be burned at the stake. Michele belonged to the Fraticelli, who had left the Franciscan order. Barefoot, clad in a wretched and unbuttoned shift, his head bowed, he was led to the stake through a vast and noisy crowd. He went past the Duomo and Baptistery, the Mercato Vecchio, Calimala and the Mercato Nuovo, to the Piazza della Signoria and the Piazza del Grano. In front of the church of the Franciscans, they pointed out the image of St Francis to him and he gazed sadly at it, asking St Francis to intercede for him. Then he turned to the friars who were standing on the steps in front of the church, looked them in the eye and began to shout: 'You swore obedience to the rule of St Francis – but the rule has been condemned along with me. Is this how you punish those who try to live according to the rule?'

The friars shrugged their shoulders or pulled their hoods down over their faces. Michele was thrust onwards through the jeering crowd, in which the occasional figure stood weeping silently, and was pushed into a little hut improvised of wood and branches and bound to a post inside. A torch was put to the roof and he began to chant the Te Deum. Then the smoke made him cough, the ropes holding him up burned through and he fell to his knees, dead.

A Note on Further Reading
and Sources

This book is not intended for specialists, though they will find here new interpretations of familiar material. Rather, I hope it will appeal to all who have an interest in this period and who are curious to understand patterns of thought in the past and to discover, perhaps, that which is of lasting value. The following suggestions for further reading, which are set out part by part, have that in mind, while readers seeking more specialist bibliographies will find them in the books and articles cited. Sources have been indicated in a general way in the text, and Shayne Mitchell has kindly listed editions useful to an English reader of most of the main works in a final section.

Part I   When the Heavens Darken

On the history of mentalities J. Le Goff's contribution to *Faire de l'histoire* (Paris: Gallimard, 1974) is essential reading; selections in J. Le Goff and P. Nora, eds., *Constructing the Past: Essays in Historical Methodology*, intro. by C. Lucas (Cambridge and Paris: Cambridge University Press and Éditions de la Maison des Sciences de l'Homme, 1985). Although written some years ago, his comments there are still valid: 'For the historian today, the new term *mentalité* is already tainted. There has been much talk of the history of *mentalités* but in practice we have few good examples . . . It is still virgin territory and much spadework remains to be done.'

Le Goff cites some of these good examples; in addition, any of his writings or those of E. Le Roy Ladurie can be recommended, as well as J.-C. Schmitt's *The Holy Greyhound: Guinefort, Healer of Children since the Thirteenth Century*, trans. M. Thom (Cambridge: Cambridge University Press, 1982). The value of these writings lies, I believe, in their analysis of specific phenomena from both 'high' and 'low' culture against the particular historical context and social background. In this they differ from studies which seek to provide a more general survey and which concentrate on patterns of behaviour which are common to different groups within society and which have a *longue durée*. Such studies are of course also necessary as they provide a context against which particular phenomena can be better understood.

The theory of the division of society into three orders (a notion not unique to the Middle Ages or to western Europe) and the historical circumstances which gave rise to it are discussed by G. Duby in his *The Three Orders: Feudal Society Imagined*, trans. A. Goldhammer (Chicago and London: University of Chicago Press, 1980). J. Le Goff's 'Les trois fonctions indo-européennes. L'historien et l'Europe féodale', *Annales Economies, Sociétés, Civilisations (E.S.C.)* 34.6 (1979), pp. 1187–215, and O. Niccoli's *I sacerdoti, i guerrieri, i contadini. Storia di un'immagine della società* (Turin: Einaudi, 1979) are also useful.

The intimate relationship, amounting almost to identification, with the natural world in the Middle Ages is discussed by A. Ja. Gurevich in *Categories of Medieval Culture*, trans. G. L. Campbell (London: Routledge and Kegan Paul, 1985; original Russian edition Moscow, 1972). Its importance lies in its stress on the distinction between high and low, popular and elite, culture, although Gurevich pays insufficient regard to the differences between the early and late Middle Ages and to the varying rates of change within Europe, notably in areas where the periodization commonly applied to western Europe is inappropriate. There is a vast range of studies of magic and science in the Middle Ages; an indication of its richness can be gained from Gurevich's bibliography.

Legends and the climate of fear and pagan beliefs in the early Middle Ages, as well as high culture, are treated by V. Fumagalli in *Il Regno italico* (Turin: UTET, 1986), pp. 24–5 and *passim*. Apparitions of the dead are described and set in their historical context by V. Fumagalli, 'Il paesaggio dei morti. Luoghi d'incontro tra i morti e i vivi sulla terra nel Medioevo', *Quaderni storici* 17.2 (1982), pp. 411–25. Visions and the image of the next world between the sixth and eleventh centuries are surveyed by M. Aubrun in 'Caractères et portée religieuse et sociale des *Visiones* en Occident du VIe au XIe siècle', *Cahiers de civilisation médiévale* 23.2 (1980), pp. 109–30, and by G. Le Don in 'Structures et significations de l'imagerie médiévale de l'enfer', *Cahiers de civilisation médiévale* 22.4 (1979), pp. 363–72. The warriors with dogs' heads, the cynocephali, are discussed by C. Lecouteux in 'Les Cynocéphales. Étude d'une tradition tératologique de l'Antiquité au XIIe siècle', *Cahiers de civilisation médiévale* 24.2 (1981), pp. 117–28. For attitudes to wolves, with much detail on the cultural background and on animal behaviour, see G. Ortalli, 'Natura, storia e mitografia del lupo nel Medioevo', *La Cultura* 11 (1973), pp. 257–311.

Thought-provoking and informative studies of the image of death, with full bibliographies, are found in P. Ariès, *Images of Man and Death*, trans. J. Lloyd (Cambridge, Massachusetts, and London: Harvard University Press, 1985), and in C. Frugoni, 'La protesta affidata', *Quaderni Storici* 17.2 (1982), pp. 426–48; the latter work profits greatly from Frugoni's familiarity with the iconography of the dead and of death between the twelfth and fifteenth centuries. C. Ginzburg's *The Night Battles: Witchcraft and Agrarian Cults in the Sixteenth and Seventeenth Centuries*, trans. A. Tedeschi and J. Tedeschi (London: Routledge and Kegan Paul, 1983), is valuable not only for its investigation of the Benandanti but also for its considerations on witchcraft practices in general and on the changing attitude of the elite towards them. For the development of the portrait and its implications for how people perceived themselves, E. Buschor's *Das Porträt* (Munich: Piper, 1960) is indispensable. An overview of attitudes to the family, relationships, women and sexuality can be found in R. Fossier, *Enfance de l'Europe*, vol. 2 (Paris: Presses Universitaires de France, 1982), pp. 905–50, with an excellent bibliography; see also his *Peasant Life in the Medieval West*, trans. R. Vale (Oxford: Blackwell, 1988), and his *The Village and the House in the Later Middle Ages*, trans. H. Cleere (London: Batsford, 1985). G. Vinay's *Alto Medioevo latino* (Naples: Guida, 1978) is stimulating; his books are valuable not only for their understanding of the historical and cultural background of individual writers but also for their attention to details which cast light on the writer, such as the passage in Paul the Deacon's *History of the Langobards* where he describes his forebears. K. Schmid's 'Über das Verhältnis von Person und Gemeinschaft im früheren Mittelalter', *Frühmittelalterliche Studien* 1 (1967), pp. 225–49, is fundamental for an understanding of the relationship between the individual and society.

During late antiquity and the early Middle Ages a largely silvo-pastoral economy developed. After the first piecemeal clearances between the seventh and the tenth centuries, the rate of clearance increased enormously as a result of deep-seated economic, social and even cultural changes. The task was enormous: nearly everywhere was wilderness and it was to take a long time, even with the new economic and social structures, to make much impact on it. Nonetheless, the countryside was steadily transformed. At the same time attitudes to nature, to the countryside and to the remaining areas of wilderness were changing and wild areas were less and less tolerated.

On the limitations of *Kulturgeschichte* see G. Tabacco, 'Problemi di insediamento e di popolamento nell'alto Medioevo', *Rivista Storica Italiana* 79.1 (1967), pp. 67–110; compare his *Struggle for Power in Medieval Italy: Structures of Political Rule*, trans. R. B. Jensen (Cambridge: Cambridge University Press, 1989). A useful overview of current thinking on perceptions of distance and space is R. Comba's 'Il territorio come spazio vissuto. Ricerche geografiche e storiche nella genesi di un tema di storia sociale', *Società e storia* 11 (1981), pp. 1–27. V. Fumagalli's *Il Regno italico*, pp. 57–100, examines the Italian countryside in the early Middle Ages in the general European context and includes the relevant sources and a full bibliography on pp. 305–14.

The writings by members of the Cluniac reform movement, on which I have drawn extensively not only for their content but also for what they reveal of contemporary thinking, have been studied by P. Lamma, *Momenti di storiografia cluniacense* (Rome: Istituto Storico Italiano per il Medio Evo, 1961), see especially p. 21, n. 4; by V. Fumagalli, 'Note sulla *Vita Geraldi* di Odone di Cluny', *Bullettino dell'Istituto Storico Italiano per il Medio Evo* 76 (1964), pp. 217–40; and by J.-C. Poulin, *L'idéal de sainteté dans l'Aquitaine carolingienne. D'après les sources hagiographiques (750–950)* (Quebec: Les Presses de l'Université Laval, 1975), with a full list of sources and bibliography on pp. 167–201. B. H. Rosenwein's *Rhinoceros Bound: Cluny in the Tenth Century* (Philadelphia: University of Pennsylvania Press, 1982) is unfortunately marred by omissions and serious misunderstandings of the earlier literature.

On freemen and their gradual loss of liberty, and the emergence of the aristocracy and their increasing domination of both warfare and government, see J. Fleckenstein, 'Adel und Kriegertum und ihre Wandlung im Karolingerreich', in *Nascita dell'Europa ed Europa carolingia: un'equazione da verificare*, vol. 1 (Spoleto: Centro Italiano di Studi sull'Alto Medioevo, 1981), pp. 67–94, and V. Fumagalli, 'Le modificazioni politico-istituzionali in Italia sotto la dominazione carolingia', in ibid., pp. 293–317; see also Fleckenstein's *Early Medieval Germany*, trans. B. S. Smith (Amsterdam and Oxford: North Holland, 1978).

St Odo of Cluny and St Gerald of Aurillac are discussed, with particular reference to their earlier life as laymen and their spiritual crises, by V. Fumagalli in 'Note sulla *Vita Geraldi* di Odone di Cluny', *Bullettino dell'Istituto Storico Italiano per il Medio Evo* 76 (1964), pp. 217–40, especially pp. 219–21. The importance of hunting in the lives of both laymen and ecclesiastics is stressed by M. Montanari in his chapter on 'Caccia e vita signorile: cultura e atteggiamenti mentali' in *L'alimentazione contadina nell'alto Medioevo* (Naples: Liguori, 1979), pp. 261–8. On royal and imperial hunting estates, K. Brühl's *Fodrum, Gistum, Servitium Regis. Studien zu den wirtschaftlichen Grundlagen der Königtums im Frankenreich und in den fränkischen Nachfolgestaaten Deutschland, Frankreich und Italien vom 6. bis zur Mitte des 14. Jahrhunderts*, vol. 1 (Cologne-Graz: Böhlau, 1968), is indispensable (see especially pp. 392–451). The association between violence in everyday life and in warfare is investigated by G. Duby in *The Early Growth of the European Economy: Warriors and Peasants from the Seventh to the Twelfth Century*, trans. H. B. Clarke (London, 1974; original French edition Paris: Gallimard, 1973). The emergence of the aristocracy and its increasing monopoly of defence, as well as the growing subjection of freemen, are charted in V. Fumagalli's 'Le modificazioni politico-istituzionali in Italia sotto la dominazione carolingia', in *Nascita dell'Europa ed Europa carolingia: un'equazione da verificare*, vol. 1, pp. 293–317. Instances of spiritual crises and withdrawal to monasteries among the aristocracy are discussed in V. Fumagalli, *Il Regno italico*, pp. 121–3. For the social nuances of canonization in the Middle Ages, see P. Delooz, *Sociologie et canonisations* (La Haye: M. Nijhoff, 1969), *passim*, and its extensive bibliography.

Finally, thanks go to UTET, Turin, for kind permission to use in part I passages from Vito Fumagalli, 'Atteggiamenti mentali e stili di vita', in *Il Medioevo*, vol. 1 of *La Storia: I grandi problemi dal Medioevo all'Età Contemporanea*.

Part II The Living Rock

Towns played a crucial role in the changes in the countryside and attitudes to the natural world in the Middle Ages. This is true especially of Italy, especially after AD 1000, a date which as well as marking the millennium does in fact represent a crucial watershed in so many areas of history. A useful summary of the current state of research on attitudes to territory and distance is R. Comba, 'Il territorio come spazio vissuto. Ricerche geografiche e storiche nella genesi di un tema di storia sociale', *Società e storia* 11 (1981), pp. 1–27. Comba cites works by G. Duby, J. Le Goff, G. Bertrand, R. Fossier, M. Lefebvre, M. T. Lorcin, G. Sivéry, P. Toubert, and a special issue of *Revue du Nord* (no. 244, 1980) devoted to the topic and entitled *Le paysage rural: realités et représentations*. In this area G. Ricci's *Bologna* (Bari: Laterza, 1980) and C. Frugoni's *A Distant City: Images of Urban Experience in the Medieval World*, trans. W. McCuaig (Princeton: Princeton University Press, 1991), are outstanding. The works by P. L. Cervellati referred to by Ricci are also worthy of mention.

In part II of this book my concern has been to demonstrate how the complex interplay of economic, social and political factors moulded attitudes to the countryside in both town and country. Once the city, the urban mentality, had emerged as a powerful force, it, like all dominant forces within society, sought to attain a balance between these factors; but this of course resulted in social tension and identity crises and disrupted the balance of nature in towns as well as in the country. Throughout the Middle Ages this was especially true of the Italian city-republics and the towns of northern Europe. The literature on medieval towns is vast and I shall limit myself to a preliminary bibliography. The first postwar monograph on the subject in Italy is E. Sereni, *Storia del paesaggio agrario italiano* (Bari: Laterza, 1961), still essential reading for its meticulous attention to change and for its careful and sensitive re-creation of the pattern of rural life and of agriculture inside and outside the towns. Also useful, although it takes a different approach, is L. Gambi's *Una geografia per la storia* (Turin: Einaudi, 1973). For the wider European picture, see G. Duby, *The Early Growth of the European Economy: Warriors and Peasants from the Seventh to the Twelfth Century*, trans. H. B. Clarke (London, 1974; original French edition Paris: Gallimard, 1973). The world of the aristocracy is well treated by F. Cardini in *Alle origini della cavalleria medievale* (Florence: La Nuova Italia, 1981).

On the economic decline of the late antique and early medieval period see L. Ruggini, *Economia e società nell' 'Italia Annonaria'* (Milan: Giuffrè, 1961), and A. Giardina, ed., *Società romana e impero tardoantico*, vol. 1: *Istituzioni, ceti, economie* (Bari: Laterza, 1986). On the notion of the sacred, and especially the reverence felt for ruins, see E. Benveniste, *Indo-European Language and Society*, trans. E. Palmer (London: Faber and Faber, 1973; original French edition Paris, 1969), and A. Ja. Gurevich, *Categories of Medieval Culture*, trans. G. L. Campbell (London: Routledge and Kegan Paul, 1985), with a good bibliography (original Russian edition Moscow, 1972). An up-to-date discussion of the plant remains found in medieval towns, techniques for their analysis and conclusions to date can be found in U. Willerding's 'Zur paläo-ethnobotanischen Erforschung der mittelalterlichen Stadt', in *Braunschweigische Wissenschaftliche Gesellschaft. Jahrbuch*, 1987, pp. 35–50. The essays edited by B. Andreolli and M. Montanari in *Il bosco nel Medioevo* (Bologna: Clueb, 1988) draw on this as well as on other works. On the environment itself, C. Higounet's 'Les forêts de l'Europe Occidentale du Ve au XIe siècle', in *Agricoltura e mondo rurale in Occidente nell'Alto Medioevo* (Spoleto: Centro Italiano di Studi sull'Alto Medioevo (Cisam), 1966), pp. 343–98, is indispensable, while P. Keller's 'Storia postglaciale dei boschi dell'Italia Settentrionale', *Archivio botanico* 8.1 (1932), pp. 1–24 (original German edition: *Die postglaziale Entwicklungsgeschichte der*

Wälder von Norditalien, Berne: Veröffentlichungen des Geobotanischen Institutes Rübel in Zürich 8, 1931), deals specifically with Italy. A useful general guide, not only for Italy, is V. Giacomini and L. Fenaroli, *La flora* (Milan: Touring Club Italiano, 1958).

Towns are treated in *La città nell'alto Medioevo* (Spoleto: Cisam, 1959); in R. S. Lopez, 'Le città dell'Europa postcarolingia', in *I problemi comuni dell'Europa postcarolingia* (Spoleto: Centro Italiano di Studi sull'Alto Medioevo, 1955); in A. Sapoti, *La mercatura medievale* (Florence: Sansoni, 1972); in M. Sanfilippo, ed., *La città medievali* (Turin: Sei, 1973); in *Topografia urbana e vita cittadina nell'alto Medioevo in Occidente* (2 vols, Spoleto: Centro Italiano di Studi sull'Alto Medioevo, 1974); and in E. Ennen, *Storia della città medievale* (Bari: Laterza, 1975) (German edition: *Die europäische Stadt des Mittelalters,* Göttingen: Vandenhoeck and Ruprecht, 1979). See also H. A. Miskimin, D. Herlihy and A. L. Udovitch, eds., *The Medieval City: Essays Written in Honor of Robert S. Lopez* (New Haven: Yale University Press, 1977). For Italian towns see G. Fasoli and F. Bocchi, eds., *La città medievale italiana* (Florence: Sansoni, 1973). As for individual cities, Milan is discussed by C. Violante in *La società milanese nell'età precomunale* (Bari: Laterza, 1953), Pisa by E. Cristiani, *Nobiltà e popolo nel comune di Pisa* (Naples: Istituto Italiano per gli Studi Storici, 1963), and Florence by F. Sznura, *L'espansione urbana di Firenze nel Dugento* (Florence, 1975). An invaluable and up-to-date bibliography can be found in R. Bordone, ed., *La società urbana nell'Italia comunale (secoli XI–XIV)* (Turin: Loescher, 1984). The monographs and articles cited there by P. Cammarosano, A. Castagnetti, G. Chittolini, A. I. Pini and G. Rossetti are especially important. Southern Italy is covered by S. Tramontana in the chapter on 'La monarchia normanna e sveva' in *Storia d'Italia,* vol. 3 (Turin: UTET, 1983), pp. 436–568, with an excellent bibliography.

Information on art, with exhaustive bibliographies, can be found in X. Muratova, 'L'arte romanica', and in R. Recht, 'L'arte gotica', both in *La Storia,* vol. 1 (Turin: UTET, 1988), pp. 627–52 and pp. 653–79. Recht has contributed to L. Grodecki, ed., *Gothic Architecture* (London: Faber and Faber, 1986). E. Guidoni's *Arte e urbanistica in Toscana 1000–1315* (Rome: Bulzoni, 1970) is valuable. A good guide to science and technology in the period and their social implications is M. Parodi's 'Scienza e tecnica nel Medioevo', in *La Storia,* vol. 1, pp. 681–700, with an up-to-date bibliography.

The poor and the marginalized, the lower groups in society and rural and urban revolts are discussed by V. Rutenburg, *Popolo e movimenti popolari nell'Italia del '300 e '400* (Bologna: Il Mulino, 1971; original Russian edition Moscow–Leningrad: Academy of Sciences, 1958); by M. Mollat and P. Wolff, *The Popular Revolutions of the Late Middle Ages,* trans. A. L. Lytton-Sells (London: Allen and Unwin, 1973); by L. Martines, ed., *Violence and Civil Disorder in Italian Cities, 1200–1500* (Berkeley/Los Angeles/London: University of California Press, 1972); by P. Camporesi, *Il libro dei vagabondi* (Turin: Einaudi, 1973); by M. Mollat, ed., *Études sur l'histoire de la pauvreté. Moyen Age – XVIe siècle* (2 vols, Paris: Publications de la Sorbonne, 1974); by M. Mollat, *The Poor in the Middle Ages: An Essay in Social History,* trans. A. Goldhammer (New Haven: Yale University Press, 1986); by G. Cherubini, *Si-*

gnori, contadini, borghesi (Florence: Sansoni, 1974); by B. Geremeck, *Les marginaux parisiens aux XIVe et XVe siècles* (Paris: Flammarion, 1976); and by M. S. Mazzi, 'Gli inutili: miserabili e vagabondi', in *La Storia*, vol. 1, pp. 275–96, with a full bibliography.

Attitudes to money are discussed in O. Capitani, ed., *L'etica economica medievale* (Bologna: Il Mulino, 1974) and in J. Le Goff, *Your Money or Your Life: Economy and Religion in the Middle Ages* (New York: Zone Books, 1988). For an excellent panorama of the agricultural history of Europe, see B. H. Slicher van Bath, *The Agrarian History of Western Europe AD 500–1850*, trans. O. Ordish (London: Edward Arnold, 1963). For Italy see B. Andreolli, V. Fumagalli and M. Montanari, eds., *Le campagne italiane prima e dopo il Mille. Una società in trasformazione*, with articles by B. Andreolli, T. Bacchi, A. Castagnetti, P. Galetti, M. Montanari, G. Pasquali and V. Fumagalli and full bibliography. Vito Fumagalli's contribution, 'Il paesaggio si trasforma: colonizzazione e bonifica durante il Medioevo. L'esempio emiliano', pp. 95–131, discusses the relationship between town and country, clearances, floods and deliberate breaches of riverbanks, and cites publications by F. Cazzola and G. Poni and MA theses by A. Amaducci, A. Bonacini, G. Barbieri, M. Bentivogli, M. B. De Capoa, E. Guidoboni, R. Savioli and G. Serrazanetti. An authoritative study of the relationship between landowners living in the town and their estates in the countryside is G. Cherubini and R. Francovich's 'Forme e vicende degli insediamenti nelle campagne toscane dei secoli XIII–XV', *Quaderni Storici* 8 (1973), pp. 879–904. The climate in the period is discussed by P. Alexandre in *Le climat en Europe au Moyen Age* (Paris: Éditions de l'École des Hautes Études en Sciences Sociales, 1987).

On attitudes to animals, see *L'uomo di fronte al mondo animale nell'alto medioevo* (2 vols, Spoleto: Centro Italiano di Studi sull'Alto Medioevo, 1985). On changing attitudes to the dead in the Middle Ages, see V. Fumagalli, 'Il paesaggio dei morti. Luoghi d'incontro tra i morti e i vivi sulla terra nel Medioevo', *Quaderni Storici*, 50 (1982), pp. 411–25; C. Frugoni, 'La protesta affidata', ibid., pp. 426–48; and J. Chiffoleau, 'Perchè cambia la morte nella regione di Avignone alla fine del Medioevo', ibid., pp. 449–65.

Part III   The Solitude of the Flesh

A wide-ranging study is U. Ranke-Heinemann, *Eunuchs for Heaven: The Catholic Church and Sexuality*, trans. J. Brownjohn (London: André Deutsch, 1990; original German edition Hamburg: Hoffmann and Campe, 1988) but it relies on a rigid and uncompromising interpretation of the Church's teaching on sexual matters. J. A. Brundage, *Law, Sex and Christian Society in Medieval Europe* (Chicago/London, University of Chicago Press, 1987) provides valuable information on sources and secondary works. P. Ariès and A. Béjin, eds., *Western Sexuality: Practice and Precept in Past and Present*, trans. A. Forster (Oxford: Basil Blackwell, 1985), with contributions by P. Ariès, R. Fox, M. Foucault, P. Veyne, M. Pollak, J. Rossiaud, J.-L. Flandrin, A. Béjin and H. Lafont, is essential reading. Also important is G. Miccoli's chapter on 'La storia religiosa' in *Storia d'Italia*, vol. 2: *Dalla caduta dell'Impero romano al secolo XVIII* (Turin: Einaudi, 1974), pp. 431–1079. G. G. Merlo, *Eretici ed eresie medievali* (Bologna: Il Mulino, 1989) is a balanced study, covering a much wider area than the title might suggest; the excellent bibliography includes works on religion in the Middle Ages as well as on heresy.

On the history of the aristocracy and its relationship with the Church and with the religious houses, see A. Berbero, *L'aristocrazia nella società francese del Medioevo. Analisi delle fonti letterarie (secoli X–XIII)* (Bologna: Cappelli, 1987) which has a very full bibliography and extensive quotations from the sources. V. Fumagalli, *Terra e società nell'Italia padana. I secoli IX e X* (4th edn, Turin: Einaudi, 1990) is useful also for events outside Italy.

A bibliography and list of sources for religiosity in the thirteenth century and later can be found in V. Fumagalli, 'Motivi naturalistiche e aspirazioni alla pace: l'"Alleluja" del 1233', in *Uomini e paesaggi medievali* (2nd edn, Bologna: Il Mulino, 1990), pp. 143–59. R. Lambertini and A. Tabarroni, *Dopo Francesco: l'eredità difficile* (Turin: Edizioni Gruppo Abele, 1989) is a valuable study with an excellent bibliography of both primary and secondary sources. C. Frugoni's *Francesco. Un'altra storia* (Genoa: Marietti, 1988) includes among much useful material a study of the iconographical tradition of St Francis. C. Ginzburg's *Ecstasies: Deciphering the Witches' Sabbath*, trans. R. Rosenthal (London: Hutchinson Radius, 1990), an outstanding study of marginalization, is important for the history of intolerance towards Jews, lepers and witches, and has an extensive bibliography.

The darker side of the Renaissance world picture is discussed by E. Garin in *La cultura del Rinascimento* (Bari: Laterza, 1967); by R. Romano and A. Tenenti in *Alle origini del mondo moderno* (Milan: Feltrinelli, 1967), translated into German as *Die Grundlegung der modernen Welt. Spätmittelalten, Renaissance* (Frankfurt-am-Main, 1967); in A. Tenenti, *L'amore della vita e il senso della morte nel Rinascimento* (2nd edn, Turin: Einaudi, 1989); and in *Guido Reni, 1575–1642*, catalogue of an exhibition jointly organized by the Pinacoteca Nazionale of Bologna and the Los Angeles Museum of Art (Los Angeles: Los Angeles Museum of Art, 1988).

A. Vauchez, *La sainteté en Occident aux derniers siècles du Moyen Age* (Rome: École Française de Rome, 1981) covers a wider area than its title might suggest and is informative over a wide area. On holy women both in Italy and elsewhere see G. Pozzi and C. Leonardi, eds., *Scrittrici mistiche italiane* (Genoa: Marietti, 1988), especially C. Leonardi's contribution, 'La santità delle donne', pp. 43–57. G. Zarri, 'Le sante vive. Per una tipologia della santità femminile nel primo Cinquecento', *Annali dell'Istituto Storico Italo-germanico in Trento* 6 (1980), pp. 371–445, is perceptive. J. Delumeau, *Le péché et la peur. La culpabilisation en Occident XIIIe–XVIIIe siècles* (Paris: Fayard, 1983) is also useful.

The quotation from Nicola Abbagnano on p. 189 comes from his *Ricordi di un filosofo* (Milan: Garzanti, 1990), while for a vigorous and detailed evocation of the world of the Franciscans in the fourteenth century, Umberto Eco, *The Name of the Rose*, trans. W. Weaver (London: Secker and Warburg, 1983), can be recommended.

Some Sources in English and Original Texts

MGH: Monumenta Germaniae Historica

The *Confessions* of St Augustine have been translated by H. Chadwick (Oxford, 1991) and the *Dialogues* of Gregory the Great by O. J. Zimmermann (New York, 1959). Cassian can be found in W. O. Chadwick, *Western Asceticism. Selected Translations* (London, 1958).

The letters of Sidonius Apollinaris are translated by O. M. Dalton (2 vols, Oxford, 1915). For St Columbanus, see his life by Jonas of Bobbio, *Vitae sancti Columbani abbatis*, ed. B. Krusch, *MGH. Scriptores*, IV. The story of St Wandrille at Fontenelle is recounted in the *Vita Wandregisili* in *MGH. Scriptores rerum Merovingicarum*, V.

Gregory of Tours's *Poems and Letters* are published with an accompanying English translation by W. B. Anderson (2 vols, London: Loeb Classical Library, 1936). See also his *History of the Franks*, trans. L. Thorpe (London: Penguin, 1974). The edition of Bede's *Ecclesiastical History of the English People* by B. Colgrave and R. A. B. Myers (Oxford, 1969) has parallel Latin and English texts. See also J. M. Wallace-Hadrill, *Bede's History of the English People. A Historical Commentary* (Oxford, 1988).

There is an English translation by W. D. Foulke of Paul the Deacon's *History of the Langobards*, ed. E. Peters (Philadelphia, 1974, facsimile of Philadelphia 1907 edn); a facing German translation is in *Scriptores rerum Germanicarum in usum scholarum, ex MGH*, ed. G. Waitz. See also W. Goffart, *The Narrators of Barbarian History (AD 550–800). Jordanes, Gregory of Tours, Bede and Paul the Deacon* (Princeton, 1988).

The Lombard laws are edited by F. Bluhme in *Edictus ceteraeque Langobardorum leges* in *Scriptores rerum Germanicarum. Leges*, IV, and by F. Beyerle in *Leges Langobardorum* (Witzenhausen, 1962). There is an English translation, *The Lombard Laws*, by K. F. Drew (Philadelphia, 1973).

The adventures of the relics of St Genesius at Brescello are told in *Ex Miraculis Sancti Genesii*, ed. G. Waitz, *MGH. Scriptores*, XV, 1. Andreas of Bergamo's *Historia* is edited by G. Waitz, *MGH. Scriptores rerum Langobardicarum*, and Donizo's *Vita Mathildis* by L. Bethmann, *MGH. Scriptores*, XII. The description of Verona *circa* 800, the so-called *Versus de Verona*, is in *MGH. Poetae*, I, pp. 119–22 (ed. Pighi); likewise the description of Milan, the *Laudes Mediolanensis Civitatis* (pp. 24–6).

The chronicle of St Agobard, Archbishop of Lyons, the *Annales Lugdenenses*, is in *MGH. Scriptores*, I. The works of Liutprand of Cremona have been translated by F. A. Wright (London, 1930). The *Gesta Berengarii imperatoris*, ed. E. Dummler, is in *Beiträge zur Geschichte Italiens im Anfange des zehnten Jahrhundert* (Halle, 1871). The chronicle of the monastery of Novalesa in Piedmont (*Chronicon Novaliciense*, ed. L. C. Bethmann) is in *MGH. Scriptores*, VII. Salimbene is edited by J. L. Baird, G. Baglivi and J. R. Kane, as *The Chronicle of Salimbene de Adam* (Binghamton, New York, 1986) (Medieval Texts and Studies 40). The Latin text is in *MGH. Scriptores*, XXXII.

Einhard is translated by B. W. Scholz with B. Rogers (*Royal Frankish Annals*, Ann Arbor, 1970). The Latin text, the *Annales regni Francorum*, with a facing German translation, is in *Scriptores Rerum Germanicarum in usum scholarum, ex MGH*. For Alcuin's poetry see his *Opera omnia* in *Patrologia Latina*, ed. Migne, C and CI, 1863; also *MGH. Poetae*, I.

The quotation from Marc Bloch about Viking longships is from his *Feudal Society*, trans. L. A. Manyon (2nd edn, London, 1969). Dudo of Saint-Quentin's *Historia Normannorum* is edited by G. Waitz, *MGH. Scriptores*, IV, and Folcuin of Lobbes' history of the abbots of Saint-Bertin is in *Patrologia Latina*, ed. Migne, CXXXVI.

For Odo of Cluny see *St Odo of Cluny; Being the Life of St Odo of Cluny by John of Salerno, and the Life of St Gerald of Aurillac*, trans. G. Sitwell (London, 1958). Odo's writings are in *Patrologia Latina*, ed. Migne, vol. 133. John of Rome's life of St Odo of Cluny is in *Patrologia Latina*, ed. Migne, vol. 133.

Abbot John of Metz's life of St John of Gorze is in *MGH. Scriptores*, IV. The life of King Wenceslas of Bohemia by Gumpoldus, Bishop of Mantua, is in *MGH. Scriptores*, IV.

For Orderic Vitalis see the *Ecclesiastical History of Orderic Vitalis*, ed. and trans. M. Chibnall (6 vols, Oxford, 1969–). Reginus of Prüm's *Chronicon*, with a facing German translation, is in *Scriptores rerum Germanicarum in usum scholarum*. German translations of passages are in *Quellen zur Geschichte der sächsischen Kaiserzeit*, ed. A. Bauer and R. Rau (Darmstadt, 1971). The *Annales* of the French chronicler Flodoard are in *MGH. Scriptores*, III. For Rudolf Glaber see *The Five Books of the Histories*, ed. and trans. J. France (Oxford, 1989). Alpert of Metz's *De diversitate temporum* is in *Patrologia Latina*, ed. Migne, vol. 140.

For Marie de France see *The Lais of Marie de France*, trans. and introduced by G. S. Burgess and K. Busby (London: Penguin, 1986). For Abbot Suger see *The Abbey Church of Saint-Denis and its Art Treasures*, ed. and trans. E. Panofsky, parallel Latin and English texts (2nd edn, Princeton, 1979). Jean de Joinville's life of St Louis can be found in *Chronicles of the Crusades*, trans. M. R. B. Shaw (London: Penguin, 1963); the French text is edited by L-F. Flutre, *Histoire de Saint Louis* (Paris, 1942). Saint-Simon's comments on Louis XIV and hunting are in chapters 51–9 of his *Mémoires*.

The thirteenth-century laws of Reggio Emilia are in *Consuetudini e Statuti Reggiani del secolo XIII*, ed. A. Cerlini, vol. 1 (Milan, 1933) (*Corpus statutorum Italicorum*); those of Imola in *Statuti di Imola del secolo XIV (1334)*, ed. S. Gaddoni, vol. 1 (Milan, 1931) (*Corpus Statutorum Italicorum*); those of Modena in C. Campori, *Statuta civitatis mutinae anno 1327 reformata* (Parma, 1864); those of Piacenza as *Statuta varia civitatis Placentiae* in *Monumenta historica ad provincias parmensem et placentinam pertinentia* (Parma, 1860); and those of Bologna in *Statuti di Bologna dell'anno 1288*, ed. G. Fasoli and P. Sella (2 vols, Vatican City, 1937–9) (Studi e Testi 73, 81).

For St Francis see *St Francis of Assisi. Writings and Early Biographies*, trans. R. Brown et al. (3rd edn, London, 1979), and G. G. Coulton, *From St Francis to Dante. Translations from the Chronicle of the Franciscans, 1221–88*, 2nd edn, introduction by E. Peters (Philadelphia, 1972; reprint of 1907 edn).

Bonvesin dela Riva's *De magnalibus Mediolani* is published with a facing Italian translation by G. Pontiggia and an introduction by M. Corti (Milan, 1974). For Giovanni Villani see *Villani's Chronicle, Being Selections from the First Nine Books of the Croniche Fiorentine*, trans. R. E. Selfe and ed. P. H. Wicksteed (2nd edn, London, 1906).

There is an English translation of *Il Novellino. The Hundred Old Tales* by E. Storer (London, 1925); for the original see *Il Novellino*, ed. G. Favati (Genoa, 1970). Franco Sacchetti's *I trecentonovelle* are edited by V. Pernicore (Florence, 1946). Boccaccio's *Decameron* is well translated and introduced by G. H. McWilliam (London: Penguin, 1972).

For Paolo da Certaldo see *Mercanti scrittori. Ricordi nella Firenze tra Medioevo e Rinascimento. Paolo da Certaldo . . .*, ed. V. Branca (Milan, 1986).

Edward Fairfax's translation of Tasso's *Gerusalemme liberata* (*Godfrey of Bulloigne, or the Recovery of Jerusalem. Done into English heroicall verse by E. Fairefax*, London, 1600) was reprinted with an introduction by R. Weiss (London, 1962). Giorgio Franchi's 1544 chronicle is edited by G. Bertozzi, as *Poveri homini. Cronaca parmense del secolo XVI. 1543–1557* (Rome, 1976).

For William of Ockham see *Philosophical Writings. A Selection*, ed. and trans. P. Boehner (with Latin text) (London, 1957). English translations of the principal sources for St Dominic are in *St Dominic. Biographical Documents*, ed. F. C. Lehner (Washington, 1964). Leandro Alberti's life of Giovanni da Vicenza is in *De viris illustribus Ordinis Praedicatorum* (Bologna, 1517). On Thomas of Cantimpré see L. Thorndike, *A History of Magic and Experimental Science*, vol. 2 (New York, 1923) pp. 372–400.

St Catherine of Siena's letters have been translated and introduced by S. Noffke (Binghamton, New York, 1982). For Angela da Foligno see *Il libro della Beata Angela da Foligno*, ed. L. Thier and A. Calutetti (2nd edn, Grottaferrata, 1985). Joan of Arc is treated by M. Warner, *The Image of Female Heroism* (London, 1981) and by D. Fraioli, *The Image of Joan of Arc in Fifteenth-Century French Literature* (Ann Arbor, 1983).

On St Luigi Gonzaga see *The Life of Blessed Aloysius Gonzaga by V. Cepari*, trans. R. S. S[tanford] (Ilkley, 1974; facsimile of 1627 edn). The sources for the life of St Philip Neri are listed and discussed in L. Ponnelle and L. Bordet, *St Philip Neri and the Roman Society of his Times (1515–1595)*, trans. and introduced by R. E. Kerr (London, 1979), and in A. Capecelatro, *The Life of St Philip Neri*, trans. T. A. Pope (new edn, 2 vols, New York, 1926).

For St Teresa see *The Letters of St Teresa of Jesus*, trans. E. Allison Peers (2nd edn, London, 1980), and *The Collected Works of St Teresa of Avila*, vol. 1 (*The Book of her Life, Spiritual Testimonies, Soliloquies*), trans. K. Kavanagh and O. Rodriguez (Washington, 1976). The *Lauds* of Iacopone da Todi have been translated by E. Hughes and S. Hughes (New York, 1982).

Maupassant's story 'Le loup' is in *Contes et nouvelles*, ed. L. Forestier (Paris, 1974). See also *The Complete Short Stories of Guy de Maupassant* (London, 1970). The quotation from Thomas Mann's *The Magic Mountain* is from the translation by H. T. Lowe-Porter (2 vols, London, 1927). For Proust's *The Guermantes Way* and *Cities of the Plain*, see now the translation by C. K. Scott

Moncrieff and Terence Kilmartin, revised by D. J. Enright (London, 1992); also R. Bales, *Proust and the Middle Ages* (Geneva, 1975).

Marc Bloch's *Strange Defeat* was translated by G. Hopkins as *Strange Defeat. A Statement of Evidence Written in 1940* (London, 1949).

Index

Index by Isobel McLean